History and Ideology in Ancient Israel

Giovanni Garbini

History and Ideology in Ancient Israel

Crossroad • New York

1988

The Crossroad Publishing Company
370 Lexington Avenue, New York, N.Y. 10017

Translated by John Bowden from the Italian
Storia e Ideologia nell'Israele Antico
© Paideia Editrice 1986

Translation © John Bowden 1988

Printed in the United States of America

Library of Congress Cataloging-in-Publication Data

Garbini, Giovanni.
    [Storia e ideologia nell'Israele antico. English]
    History and ideology in ancient Israel/Giovanni Garbini;
[translated by John Bowden from the Italian].
        p. cm.
    Translation of: Storia e ideologia nell'Israele antico.
    Includes index.
    ISBN 0-8245-0887-4
    1. Bible. O.T.—History of Biblical events. 2. Jews—History—To
586 B.C. 3. Judaism—History—To 70 A.D. I. Title.
BS1197.G3713 1988
221.9'5—dc19   88-3859
                                                             CIP

To Paolo and Enrica

CONTENTS

Contents

PREFACE TO THE ENGLISH EDITION

Because of the short time that has elapsed between the Italian edition and this English edition I have been dissuaded from producing a text different from that of the original. Filling some gaps in the bibliography and bringing the text up to date where that was indispensable have added a few lines to not more than five or six footnotes. Having pointed that out, as an Italian author now addressing an English-speaking public I feel that I should say a few words by way of justification.

Planned in Italy, this book is obviously influenced not so much by Italian bibliography, which is extremely scarce at an academic level in connection with ancient Israel, as by the cultural ambience of Italy. That explains why, for example, alongside the great name of Benedetto Croce mention is made of mediocre nineteenth-century historians like Cesare Cantù and Cesare Balbo, or a brilliant but superficial biblical scholar like Giuseppe Ricciotti is given such prominence, albeit in a negative way. Notwithstanding some inevitable but limited references to Italian authors, it will be evident to the reader that the dialogue and, perhaps too often, the polemic is almost always carried on with non-Italian scholars. The fact of the matter is that up to the present day Italy has remained substantially on the periphery of biblical studies, which have been cultivated particularly in Germany; however, I have a strong suspicion that this peripheral status of a country which has created a literary language and has produced a not insignificant literature, even if it has not known prestigious and influential versions of the Bible like the Authorized Version of King James and the *Gantze Heilige Schrift Deudsch* of Martin Luther, has been more an advantage than a disadvantage for Italian culture. Unlike what usually happens outside Italy, in Italy it is possible to be a semitic scholar without being primarily a biblical scholar: one need only think of Ignazio Guidi and Giorgio Levi Della Vida (though in Great Britain there has also been G.R.Driver). This also means being psychologically freer towards the Old Testament.

I remember with great affection Professor H.H.Rowley, who in the last years of his life was kind enough to send his books to the young Italian semitic scholar who had begun to recognize the problems of the Hebrew Bible through a valuable small book, *The Growth of the Old Testament*, which saw the light in 1950, the year in which that author entered university for the first time. For many years Professor H.H.Rowley has been an essential point of reference for me; later, I found refined tools for research in the writings of my friend Professor James Barr. In one sense I therefore feel myself to be a pupil of the best British biblical school, which has perhaps passed on to me something of its healthily empirical attitude.

I said at the beginning that it has not seemed to me appropriate to introduce changes in the original text of this book. But there is one argument which might have deserved some touching up. In Chapter 4 Yahwism is considered to be virtually synonymous with monotheism, and monotheism to be the ideal and conclusive outcome of the development of religious thought: this is a point of view which for a number of years I continued to regard as sound (I should explain that the substance of this chapter consists in two lectures which I gave in 1979 and 1981 respectively). Today, however, this position seems to me to be inadequate. The concept of monotheism may be satisfying from the perspective of Aristotelian philosophy, but it remains to be seen whether that is equally true from a strictly religious perspective. We must not forget that a religion with a dualistic basis like Mazdaeanism or with an essentially pantheistic conception like Hinduism has satisfied, and continues to satisfy, the religious demands of a very great many individuals, without the intellectual disputes provoked by the problem of evil when it is raised in a monotheistic religion. However, the essential point is not the more or less absolute value of monotheism but the legitimacy of a substantial identification of Yahwism and monotheism.

Biblical Yahwism certainly reflects a monotheistic conception, but at the same time it is something less and something more than monotheism. If we leave aside the message of Deutero-Isaiah, Yahwism seems to be something less than monotheism: God is certainly one, but he is essentially the God of just one people and he acts only with them. If we reflect on this aspect, which is the central nucleus of the Old Testament, we discover that here we have what the historians of religions call henotheism rather than monotheism. On the other hand Yahwism is also, and perhaps above all, an extremely rational vision of the world and of the privileged position that the people of Israel occupies in the world. So it would be legitimate to ask whether one could consider as a real 'religion', with all that this word implies for the individual who professes it, a doctrine like that taught in the Old Testament in the first millennium BC which denies the survival of the spirit. Without what I have defined as a rational vision, but can simply be called ideology, it would be impossible to explain how a 'religion' which attributes an essential importance to the liturgical practices celebrated in the Jerusalem temple, and only in it, could have survived and also spread, even after the destruction of that temple. And it would also be impossible to understand how in 1949 a non-believing Jew, i.e. one without religion, like Erich Fromm, could have written a book like *You Shall Be as Gods*.

I am well aware that more than one reader may find these ideas, like various pages of this book, hard to understand and even provocative. A very great many books about the Old Testament have been written from a similar point of view; here the perspective is different, but I hope that it is also more correct.

It is a pleasure for me to thank Dr John Bowden, who has skilfully translated (and sometimes improved) my Italian text.

G.G.

INTRODUCTION

I began to concern myself directly with problems relating to ancient Hebrew history writing only a few years ago, namely from the point when my linguistic interests took on a more markedly philological dimension; this happened to coincide, in a relationship of cause and effect which is not clear even to me, with the beginning of the publication of the journal *Henoch*, which has on its masthead the phrase 'Historico-philological Studies on Judaism'; I was invited to be its co-editor by my friend Professor Paolo Sacchi. My first study in this area appeared in *Henoch* in 1979; it was on the so-called 'Succession Narrative', and while expressing some personal points of view it took a decidedly traditional line; in other words, it presupposed that a narrative had been written at a time still very close to the events narrated. However, only a few months later my attitude had changed radically.

In 1980 I was invited to contribute a short article to a 'History of Jesus' People', published in the monthly journal *Jesus*. While I was trying to understand the meaning of that somewhat hallucinatory story of the episode of the Golden Calf (Exodus 32), I was struck by the detail that the tables of the law were written on two surfaces, as the text emphasizes, and were broken so easily by Moses. Although it is said that they were of stone, these tablets seem to have been the small terra cotta tablets on which the Babylonians wrote. And given that cuneiform tablets had disappeared from Egypt and Palestine by the end of the thirteenth century BC (they were only reintroduced by the Assyrian administration), the story of the golden calf, written by someone who was familiar with such tablets, must have been composed by an author who was or had been in Babylon. At this point, for me, as they already were for some others, the classical 'sources' of Wellhausen became nothing more than splendid antiques, to be viewed in a glass case. I arrived at this radical conclusion only apparently unexpectedly: the exilic or even post-exilic dating of a text which for the most part is usually attributed to the Elohistic source represented the logical corollary of the observation, made a long time ago, of the presence of Babylonian words in the Yahwistic source; not to mention the personal interpretation that this latter Hebrew writer had made of Babylonian texts (the creation of the world) of a relatively late date (not before the end of the second millennium BC for the earliest) which can only have been known during the exile.

From 1980 I have been concerned with biblical matters with some frequency, presenting the results of my researches especially at congresses and seminars which, with their varied themes, gave me the possibility of investigating one or other aspect of the remarkable historical happenings narrated in the Old Testament. When the possibility of publishing my studies in one volume was raised, I left unedited those which I was working on at the time, namely the final chapters (11-14) and the fourth section of chapter 3. The others, which have appeared previously, have been revised and quite often been considerably changed in structure; none of them has been published in its original form. Although the individual pieces of research are all different, from the beginning I have had a single aim: to investigate how far the legacy of the ancient Hebrew historical tradition is history and how far it is ideology (and of what kind). For me, too, this research is only beginning: had this book been published a few years later it would certainly have been much larger and would have had more specific conclusions, perhaps different from those it now contains. However, as things are, it already seems to me sufficient to outline in a broad sweep the development, if not of Hebrew history, at least of the way in which the Hebrews presented their history.

History: the ambiguity of the Italian (and English) language over this word (history/*storia* can denote both a succession of events and historiography, and I am deliberately leaving aside the philosophical debate over the identity of history and historiography) has made it possible for me to give this book a title with only two terms. The title 'History and Ideology' is in fact meant to indicate two different things that are being studied: how ideology has conditioned Hebrew history writing, but also how the ideology has created a historical past; to be precise, I should have entitled the book 'History, Historiography and Ideology in Ancient Israel'. Because to present the accession of Solomon in a certain way is the expression in historiography of an anti-monarchical ideology; to have a military conquest of Palestine by the Hebrew tribes under the leadership of Joshua is to create a fictitious historical datum to meet the ideological demands of a frustrated nationalism.

This book talks especially about the influence of ideology on historiography, and there is not much in it about the events of history (and I can also explain why). It was not my intention to write even a sketch of the history of ancient Israel, and in fact that is not what I have done. The order in which the various chapters follow one another does, however, show how such a history could have been written: David before Abraham and Moses, Joshua after Darius, Ezra after Simon the Just; whereas it is no coincidence that only for the period before the exile can one talk of historical problems in the strict (or, if you like, traditional) sense. It is obvious that the dating of the biblical texts followed here is later than what one generally finds: sometimes it is discussed explicitly; at other times it is presupposed. It would not be inappropriate to remind anyone who is surprised at this that so far there is *no evidence* to provide a basis for the usual datings (those which can be found in the textbooks); they are only chronological hypotheses, when they are not merely wishful thinking.

It is often said that the Bible is a religious book and not a history book. That is true, but it is still rather vague. Certainly the Bible is the foundation of the Christian religion, and the Old Testament is the foundation of the Jewish religion. But what is not thought about enough is that when the Old Testament was written as a book of religion, the concept of religion was different from ours; that is the case not only because more than two millennia have passed since then but because after the Old Testament, the New Testament has modified the very concept of religion, providing the beginning of that way of looking at things which is still essentially ours today. In some cases to talk of ideology is tantamount to talking of theology, but the two terms are not always interchangeable, because Hebrew religion (like all the religions of the Near East, whether ancient or not) included things which today seem to us to be external to religion. Historical conceptions, political reports, rivalries between priestly castes can only seldom be considered expressions of a 'religious' view of life – at least from our point of view; but when a people becomes 'holy', every action in everyday life and every political event becomes a religious phenomenon – from its point of view. So in the Old Testament it is difficult, I would say impossible, to draw a dividing line between what is 'history' and what is 'religion', because its 'religion' is not our 'religion' and its 'history' is not our 'history', at least as an object of analysis. Once one becomes aware of this diversity, which simply means adopting a historically critical attitude, it becomes relatively easy to define the 'historical' conception of the Old Testament: that political thought which identifies itself with religious thought (the prophets) and that religious thought which makes itself historical thought (the history writers) and creates a fictitious but sacral history come together in a circularity which in our all too knowing language is no longer politics or religion or history – but only ideology.

The title I have chosen for this book deliberately recalls that of a thought-provoking volume published in 1924 by Giorgio Levi Della Vida, *Storia e religione nell'Oriente semitico*, Rome 1924. On the centenary of the birth of this great scholar it seems to me right that these pages, written in the shadow of a scientific tradition of which Levi Della Vida was one of the most illustrious figures, should bear a recollection of his name and his work.

Finally, particularly warm thanks to Dr Marco Scarpat, for being willing to publish this by no means easy volume.

Giovanni Garbini

Chapter 1

The History of Israel

The ancient Near East, with its civilization and its history, has been rescued from the oblivion of time by just over a century of European science. With it have appeared the remotest roots of Western civilization: before Paris, Rome, Athens and Jerusalem there were Babylon and Uruk. This last name is certainly unfamiliar to many people; but in this most ancient city of southern Iraq our civilization learned to write, to build cities, to organize a state – and did so more than five thousand years ago. Historical knowledge of this now long past of ours, i.e. the capacity to recover it, grows progressively less the further back we go in time; the record becomes increasingly more faded the further back we trace the route from West to East, from Europe to Asia. Perhaps it is not just chance that the clearest break between what is well known and what is little known comes half way, around the sixth century BC, when the creative force of this civilization was passing from Asia to Europe.

In the trajectory so far followed by our civilization, Israel is the central point, the link between Asia and Europe. Their stay in Babylon, the brilliant heir to Uruk, in the transitional phase from the Chaldaeans to the Achaemenids, allowed the Hebrews to gather both the ripe fruits of an ancient thought which had come down over millennia and the bitter fruits of a vision of the world developed by a new people. The unexpected horizons which opened up to men shaped by contact with Egyptian culture were viewed by the Hebrew exiles in the light of a message, the prophetic message, which they had received earlier but which was only now fully understood and appreciated: Israel returned to Jerusalem enormously enriched and transformed. When Greek culture arrived there, Hebrew thought was in a stage of further revision, the final result of which was transmitted to Europe by some brilliant men. This was the historical function of Israel: but what do we really know about this people? We know a good deal about Rome and Athens, much less about Uruk and Babylon, with alternate phases of light and shade; great historians have written about Greece and Rome, but only some specialists have examined one or other feature of the ancient Near East, mostly from a philological perspective. Once again, Israel is half way.

Israel is part of a geographical and cultural area, that of Syria and Palestine, which was relatively autonomous over against Mesopotamia and Egypt; but it was also, after all, culturally much poorer. That meant that it wrote less and therefore we know less about it. Limiting the discussion to the period that sees the rise and establishment of the Hebrew people (the so-called Iron Age, from 1200 BC onwards) one must say that political fragmentation and the scarcity of sources no longer allow a unitary historical view except in very broad outline;[1] whereas the ethnic fragmentation, often corresponding to political fragmentation, has encouraged a historical view in modern times centred on ethnic individuality, not always defined correctly, rather than on more complex historical reality. In this way syntheses have come into being, very full of gaps, relating to the Phoenicians and the Aramaeans, on the basis of Akkadian, Hebrew, Greek and Latin sources and on a by no means insignificant basis of epigraphy and archaeology; the enormous gaps in the overall picture are also highlighted by the fact that each new historical inscription that is discovered reveals names of previously unknown rulers and even kingdoms. Against this background of a general lack of evidence there emerge, as a happy exception, the Hebrews, who have succeeded in preserving down to the present day not only a degree of identity but also their ancient tradition of history writing. Thanks to a complex of reasons which we need not recall here, this tradition has been handed over to modern historians who have considered it *de facto* complete, because it has all the essentials: events, historiographical reflection and theological, i.e. philosophical, reflection. For these historians all that needed to be done was to make this history writing their own, and this is what they have done; often to the point of neglecting even the few pieces of information that epigraphy and the Akkadian sources have put at their disposal, so as not to interrupt the smoothness of the historical picture presented by the Bible.

At this point it is necessary to be rather more precise: all those who have been occupied with and have written about the story of the ancient Hebrews are not historians by profession, though for the sake of brevity I have called them 'historians'; almost without exception they are all professors of theology. They are *Alttestamentler*, professors from German theological faculties, who regard the writing of a *History of Israel* as the culmination of their study of the Old Testament. So the *History of Israel* appears as a modern literary genre born in Germany in the last century from the encounter of historicism with theology. The monumental and now forgotten *Geschichte des Volkes Israel* by H.A.Ewald, published between 1843 and 1868, and the work with the same name, still quoted, by R.Kittel, the first volume of which appeared in 1888 and the last edition of which was published in 1932, represent the two pillars around which grew up a forest of analogous and less pretentious histories. A partially new voice, free from dogmatic ties, was heard in 1878 with the first volume of the *Geschichte Israels* by Julius Wellhausen who was then still a professor of theology;[2] the volume remained a solitary one and was reprinted subsequently with the title *Prolegomena zur Geschichte Israels*. Wellhausen gave a strictly historical exposition in 1881 in his article 'Israel' for the *Encyclopaedia Britannica*; his treatment began with the exodus from Egypt. However, the patriarchs soon reappeared with Kittel who, not to leave anything out of his history, began his account with the palaeolithic age. Wellhausen had a follower, B.Stade, who was also author of a *Geschichte des Volkes Israel*, which appeared in two volumes in 1887 and 1888.[3] The *Histoire du peuple d'Israël* by Ernest Renan, published in five volumes between 1887 and 1893, has a place of its own; the last effort of the French man of letters, it has been rightly forgotten by scholars, even if it could still be of interest because of its sometimes emphatic and sometimes journalistic style and because of its freedom of thought.

Over recent decades the 'Histories of Israel' have multiplied,[4] all going back in a way to an ideal model, Martin Noth's *Geschichte Israels*, which appeared in 1950; this is at least a model in terms of size, since modern treatments have lost the monumental character of the earlier ones. Now it is interesting to see Noth's judgment on the history of Israel: ' "Israel" still appears a stranger in the world of its own time, a stranger wearing the garments and behaving in the manner of its age, yet separate from the world it lived in, not merely in the sense that every historical reality has its own individual character, and therefore an element of uniqueness, but rather that at the very centre of the history of "Israel" we encounter phenomena for which there is no parallel at all elsewhere, not because the material for comparison has not yet come to light but because, so far as we know, such things have simply never happened elsewhere.'[5] The attitude thus clearly expressed by Noth puts the German scholar firmly in that group of theologians who a few years after these words were written formed the object of the powerful but salutary criticism of James Barr.[6] Therefore there is no cause for amazement at the inability demonstrated by Noth, some lines after the passage which I have quoted, to give any sort of historical explanation of one of the most important external sources for Hebrew history, namely the Merneptah stele; this earliest mention of 'Israel', which does not fit either the biblical data or the particular theory developed by Noth himself (the theory of the amphictyony), calls for a different critical attitude from that cultivated in the theological faculties of the German universities. Noth, for whom Israel 'cannot really be grasped as a historical entity until it becomes a reality living on the soil of Palestine' (53), has no difficulty in accepting that 'there can be no doubt that (the Pentateuch) sets out to relate events that have happened and that it contains a good deal of material relating to historical traditions' (43); it would have been interesting to ask Noth what example he would give of what he claimed to be 'events that have happened' other than the exodus from Egypt, 'a historical fact the premises and external circumstances of which it is not difficult to recognize'.[7] This point is illuminating for Noth's 'historical' method: he begins from a 'profession of faith' (the definition of which is only an invention of some modern theologian) for which he recognizes a fully historical basis (see the words quoted above); he then gives a broad illustration of the general historical situation to demonstrate the plausibility of the 'concrete foundation' for the presence of north-west Semites in Egypt. It is 'no longer possible to discover any historical details' about the exodus (115); but Noth nevertheless diligently recapitulates the biblical story, endorsing it with contemporary geographical information and, we should add, some historical errors. To say that the flight 'certainly occurred on the eastern border of the Delta where the Israelites were bound to attempt to leave the sphere of direct Egyptian suzerainty' (115) is to forget that Ramesses II (in whose reign Noth puts the exodus) had an Asiatic empire which extended as far as Syria (and moreover Ramesses IV was still in control of Sinai). The only point on which the German scholar differs from the Old Testament is over the protagonists of the narrative: they were certainly not the 'Israelites', who did not yet exist as such, nor a large group of tribes, nor even any tribe as such, given that 'the later tribes did not exist at all' (119); these were only 'elements which became part of the tribes which were formed when the land was occupied. They were probably not absorbed by a single tribe, or even a single group of tribes, but by the whole range of the Israelite tribes' (119). How a few people who escaped from Egypt succeeded in relating to all the Israelite tribes and imposing on them their own 'profession of faith' is to be considered an even greater miracle than the passage through the Red Sea: what is striking is that the history which the Old Testament attributes to the Israelites corresponds in an impressive way, miracles apart, to that of the Philistines, who happened to give their name to the land which other exiles from Egypt claimed for themselves.

But I shall not dwell further on this mother of modern 'histories of Israel'. Instead I shall look at two recent German 'histories', the first of which has been translated into Italian and English and the second into Italian. The *Geschichte Israels in alttestamentlicher Zeit*, by Siegfried Herrmann, first published in 1973, is dedicated to A.Alt; it is quite long, above all in its enlarged second edition (456 pages),[8] and implicitly sets out to be the heir to Noth's *History*. Its plan is the classic one: the geographical and historical context, archaeological references, narration of events from the patriarchs, in the first edition to Alexander the Great and in the second to the New Testament period. The choice of starting point (the patriarchs) immediately indicates the author's attitude to the content of the Bible: total adherence to and acceptance of every detail. Let us listen directly to Herrmann: 'The history writing which Israel produced in the period of David and Solomon was the first writing deserving of the name from a cultured nation; it can even claim a high degree of excellence' (32). 'The three great figures of Abraham, Isaac and Jacob, who are associated in a series of father-son relationships, are hardly literary inventions... There is evidence that Abraham at least is rooted in the northern group from Upper Mesopotamia' (46). The author's trust in his sources cannot be shared by the reader, who would prefer to know where the evidence is for rooting Abraham in history, but it is certainly admirable in its simplicity: 'Jericho itself was captured, not by military power but most probably by a ruse' (87); even if 'the degree to which the theme of the "harlot story" is involved here is quite a separate question', it is certainly 'unnecessary to seek to check the detail about the falling walls from the archaeological evidence' (95). 'At the least, the acclamation of the people means that the king could not rule on the narrow basis of a decision which had been made by only a few people. From the beginning, an absolute monarchy in Israel was ruled out' (136). 'The great originality of the stories about David which we now possess cannot be denied. They took shape only a short time after the events themselves, and in any case soon after the death of David' (151f.). 'Solomon, too, is said to have reigned for forty years (I

Kings 11.42). Given that Solomon died about 930 BC, it may be said that David's rule should be put about 1000 BC' (167). 'Only Chronicles reports this [the fortification of some cities of Judah], but the list is certainly based on official documents, especially as the details give an astonishing glimpse of the territorial possessions of Judah' (197).⁹

In short, Herrmann's *History of Israel* is also a theologian's history. What can be discovered from reading the volume is, moreover, explicitly admitted by the author, who at one point in the introduction states: 'The Old Testament is a collection of sources from all periods of the history of Israel, which have been assembled not to present an unbroken history but consistently to present the acts of Yahweh, the God of Israel, who at all times showed himself to be living, present and uniquely powerful' (31) and ended the first edition of his history by saying: 'It is beyond doubt a theological task to see the reflection of knowledge of the world and of God in the mirror of Israel; now more than ever this has become a question posed to every thinking man. The presuppositions for understanding Israel lie in the Old Testament and its history' (326).

If Herrmann's book is immediately under the shadow of Noth's *History*, Georg Fohrer's *Geschichte Israels. Von den Anfängen bis zu Gegenwart*, which appeared in 1977, was written with a more popular audience in mind; in 336 pages, after a historical profile of the ancient Near East, we find the history of Israel brought down to the present time, specifically to Sadat's visit to Jerusalem in 1977. Here, too, the author is a theologian (he was Professor of Old Testament in the University of Erlangen until he retired to Jerusalem).

To go by some of the things he says, Fohrer's approach to the sources seems particularly critical: 'The traditions about the patriarchs contained in Genesis must be considered to be substantially a novellistic heritage. Their historical content is very thin; it consists mainly of some names and some comments on the life-style and beliefs of the proto-Israelites' (30). 'There is no doubt that the narrative in the Book of Joshua does not correspond at all to the historical facts' (44). However, that goes only for the earliest phases, because we are then told that 'the narratives in the book of Judges have a more historical basis than those of the previous period' (67); obviously the accounts relating to David are now completely historical (92). But then the earliest traditions are in fact themselves accepted: 'ancient and trustworthy sources associate the Israelites with the Aramaeans' (24); 'in Num.1.5-15 we have an ancient list with figures inserted at a later stage...: in Num.26.5ff. a long list of tribes has been handed down... probably going back to the period before the state' (46);

the song in Exodus 15 is 'important not only because it is historical evidence of the episode of the rescue but also because it reveals what happened under the sign of faith in Yahweh' (60); 'from these traditions relating to Saul] in which at least the names of the sanctuaries and the definitions of the ritual acts derive from early reminiscences, one may infer that Saul was probably not proclaimed king of the Israelite tribes in a single act, but was approved in this capacity by one tribe after another. It seems that only the tribe of Judah did not follow him' (85). I shall stop here so as not to bore with other quotations the reader who will have now realized that in Fohrer's book, as in that of Herrmann, he or she will find no more than a paraphrase of the biblical text.[10]

The lack of a real historical approach, even where the biblical data are only partly accepted, is also clear from the vagueness in which certain situations are shrouded. It is difficult to understand how the 'Moses group' did not succeed in entering Palestine (64) at the end of the thirteenth century BC (for Fohrer, Merneptah is the Pharaoh of the exodus) when all or almost all the Israelite tribes were already there (55); the situation of calm implicitly described by the author when he states: 'subsequently the group, deprived of its leader, crossed the river and found a new home near the tribes of central Palestine' (64), existed before the death of Moses; this is all the more problematical since Fohrer had said earlier that 'the pattern of the settlements of the Israelite tribes indicates that they established themselves in parts of Palestine which up to that time had been either sparsely populated or uninhabited' (53). The historical fragility of the hypothesis of the 'Moses group' which comes to join the Israelite tribes is also revealed by a feature of nomenclature; according to Fohrer, the Yahwistic religion was introduced into Palestine by the 'Moses group' (64), which became integrated with the Joseph tribes commanded by Joshua; since there was no other contact between Moses and Joshua (66) and the latter with his tribe became an adherent of the new religion only after the battle of Gibeon (68), how do we explain Joshua's own name (which presupposes knowledge of the name of Yahweh)? Then there are the Philistines: on pp.97f. we read that 'from the time of David the Philistines ceased to play a political role in Palestine. The power of the dominant class was exhausted, having been absorbed into the Canaanite population. The Philistine city states became vassals of David'; however, on p.129, in connection with the political division of the Hebrew state, it is said that the 'Philistine vassals will also have remained independent, though they had not exercised any important political function for a long time'; and

Nadab son of Jeroboam died in battle 'during the siege of a Philistine city... The expedition against the Philistines allows us to suppose that there were perhaps also attacks against Israel from there' (130); when the city of Libnah rebelled against Jerusalem 'it joined forces with the Philistines' (139); the Philistine cities were engaged in organizing the revolt against the Assyrians under Sargon (160) and Sennacherib (161-2); and after the latter had defeated the coalition and assigned part of the possessions of Judah to the Philistines, Fohrer comments: 'in this way ancient claims of the Philistine cities from the period before David were satisfied, relating to the sovereignty of their eastern hinterland as part of their sovereignty over all Palestine, which will have affected the Philistines as successors of the Egyptians' (164). Quite apart from the question of the explanations offered by the German scholar for the Philistine 'claims', after such a scanty enumeration of events, we must ask what Fohrer means by 'political role', since he denies it to the Philistines from the time of David on.

It does not take much to realize that Fohrer's attitude to the Philistines has its origin not in a historical evaluation but in a position of an apologetic kind. And it is into this context that there is inserted the acceptance of the fable, put into circulation by Albright, of 'progressive Canaanite decadence' (21), even if the blame is now laid on 'Egyptian malgovernment'; and it is also in this climate that the author comes to talk of waves of 'pantheistic Enlightenment and naturistic mysticism' (16) in connection with the religious reform of Amenophis IV: a monotheistic precedent is too uncomfortable.

If this is the situation in German historiography relating to ancient Israel, things are not much better outside Germany. In the United States, where John Bright's *History of Israel* (1958, [2]1972, [3]1980) has become a classic, the predominant strand is the apologetic one with an archaeological basis initiated by the various works of W.F.Albright;[11] M.Liverani and P.Sacchi have passed equally severe judgments on the incomplete *The Early History of Israel* (1971-1973) by R.de Vaux[12] and the composite work *Israelite and Judaean History* (1977) edited by J.H.Hayes and J.M.Miller.[13] And so finally we come nearer home.

In Italy, the problem of the history of Israel was already present in the mind of the historians of the nineteenth century. The *Storia universale* of Cesare Cantù, which began to appear in 1838, naturally devoted a significant amount of space to the history and the culture of the Jews; the exposition faithfully followed the information in the Old Testament and the position of the author was clearly expressed in the first note of

Volume II, which reads: 'The best sources for Hebrew history are the holy books.'[14] We find a similar position in the Guelph Cesare Balbo, who in the first volume of his *Meditazioni storiche*, which appeared in 1842, wrote in connection with the historical validity of the Old Testament: 'This history is the one that we have already found to be the truest, the only true, only credible, only simple history in its cosmogonical narrative with which these facts are directly connected; it is that which in all the following narratives proves equally credible for the same historical virtues, and for its agreements with itself and with the best histories of later times; it is the earliest of the histories and therefore nearest to the facts that are narrated here';[15] with these words Balbo was alluding to Moses. A good Catholic, Cesare Balbo did not limit himself to following the Bible in the narrative of the history of Israel but also put what the Bible says on the foundation of the history of the other peoples of the ancient Near East, attacking those scholars who preferred the external sources to the Bible: 'But I believe that it can be claimed that here as usual the expositors, commentators and sacred historians certainly put the Bible above the other sources but do not go on to draw the consequences of this proposition in the details of secular history since that is not their task; that the sacred historians all more or less explicitly or implicitly attributed the greatest authority to the secular sources; that Volney, Gesenius and the other rationalists took this kind of criticism to the extreme, correcting the Bible by the sources; that precisely as a result of the work done most recently, that is, by the new agreements and even more by the disagreements that have been found, the historical superiority of the Bible stands out incontrovertibly; and that there follow from this such new certainties and clarities that it is now definitely possible to do the work required, the true history of Western and Central Asia from Nimrod or at least from Ninus to Cyrus.'[16] This apologetic position, somewhat irritating in tone and inconclusive in its repudiation of the historical method, has been dominant a long time in Italy, and we find it again in Giuseppe Ricciotti's *History of Israel*.[17] Criticizing the phrase of W.Robertson Smith (from his preface to the English edition of the *Prolegomena*), 'The Old Testament does not offer us a history of Israel, but it does furnish the materials from which that history can be constructed', our biblical scholar accepts the second part of the statement but rejects the first, which he describes as 'typical of Wellhausen'; the scholar who wants to write the 'authentic' history of Israel must keep to the general lines provided by the Bible 'and order the material accordingly, after testing it critically. Certainly, it should be tested critically, but that is not to say that the only criticism possible is that based on the philosophical principles presupposed by Wellhausen's theory' which, above all, 'would do away with a very great deal of the material' that the Bible provides. 'How imprudent those mass rejections are, even from a critical perspective, appears from the fact, already mentioned, that what yesterday was fable today turns out to be authentic history and that the archaeologists of today carefully make use of much biblical material which was scornfully discarded by the Wellhausen followers of yesterday.' Ricciotti concludes: 'It is certainly risky to forecast the future attitudes of critics, but it does not seem risky to assert that any future critical history of Israel that does not want to be a simple attempt destined to be here today and gone tomorrow, must take account of the basic lines of that history as they are laid down in the Bible. Not that everything is simple and clear in it; on the contrary, question marks arise in many parts of the narrative. But in no science has a question mark ever justified an amputation. This is therefore the scientific reason on the basis of which we feel obliged to follow the thread of the biblical narrative step by step, in obscure points looking to light from future science.'[18] Ricciotti's statements are significant because although they were written at the beginning of the 1930s, they already introduce that atmosphere which was to be dominant some decades later: enthusiasm for archaeology (obviously 'biblical'), the charge that the philological method is an expression of 'philosophical principles' (as if being inspired by a philosophy were a fault), and absolute trust in the letter of the Bible. Moreover, Ricciotti shows that he has a very special idea of 'scientific reason'.

The Catholic position already appears to be more subtle and aware with Alberto Vaccari who, when introducing in 1957 the second volume of the *Sacra Bibbia* translated from the original texts with notes by the Pontifical Biblical Institute, wrote: 'More than anything, however, to appreciate the historical books of the Old Testament properly it is necessary to consider the aim of their authors and the spirit which animated them in writing their books. For the biblical writers the historical narrative is not an end in itself; they do not tell their story to satisfy an urge to know. In the facts that they record they want to show the action of God in directing human society to the high ends of his providence, especially as regards religion and the salvation of the human race; theirs is a religious history, not a civil one... But at all events they provide excellent material for the reconstruction of the civil history of those times';[19] here, if his approach is that of a Catholic, he is a good philologist, and can calmly accept the whole of the statement by the Protestant and 'Wellhausenian' Robertson Smith.

With the recent *History of Israel* by J.Alberto Soggin, which has also been translated into English,[20] Protestant historiography of a German type has also made its appearance in Italy. Soggin is sensitive to the critical demands which have been made in many quarters in Italy recently, but while allowing them a certain weight in fact he does not take account of them. His exposition begins with David, but the presentation, with full discussions, of the period from Abraham to the Judges, is merely postponed, to after Solomon; almost a third of the 'history of Israel' is devoted to the ancient traditions, which are held to be substantially valid and are therefore substantially accepted as historical. In fact Soggin affirms: 'What does seem improbable, though, is that the redactors created a considerable number of texts from scratch, presenting them as though they were ancient and thus filling in gaps in the content with their imagination. Certainly there are texts the late character of which is now generally recognized: Gen.14 and 24; Ex.19.1ff. and a great many others like I Sam.17; however, it is not easy to show that these were created by the redactors. At all events we need to recognize that even these texts are the exception and not the rule, and it would not be strange if the redactors had drawn from contemporary temple traditions or popular traditions the material which our analyses prove to be late' (28f.; we read almost identical words again on p.31). So these are reliable traditions, and also ancient: 'So we must conclude that, leaving aside the possibility of rereadings and later reinterpretation, the nucleus of the patriarchal narratives can be traced back without any difficulty to the period of the united monarchy' (90), i.e. to the tenth century BC.

The beginning of history proper is with David, because only with him are the methodological demands of the historian satisfied, i.e. when the 'material in the tradition begins to offer credible accounts, information about individuals who existed and events which happened or are at least probable, when it indicates important events in the economic and political sphere, and their consequences' (26). In the biblical account relating to David and Solomon, 'behind the façade of family life, we begin to find important information which the historian can use, all of which seems very plausible. That is why I think that the united reign of David and Solomon is a good point from which to begin the history of Israel' (31). It remains to be asked what the criterion is for judging material 'which the historian can use', i.e. which is valid for historical

reconstruction, certain biblical data as opposed to others; Soggin replies
here with a general statement (even if it does refer to the united
monarchy): 'the information we are given is often so important in the
political and economic sphere that it would be strange had it been
invented' (47), and with a perhaps unintentional practical example:
'Another feature seems historically certain: at the end of the so-called
edict of Artaxerxes (Ezra 7.12ff.; though its authenticity is open to
dispute) we find an important assertion: the "law" becomes the law of
the state and is administered with the aid of public powers' (277). In
short, the criterion of truthfulness is that of the importance of the
information; if it is important and true, and also if it is provided by an
unexpected text (note that the adjective 'important' is present in all the
four passages quoted).

It remains, finally, to call attention to the presence of biblical archaeology in Soggin's work. An appendix written by D.Conrad (357-67) and
briefly anticipated on 164f. first presents the problems of (Syro-)
Palestinian archaeology and then suggests a new model for the settlement
of the Hebrews in Palestine. The central hill-country (Ephraim and
Manasseh), that of Judah and the Negeb, that of Galilee and Transjordan
(Gilead) – and therefore the whole of Palestine with the exception of
the valley of Esdraelon – seems to have been populated, at the beginning
of the Iron Age, with 'countless new villages, largely unfortified'; there
is a 'vigorous activity of settlement throughout the country'. However,
'nothing can yet be said on the basis of archaeological evidence about
the origin of these settlers or the ethnic groups to which they belonged'
(364); 'It remains amazing how quickly in this new society people could
come to worship a common God YHWH' (510). What is amazing,
rather, is the fact that Soggin has included this last discovery of biblical
archaeology in his book and has fully accepted it on p.163 having written
on pp.161f.: 'One of the facts that we may consider to have been
established over the last ten to fifteen years is that the transition from
the end of the Bronze Age to the beginning of the Iron Age in Syria and
Palestine was not characterized by any breaks in continuity worth noting.
The only true element is provided by Philistine pottery... Moreover, and
I have stressed this often, there are no relevant traces of the settlement
of a new population in the region.'[20b]

This attitude of trust in the historical validity of the biblical sources
does not appear, in Italy as elsewhere, to be limited to confessional
circles. In February 1920, Giorgio Levi Della Vida gave an inaugural
lecture on the history of Israel.[21] In it, having paid a frankly undeserved

tribute to 'biblical science',[22] the scholar acutely hit on the fundamental character of the 'history of Israel': 'What both schools, the dogmatic and the critical, are concerned to understand and narrate is not the life of the people of Israel in its entirety, but the origin and development of its religion.' Going on to pursue his theme, the secular character of the history of Israel, Levi Della Vida showed that he accepted current (Protestant) opinions on the reconstruction of the events of Hebrew history: 'Whether the picture of patriarchal life has a purely legendary character or reflects real historical events, it is certain that the framework in which it is to be put has been verified by recent archaeological investigations'; 'with David it [viz.Israel] achieves complete independence, definitively defeating the Philistines and subjecting the Edomites...; with Solomon, heir and continuer of his father's fortune, access is opened to the sea by establishing peaceful relations with the Phoenician cities and through the territory of the Edomites reaching the port of Aqaba on the Red Sea. During the reign of Solomon Israel exercised unchallenged its supremacy over neighbouring states; for rather more than a quarter of the century it was the dominant power in the south-eastern Mediterranean basin.' A little later, in his article on 'Hebrews' in the *Enciclopedia Italiana Treccani* (1913),[23] Levi Della Vida defined the book of Samuel as a 'collection of sources of the first order' and in connection with the histories of David and Solomon considered that these facts were 'mainly narrated on the basis of chronicles and contemporary documents' having 'for the most part the character of a primary source'. Other scholars who have been concerned to trace the history of the Hebrews in the context of a universal history[24] or to include it in a textbook of the history of the ancient Near East have been guided by similar criteria.[25] The perceptive study by G.Buccellati of the political institutions in the area of Syria and Palestine,[26] carried out with those of Israel particularly in mind, nowhere raises the question of the value of the Hebrew sources, using them as they appear in the Bible. The illuminating parallel which Arnaldo Momigliano has put forward between the autobiographies of Nehemiah and Ezra and the beginnings of Greek historiography[27] also begins from the presupposition of the total authenticity and antiquity of the biblical texts.[28] Nor was the attitude of F.Pintore,[29] a scholar who died prematurely, any different in using the data provided by the Old Testament.[30]

However, for some years past, particularly in Italy, there has been some impatience with a historical reconstruction of the history of ancient Israel which in practice is limited to repeating the biblical narrative, an impatience evident not only in what one can call the lay[31] sphere but also in the Catholic sphere.[32] What is too often forgotten is that the Old Testament is a religious book and not a history book: even when we find historiography in it we must remember that this is always 'sacred' history, something much more complex than Arnaldo Momigliano would have us believe when he writes that 'the basic elements of a sacred history are in Livy as much as in the Pentateuch'.[33] A 'sacred' history has rules of its own and can easily be confused with a 'myth', but fortunately this is not the case with the history of Israel, at least from the time that Israel was settled in Palestine. Because the essential characteristic of Hebrew religion is the adoption of history as the vehicle for a myth *sui generis*; it is the historical event itself which, seen in a certain way, becomes myth; so that the earthly fortunes of the elect people are a direct manifestation of the work and the will of God.

In this perspective, which is historical and theological at the same time, there is no room for a history writing which leaves theological preoccupations out of account. We are well aware that no historiography is ideologically neutral and that every historical narrative reflects in a more or less veiled form a particular world-view. What distinguishes the history narrated by the Old Testament from all others is not the presence of an ideological motivation which controls the exposition of events but the fact that the ideological motivation has a determinative value and often conditions and directs the historical narrative itself; because of this we talk of 'sacred' history. It is the confusion of the 'sacred' character of the biblical account (a sacrality which is typologically identical to that of the 'sacred' histories all over the world, from Sumeria to the Amerindians) with a supposed 'sacrality' of the Hebrew people which has led so many theologians to fantasize over characteristics claimed to be peculiar to Israel, at the very moment when they have been claiming to make 'secular' a history which was thought of and written as 'sacred'.

Moreover, the authors of the biblical text knew very well what they were doing. When the 'Deuteronomistic historian' (or whoever) treats the Hebrew monarchy in the way with which we are familiar we can affirm that he is choosing and co-ordinating certain objective data with a view to a certain thesis. The kings were substantially the same, but chronology, undertakings, affinity and dynasty could be manipulated at will; if a ruler was forgotten it was possible to invent another one. Things begin to change when we go back to the previous period, that of the earliest Hebrew presence in Palestine, from the 'conquest' to the 'judges': a historically turbulent and obscure period for which, in contrast to that of the monarchy, there are no external points of reference (and this very lack is significant). We have no evidence that the 'judges' ever existed and that possibly they never bore the title 'king'; nor is there sure information about a Hebrew conquest. There is, however, the Merneptah stele, which attests that in the thirteenth century BC there was a group of semi-nomads in Palestine which called itself Israel. Between this tribe of Israel and the kingdom of Israel in central Palestine there must have been a historical development, a territorial, ethnic and social settlement of those who then came to form the Hebrew people – events, in short, not all that dissimilar from those narrated in the book of Judges; not all the judges of whom the memory has been handed down will have been mythical figures like the left-handed Ehud, the Hebrew Mucius Scaevola,[34] or heroes of romances like Samson. So we can say that we have here the protohistory of Israel, something analogous to the monarchical period of ancient Rome.

Going back still further in time, we come to the exodus from Egypt, preceded by the harshness of the stay there, and to the patriarchal period. On the first it is important to note that the exodus is too basic an element in Hebrew religion for us not to suspect that the theological component has come to dominate the historical component completely. In principle, it is quite probable that Semitic people first settled in Egypt and then left it, but in this case it is absolutely impossible to verify the event. As for the patriarchs, the accounts relating to them have a characteristic which distinguishes them from the others: with the exception of their origin in Mesopotamia and Abraham's mysterious war (which we shall be considering in due course), they do not provide information of a historical kind: we have family happenings, religious episodes, romance-like events. These are facts outside time, which for that very reason have been open to dating to the most varied periods by modern biblical scholars, from the middle of the third to the middle of the first millennium BC. The patriarchal period is in reality a period outside time and history, because that is what the biblical narrator wanted; by making these archetypal figures move against a background which is outside historical time (as is also the case with their superhuman longevity), the author has indicated in his own a way mythical time: the time in which God talked directly with men and came down beside them. This Hebrew myth is of course rationalized myth, which makes it as it were a prologue to the real historical development. The Bible has indicated very clearly that the time of the patriarchs was a time structurally different from that in which the Hebrew people acted later; it has been only the approximative criticism of German theologians and their like which has accepted their assertions, creating the fable of the historicity of the patriarchs.

There is no longer anything new about asserting that the Old Testament offers a series of reflections by Israel on its history rather than the history of Israel;[35] however, it must be stressed that these are not so much historical reflections (though sometimes these are there, too) as theological reflections. That means that the value of the Old Testament as a historical source is very relative and that a particular piece of information cannot be considered reliable until it has been confirmed from elsewhere. For different reasons we also find ourselves in the same position with ancient Arabic historiography relating to Arab origins and South Arabian civilization just before the rise of Islam: a 'mass of fables... which, together with the historical elements that parallels with the inscriptions [South Arabian] make incontrovertible, form the true nature of this legend: not forgetful of real glories, an expression of the vanity of the group, but also evidence of the "delight in story-telling" and the need for pious religious fraud and harmonization along with the religious demands in which the Jewish elements also share.'[36] Like the history of the ancient Yemenites, so the history of the Hebrews could be written only with the determinative help of external sources[37] which would allow us to evaluate the value of the biblical data; in using data it is not enough to establish the period of the texts from which it is drawn, as has been done hitherto far (and wrongly: the texts are all thought to be much older than they really are); it is essential to establish the nature and purpose of the biblical writings, especially the narrative ones. It is the nature, not the date of a narrative text which determines the degree of historical validity to be attached to it (it is obvious that a text always has a validity of its own, even if it narrates 'facts' which are a complete invention).

So if we turn to the question that we raised to begin with, namely what we know of the history of Israel, we must accept that the answer is rather disappointing: outside what is in the Bible, we know virtually nothing of Hebrew history. The Assyrian and Babylonian texts, the inscription of Mesha of Moab and a few Hebrew texts give us some names of kings and some events between the ninth and the sixth century BC; more detailed information is provided by the Jewish-Hellenistic literature from the time of Alexander the Great. This is a complex of data markedly inferior to what we have on the Phoenicians and the Aramaeans, from whom not one directly historical text has come down to us,[38] but from whom we possess a certain number of historical inscriptions.

This observation brings us to a problem which I believe to be of the utmost importance, even if it has hardly ever been raised, at least in terms of results. The extreme scarcity, amounting almost to the non-existence, of epigraphic evidence relating to the Hebrew people and coming from the cultures which lived in contact with them over long centuries does not cause us any surprise, so used have we become for more than a century now to be content with the inscription of king Mesha as being the only historical evidence left by the nearest of those who knew the people of the Bible. A somewhat symptomatic fact is that this same lack of wonderment can also be seen at another observation: the virtually complete absence of Hebrew epigraphy that can be described as historical in the strict sense. The empire of David and Solomon, the powerful northern kingdom, the long-lived southern kingdom with its Davidic dynasty have left not even a single document relating to their existence; not one of the forty kings, from Saul to Zedekiah, has left a direct trace of his name; we do not even have any votive inscription from the famous temple of Solomon, as we do for all the other temples of antiquity.

The virtually complete silence of epigraphy on Hebrew history seems all the more disconcerting when we compare it with the epigraphic evidence from neighbouring peoples: Phoenicians, Aramaeans, Moabites, Philistines and now even Ammonites have left more or less numerous inscriptions, if only just one, but in them we find a record of the names and actions of rulers, of relations with neighbouring peoples, of wars and works of peace. The lack of historical Hebrew inscriptions cannot be considered a matter of chance: it becomes a historical problem which must be approached as such.

Omri and his dynasty were known to Mesha and the Assyrian rulers, who will have had good knowledge of Jehu, Menahem, Pekah, Azariah, Ahaz, Hezekiah and so on. Is it possible to suppose that none of these kings, some of whom achieved greater political power than that of their neighbours, ever wrote his name on a stone, as all the other kings usually did? Frankly, that seems improbable; it seems improbable that it is mere chance which has led to the rediscovery of the inscription of one Moabite ruler of a certain importance and the loss of *all* the Hebrew royal inscriptions. It is impossible to give a definite answer to this problem. But there seems to me to be a glimpse of one possible answer: just as the present biblical text is the result of a series of choices from texts otherwise doomed to rapid oblivion (see the case of the Qumran writings) and of a series of successive revisions which usually led to the disuse of the previous text (the only exceptions are the complex of Samuel-Kings over against Chronicles and, thanks to the Christians, I Esdras), so the transformation of Hebrew and Jewish ideology in time led to the *damnatio memoriae* of the monarchy and all the documents relating to it: all the royal inscriptions, which cannot have been numerous and which were probably to be found only in the capital cities, were systematically destroyed. One pointer in favour of this hypothesis is the existence of a fragment of an inscription from a monument found in Samaria and often transcribed by epigraphists: this is a fragment of stone of a few square centimetres on which one can read only the word *'šr*, perhaps the remains of the customary formula 'stele *which* king So and So of So and So placed...' We can only guess at what led to the destruction of the inscriptions: hatred of the institution of the monarchy? That is probable. Or the need to remove information which contradicted the historical reconstruction offered by the sacred texts? That cannot be ruled out. That this sort of thing really happened is documented by one of the earliest rabbinic texts, the *Megillat Ta'anit* ('Scroll of the Fast') dated to the first century AD. Among the Jewish feast days which commemorated particularly significant events there was one, 3 Tishri, which recalled the time when 'the memory of the documents was eliminated';[39] the extremely laconic nature of the saying does not allow us to see what it is about, but this very characteristic seems suspect in relation to all the other days for which the episode celebrated is clearly specified. The day may not have been specifically about the destruction of the royal inscriptions, but if the Hebrews did celebrate a *damnatio memoriae* that means that there were others of a routine kind.

Whether or not the inscriptions were destroyed, the problem of the absence of royal epigraphy remains; there could be various solutions, but there is one that we can rule out immediately, i.e. the suggestion that the Hebrew kings never produced inscriptions for religious reasons. Everything that we know about the culture of pre-exilic Israel confirms that there were no structural or ideological differences between the Israelites and the neighbouring peoples; and all the rulers of these peoples produced inscriptions.[40]

All that has been said so far leads to an unexpected but inevitable conclusion. The Old Testament has set out a sacred history of universal value, but it is not very reliable as evidence of a secular history of the kind that the Hebrew people actually experienced. The peoples who lived alongside the Israelites (Philistines, Moabites, Ammonites, Aramaeans, Phoenicians) did not write much about themselves (but the most important Aramaean and Phoenician cities have still to be excavated), and with just one exception they never seem to have referred to their neighbours. The Hebrews were mentioned only by the Assyrians and Babylonians when they subjected them: but in the Mesopotamian texts the Hebrew kings were in good company, alongside rulers and heads of tribes much less important than they were. In short, we can note that the Israelites did not make much of an impression on those who knew them; it was not for nothing that others called the land which they inhabited by the name of the Philistines, not by that of the Israelites. And what material traces have the Hebrews left of themselves? Hebrew inscriptions are attested only between the eighth century and the first decades of the sixth century BC, for only two centuries, in a very limited area of Palestine: the boundaries of this area are fixed in the north by a line between Yabneh Yam (some kilometres south of Tel Aviv) and the northern shore of the Dead Sea, to the east by its western shore, to the south by the desert of Sinai, and to the west by the cities of the plain, all Philistine. Around this quadrilateral there are only Phoenician inscriptions (the Phoenician language was also used by the Ammonites) and Moabite, Aramaic and North Arabic inscriptions.[41] These chronological and geographical boundaries contrast with the Old Testament narrative, but confirm the decidedly secondary role that the extra-Hebraic evidence assigns to the Israelites. Only the Bible remains as evidence of what they would have liked, but did not happen.

The discussion so far has been largely about the period before the Babylonian exile; after the exile, the situation is even more strange. One would expect, as is the case with all historical evidence, that it would become progressively richer the further down in time it went. However, in the case of the Hebrews that does not happen. If before the exile we have the Mesha stele and mentions in the Mesopotamian texts, after the exile there is not a single extra-Jewish source which speaks of the Jews before the time of Alexander the Great; and even after Alexander the notices in Greek writers are as rare as they are vague, and in any case are works written in Greek by the Jews themselves. As to the extra-biblical Jewish documentation, relatively rich in Judah in the seventh and at the beginning of the sixth century BC, with the sole exception of the Elephantine papyri, which shed light on a Jewish military colony in upper Egypt during the Achaemenidean period, the epigraphic and archaeological remains are reduced to a tiny quantity until well in to the

Hellenistic period. During the Achaemenidean period and the beginning of the Hellenistic period Palestine (apart from the coast) seems almost deserted, and no one seems to note the existence of its few and poor inhabitants, far less its Jewish inhabitants: Herodotus talks of 'Syria called Palestine' (3.91) inhabited partly by Arabs (ibid.) and partly by Philistines (3.5: 'Syrians called Palestinians', *Palaistinoi*).

One last consideration to complete the picture. Hebrew culture before the exile had some form of historiography which at a later date made it possible to know the names and actions of the rulers encountered fairly precisely. From the exile to the time of Alexander the Great Judaism did not entrust the record of its happenings to any writing (for the so-called 'memorials' of Nehemiah and Ezra see Chapter 13) – two and a half centuries elapsed across which a distant history had to be recalled, and passed without history.

Chapter 2

David's Empire

Ancient Hebrew historiography set out a grandiose design of the history of Israel, from the creation of the world, as was customary at the time,[1] to 135 BC (from Genesis to I Maccabees), putting the most significant moment in the tenth century BC, when David created an empire and Solomon made it resplendent with glory and riches, like a 'Sun King' – and the deluge came after him.

It is difficult to deny that this historical framework gives the impression of being nearer to the mythical vision of an original golden age than to a convincing reconstruction of human actions; and yet it has never given rise to doubts or discussions, and has been accepted as it stands by all those – and there are a great many of them – who have been concerned with Hebrew history in one way or another. It is certainly one of the most remarkable phenomena of Western culture that a couple of centuries which have been characterized first by historical criticism (which has not often been hypercritical) on a philological basis and then by an anatomical analysis, which is nowadays one of the most vigorously waved banners, has so far left no trace on modern historiography relating to ancient Israel. Even now there is no *History of Israel* which on David and Solomon (or indeed on the whole of Hebrew history) offers anything other than a paraphrase, more or less disguised or intelligent, of the ancient biblical text with its glorious Davidic empire.[2]

The pages which follow do not claim to be a reconstruction of a century of Hebrew history; they are limited to presenting some rapid observations which might help a future historian of Israel to see rather more clearly in the all too brilliant tenth century BC.

Leaving aside I Kings 5.1,4 [EVV 4.21,25] with their exaggerated extension of the Davidic empire, which have long been recognized as late amplifications[3] (it is enough to recall, among other things, that the two verses are repeated in the Septuagint and in passages different from those in which they appear in the Massoretic text), it is impossible not to note some contradictions in the body of the narratives relating to David and Solomon. David is first presented as a page of Saul, with the task of distracting the king with his music (I Sam.16.14ff.), but then appears as the young shepherd, completely unknown to Saul, who has killed Goliath (I Sam.17). However, this latter episode is contradicted by II Sam.21.19, according to which the person who killed Goliath is said to have been not the young David but the warrior Elhanan, who is then said to have become one of David's thirty 'men of valour' (the two contradictory pieces of information have been piously harmonized by I Chron.20.5, which makes Elhanan kill a brother of Goliath!). Then there is Achish, the Philistine ruler of Gath, with whom David, who is stil a warrior, takes refuge for a year and four months (I Sam.27.2ff.); II Sam.8.1 says that David took Gath from the Philistines, but in I Kings 2.39 we find that Achish is again ruler of the city (forty-five years after his first meeting with David). Granted, these are not particularly striking contradictions, given that they have been noted in the past without any need being felt to change the general lines of the biblical narrative. And yet these contradictions are quite significant indications of the real nature of the Israelite 'historical sources'; the invention of the episode of Goliath, in open conflict with other information which no one was bothered to eliminate, is a symbolic instance: the evident falsity of the anecdote (*on ne donne qu'aux riches*) did not prevent it from acquiring a universal resonance, while no historian has asked whether any other story about David has been invented in addition to that of his victory over the giant Philistine.

Not only does the biblical account of David and Solomon contain late additions and internal contradictions; there is also information in it which is worth going into more deeply. According to I Kings 9.10ff., Hiram, king of Tyre, is still alive, and lived for twenty years after the start of the building of the temple and the reign of Solomon (which according to the biblical information lasted seven and thirty years respectively); this start took place in the fourth year of the reign of the Israelite king. So Hiram ruled at least during the first twenty-four years of Solomon's reign. But before Solomon, Hiram was a friend of his father David, for whom he built a palace after Jerusalem was conquered (II Sam.5.11). Since David transferred his residence to Jerusalem after reigning seven years in Hebron, and we know that Hiram was a friend of David 'all the days' of his reign (I Kings 5.1), we have to accept that

Hiram reigned contemporaneously with David for a minimum of thirty years; this gives us a *minimum* figure of fifty-four years for the reign of the good king of Tyre. This figure is not humanly impossible, but no one is going to accept it lightly; all the more since according to the so-called Annals of Tyre quoted by Flavius Josephus king Hiram lived only fifty-three years and reigned only for thirty-four.[4] Since the absolute chronology of the king of Tyre does not make it possible for him to be a contemporary of both the two great Israelite kings, as could easily be foreseen, Josephus opted for sacrificing the long friendship of Hiram with David, instead bringing out (as indeed does the biblical text) that of Hiram with Solomon. However, the Jewish historian had an accident in his working which led him to make a mistake while manipulating the information, with some boldness. Whereas in the *Jewish Antiquities* (8,62) he had stated that the beginning of the building of the Jerusalem temple had taken place in the eleventh year of Hiram (which would therefore correspond to the fourth year of Solomon), in *Contra Apionem* (1,126) he says that the temple was built (in the sense of being completed) in the twentieth year of Hiram (which would therefore correspond to the eleventh year of Solomon). The discrepancy of seven years between the two contradictory chronologies given by Josephus would not be so serious did it not reveal a fact the gravity of which cannot be concealed: the historian does not provide objective information, but the result of his own more or less correct calculations, aimed at matching the biblical chronology to extra-biblical information.[5] The chronology of the kings of Tyre which is displayed here with a mass of detail is aimed simply at demonstrating that 'in these [i.e. in the Annals of Tyre] it is written that in Jerusalem the temple was built by King Solomon 143 years and 8 months before Tyre founded Carthage' (*Contra Apionem* I,108), thus relying, evidently rightly, on the gullibility of readers who would have found it quite natural that what happened in Jerusalem was recorded in Tyre, not to mention calculating the year with a reference to future events. Since the year cited with such exactness in *Contra Apionem* does not correspond to that given in the *Jewish Antiquities*, it seems clear that there was virtually nothing in the Annals of Tyre about Jerusalem and its temple. Flavius Josephus, harmonizing the information in the Bible with that of the other ancient sources in his own way and without any concern to avoid contradictions, used precisely the same procedure as that followed by modern scholars who accept the biblical data without discussion, adapting everything else to them; Josephus was not a historian but simply the first *Alttestamentler* – and it is not for nothing that his

Jewish history, like the modern histories of Israel, is only a paraphrase of the biblical text.

That Josephus here to some degree also manipulated the data in the list of the kings of Tyre with their chronology is demonstrated by the fact that his version of the *Annals* conflicts with the information from non-Jewish origins – as often happens with the biblical text. Not many years ago the name of a king of Tyre appeared for the first time in an Assyrian inscription. This king lived in the period between the tenth century and the first half of the eighth century, a period for which Josephus gives the complete sequence of rulers from Hiram to Pygmalion: he was a certain Ba'limanzer, who paid tribute to Shalmaneser III in 840 BC.[6] But in the Annals, as far as Josephus is concerned, this king does not exist; supposing that Ba'li-manzer could be identified with Balezoros (which is no more than a hypothesis), the dates do not match, since the latter is said to have reigned from 855 to 850 BC.[7] Had it been another writer one might have supposed errors in the transmission of the text or something of that kind; but with a historian like Josephus with whom it is impossible to deny a not infrequent deliberate distortion of the facts for apologetic ends,[8] it is methodologically preferable to accept that this is a deliberate revision of names and figures.

In conclusion, we have come to the point of being able to affirm with absolute certainty that at least one of the pieces of information given by the biblical text in connection with Hiram of Tyre is wrong: either he was not a friend of David for a long time and therefore did not build a palace for him, or he was not a friend of Solomon for a long time, or it is not true that David and Solomon each ruled forty years and that twenty years in all were necessary for building the palace and the temple at Jerusalem. There is no doubt that for the biblical scholar the first possibility is the least loss and that, like Josephus, he will be disposed to drop the friendship with David. However, that means increasing the number of false pieces of information relating to this ruler: if David did not kill Goliath and did not have a long relationship with Hiram, it is legitimate also to begin to nurture suspicions about the rest (nor can it be forgotten that quite late psalms were attributed to the king, as for example Ps.20, which comes from the Hellenistic period).[9] On the other hand, it cannot be ignored that it was Solomon's friendship with Hiram which so greatly kindled the imagination of later Israelites, with the invention of the little story of the riddles exchanged between the two kings (a story duly reported by Joseph as true, with two sources)[10] and that of the correspondence between the two rulers kept at Tyre, according to Josephus 'down to the present day' (*Contra Apionem* 1,111). This progressive accretion of legends around the two Israelite sovereigns certainly does not favour a positive judgment on the other facts recorded by the 'historical sources'; what guarantee do we have that the rest was not also invented at an earlier stage?

Another point on which it is worth dwelling for a better estimation of the nature of the biblical sources is that of the wars fought by David, wars which are meant to justify the creation of the great empire enjoyed, and then lost, by Solomon. In his youth David, forced to defend himself against Saul, took refuge among the Philistines and under their protection made raids on his own account: in particular there is a record of one against the Amalekites (I Sam.30). When Saul died, David was anointed king in his place at the age of thirty (II Sam.5.4); for the first years of his reign, in practice the period during which he ruled in Hebron (seven years), David fought against the heirs of Saul (II Sam.3-4, 'there was a long war between the house of Saul and the house of David', 3.1). Hardly had he been chosen king of Judah and Israel than he moved the capital to Jerusalem, but immediately had to face attacks by the Philistines (II Sam.5.17). There followed a series of victorious campaigns against the Philistines, the Moabites, the Idumaeans, the Ammonites and the Amalekites (II Sam.8). The wars, obviously victorious, against the Aramaeans merit a separate mention: in II Sam.8, the chapter which is the culmination of all the military victories of David, it is said that these were over the Aramaeans of Zobah and subsequently the Aramaeans of Damascus who had come to the aid of the former, and that David established military garrisons to control the territory of Damascus. These facts, however, appear in II Sam.10 in a notably different form: David conquers and subjects (in a general way; the text says that they 'served' David) the Aramaeans of Zobah and other cities which had been claimed by the Ammonites, but there is no mention of Damascus. Since this city seems to acquire importance only after it became the capital of Rezin, an official of the king of Zobah who secured his own independence (this seems to have happened only after the death of David), the hypothesis that the presence of the Aramaeans of Damascus in II Sam.8.5-6 is a later addition, as the very structure of the whole insertion leads one to suspect, becomes quite probable.

According to the biblical narrative, then, David conquered and subjected Philistines, Edomites, Moabites, Ammonites and Aramaeans; in other words, he made himself master of all Palestine, Transjordan and the south-western part of Syria. All that happened, according to what the biblical text says, in the first years of the reign of David in Jerusalem: the Philistines were conquered when they attacked the newly united kingdom of Judah and Israel, while the war against the Ammonites (and their allies, the Aramaeans) took place soon afterwards; David took advantage of this war to seduce Bathsheba, the future mother of Solomon. Later it was no longer possible to wage important wars: the rebellion of David's son Absalom who forced him to flee Jerusalem and then the secession of Israel, which was put down, certainly did not allow imperialistic wars. Moreover, the empire of David was of short duration because already on the death of David both the Edomites and the Aramaeans regained their independence (I Kings 11.14-25); the dominion of Solomon, far from extending from the frontier of Egypt to the Euphrates (as I Kings 5.1,4 [4.21,25] has it) did not include either a spur of Syria or southern Palestine. However, we may have some doubts about the real extent of the Davidic empire, which are caused by reading the biblical text itself (note that so far our analysis has remained within that text). When we read in I Sam.14.47 that 'when Saul had taken the kingship over Israel, he fought against all his enemies on every side, against Moab, against the Ammonites, against Edom, against the kings of Zobah, and against the Philistines; wherever he turned he put them to the worse', we discover that the much-hymned empire of David is simply a repetition of the negligible empire of Saul, who after all did not have even the addition of Judah. Was Saul greater than David, then, or is this simply a literary theme applied to all the Israelite kings when they accorded with religion?

There is one way of providing an answer to this question and checking the real size of David's achievements (real, obviously, from the point of view of a biblical writer); this is to look at the great warlike deeds of David's 'men of valour', his faithful bodyguard on whom he relied (II Sam.23.8ff.). All the men of valour of whom resounding actions are recorded fought against the Philistines except for Benaiah, who distinguished himself in a war against the Moabites. All the other glorious wars fought by David find the 'men of valour' strangely absent. According to the tradition (which must be quite old) which gives the names of David's closest collaborators, these therefore fought wars exclusively against the Philistines and the Moabites, i.e. against the most immediate neighbours of Judah and Israel; and it is under the shadow of this tradition that in II Sam.7.1 we read that after entering Jerusalem 'the king dwelt in his house since Yahweh had given him rest from all his enemies round about'. So it is evident that in the Old Testament itself there were two contrasting traditions about king David: one, which was more extensive, made him a warrior king who equalled, with better fortune, the empire of his predecessor Saul; another, however, saw in David one who had succeeded in creating a modest but solid position in Jerusalem, after military victories over the powerful Philistines (and then, probably, by allying himself with them).

A simple analysis of the biblical text, without any recourse to 'higher criticism' of the sources, has clearly revealed how historically unreliable it is for the unwary scholar. The fortunate minstrel of Saul who after some vicissitudes succeeded in ascending the throne of his old master[11] is then transformed into the young national hero, the conqueror of an empire (which from the perspective of Jerusalem must have seemed enormous), the friend of a powerful and prestigious neighbour. His successor, whose inability to keep his father's heritage intact is admitted and whose figure is subsequently exalted for his religious merits (the building of the temple), is presented as the symbol of power and opulence. Does this image of Solomon stand up to criticism?

One of the high points of Solomon's reign, duly stressed by the historians, is his marriage to the Pharaoh's daughter, who brings him as a dowry the city of Gezer which her father has just conquered (and destroyed) (I Kings 3.1; 9.16). This was a city which, it should be said in passing, we should expect already to be included in the great empire of David (as the crow flies it is little more than twenty miles from Jerusalem). This marriage, apparently a secondary matter, in reality has very great political importance. Recent studies have in fact allowed us to note the quite exceptional position of the Egyptian rulers as compared to those of Asia (including the Hittites and the Babylonians) over inter-dynastic marriages:[12] the Pharaohs were the only rulers to marry foreign princesses but *never* to give Egyptian princesses to foreign rulers. In this situation, which only now has appeared in all its clarity,[13] the presence of an Egyptian princess in Solomon's harem stands out quite amazingly: this fact must have conferred an enormous prestige on Solomon in the eyes of the Israelites, but at the same time it must invite the modern historian to maximum caution.

A daughter of the Pharaoh given in marriage to an Asian king must have been such an extraordinary event that it could not pass unobserved, and in fact it has been remembered. The remarkable thing is that the protagonists of such an event have not been recorded: we do not know the name of the Pharaoh, we do not know the name of the woman who was most certainly the most illustrious spouse of an Israelite king (nor can it be said that the Bible has been niggardly with the names of queens and princesses); it has to be admitted that this is rather strange. Even if the great improbability, not to say the impossibility, of a marriage between an Asian king and the daughter of a Pharaoh has not yet been noted, the exceptional character of such an event has not escaped notice; so it is generally said that the Pharaohs of the Twenty-first Dynasty were weak in order to justify such an unusual attitude. However, it is legitimate to cast some doubt on this supposed Egyptian weakness: certainly Egypt was in a position of decadence, but this was after all the decadence of a great nation. Notwithstanding the scanty information that there is on the Twenty-first Dynasty, at any rate it is true that the fourth ruler of the dynasty, Pinedjem I, attained a considerable degree of power; given that the beginning of the dynasty is to be put at 1085 BC and that Pinedjem reigned at least sixteen years, this period of Egyptian revival is to be connected with the last decades of the eleventh century BC (in terms of biblical history that brings us to the time of Saul). Some decades later, towards the beginning of the tenth century BC, the Pharaoh Siamun, who reigned at least seventeen years, led an expedition against Palestine (and we are in the time of David or of Solomon himself); in the second half of the tenth century another great military expedition against Palestine was led by Sheshonk, the founder of the Twenty-second Dynasty, who reigned at least twenty-one years (according to I Kings 14.25 the expedition took place in the fifth year of Rehoboam, who succeeded Solomon on the throne in Jerusalem). In the light of this information provided by Egyptian documentation and confirmed by Palestinian archaeology, it becomes difficult to argue for so deep and lengthy an Egyptian weakness in order to justify a marriage to a Palestine ruler in conditions of inferiority. But there are also other considerations. Scholars are fond of saying that it was this very Pharaoh Siamun who became Solomon's father-in-law: in this way the Egyptian presence in Palestine is connected with the note about the conquest of Gezer by the Pharaoh who was Solomon's father-in-law. But how can we believe that a Pharaoh who made a military intervention in Palestine, obviously to safeguard Egyptian interests and to put down the stirrings of autonomy, should give his own daughter in marriage to one of the kings of the conquered region? And shifting the argument: is it conceivable that the dowry of a Pharaoh (a gift which should have been worthy of the person giving it) could be reduced to a destroyed city which Solomon was then forced to rebuild at his own expense (I Kings 9.17)? From whatever point of view we look at it, the marriage of Solomon to the daughter of a Pharaoh seems improbable.

Then there is the problem of the chronology of Pharaoh Sheshonk, a problem closely connected with Solomon. The passage I Kings 14.25, which has already been mentioned, fixes the Pharaoh's Palestinian expedition in the fifth year of Rehoboam. On the Egyptian side the only chronological information is that this expedition is recorded, with a wealth of details about the conquered cities, in a great relief made on the wall of a portico added to the temple of Karnak, a work which an inscription dates to the twenty-first year of the ruler.[14] The total lack of absolute chronological data has forced Egyptologists to base the chronology of the Twenty-first Dynasty exclusively on biblical parallelism, so that for a couple of centuries the Egyptian chronology is made to depend on biblical chronology.[15] The need for biblical scholars to make Sheshonk reign the least possible time alongside Solomon, indeed to leave Solomon the possibility of being for a long time a contemporary to the last Pharaohs of the 'weak' Twenty-first dynasty and even of Siamun himself, clashes with the need of the Egyptologists not to go too far from the 124 or 130 years that Manetho assigns to the Twenty-first Dynasty; if the beginning of this is put at 1085 BC, too late a date for Shoshenk, as for example that fixed by W.F.Albright (935-914 BC) who had Solomon die in 922 BC,[16] would make this dynasty last too long. To reconcile the opposed needs of biblical chronology and Egyptian chronology, on the one hand the chronology of Solomon is made as early as possible, so that the forty years of his reign are now put between 970 and 940 BC, and on the other the end of the Twenty-first Dynasty is made as late as possible, at 950 or 945 BC; the hinge is formed by the date of the Palestinian expedition which it has now been agreed to fix, in a quite arbitrary way, in the twentieth year of Sheshonk. Since, as we have seen, the twenty-first year of Sheshonk is only a *terminus ante quem*, the campaign could have taken place many years before; only the first years of Sheshonk's reign are excluded, when he had to overcome internal difficulties: it seems reasonable to suppose that the Pharaoh led his troop to Palestine at a date somewhere between the tenth and twentieth year of his reign.

According to current chronology, the fifth year of Rehoboam's reign lies in 925 BC and Sheshonk is said to have reigned between 945 and 924 BC. However, if we leave aside the biblical chronology and the inferences of the biblical scholars, fixing for Sheshonk the approximate but quite reasonable dates of 950-929 BC, also accepting that the

Palestine campaign took place in the king's twentieth year, this proves
to be during the reign of Solomon (that applies all the more if for this
ruler we follow the dates of those biblical scholars who are less concerned
with the Egyptian synchronism and who date Solomon's death around
925 BC). Even accepting the late dating of Sheshonk (945-924 BC) it is
enough to accept (quite legitimately) that the Palestine expedition took
place before the twentieth year to explode the biblical synchronism with
the fifth year of Rehoboam.

In conclusion, an analysis of the chronology completely discredits the
biblical information that Sheshonk's Palestinian expedition took place
in the fifth year of Rehoboam. The expedition took place before then;
it is enough to say that in all probability Sheshonk invaded Palestine
during the reign of Solomon and that he conquered Gezer in the time
of Solomon. In the light of all the information collected so far (the
political weakness of Solomon admitted by the Bible itself, the situation
of Egypt between the end of the eleventh century and the middle of the
tenth: Pinedjem I, Siamun, Sheshonk; the Pharaonic ideology over
inter-dynastic marriages) it proves impossible to accept that Solomon
could have married the daughter of a Pharaoh: these same data and the
chronological position moreover force us to accept that Sheshonk's
expedition could have taken place only during the reign of Solomon.
Postponing this unfortunate event to the time of Rehoboam was dictated
by the need not to dim the splendour which it was intended to create
around the reign of Solomon, while the sudden atttack by the Pharaoh
was transformed into an act of homage by means of the invention of too
prestigious a mariage. Such transformations of a situation are no novelty
for the Bible; in connection with Solomon the twenty Galilean villages
which he gave to Hiram in payment for the supply of wood (I Kings
9.11) later become twenty cities which Hiram gives to Solomon (II
Chron.8.2): and there was a Jewish historian who was able to make the
text talk of letters exchanged between Solomon and Pharaoh Apries.[17]

It is not worth dwelling on the building activity of Solomon inside and
outside Jerusalem: we know nothing about tenth-century BC Jerusalem,
and in the other three cities (Gezer, Hazor and Megiddo) to which the
attention of the sovereign was particularly directed (I Kings 9.15) the
identification of the 'Solomonic' stratum (i.e. that of the tenth century
BC), which is full of problems, cannot be considered sufficient proof
that these particular remains had anything to do with the king of
Jerusalem: it is obvious that in all the cities of Palestine (and outside it)
there must have been buildings from the time of Solomon. The point is

to demonstrate that a certain building of the 'Solomonic period' was built by the king of Jerusalem and no one else; and this has not yet been demonstrated for any Palestinian centre. It is, however, significant that at Megiddo, of all places, the city of the famous Solomonic 'stables', a stele of Pharaoh Sheshonk has been found: this is confirmation for my historical reconstruction rather than for that offered by the Bible. Nor does epigraphy give us much more help: the only Palestinian inscription of the tenth century BC that can in any way be connected with Solomon is the so-called agricultural 'calendar' of Gezer, but its peculiarities of language, morphology and vocabulary make it the product of those 'Canaanites' conquered by the Pharaoh and not of the later culture imported from Jerusalem.[18]

We have seen some improbable things among what Hebrew historiography attributes to Solomon and some probable things that this historiography did not know. Now I would like to dwell on a last point of a general kind: the commercial aspect of the reign of Solomon. It is well known that the Bible describes an extremely lively pattern of commercial activities on the part of David's son: an intercontinental fleet built with the help of Hiram of Tyre, based on Ezion-geber on the Red Sea, and a flourishing trade in chariots and horses imported from Cilicia and northern Syria (*Musri*, which erroneously became *Misrayim*, 'Egypt' in the Massoretic text, I Kings 10.11ff.). All this presupposes an intense commercial exchange on an international level (Phoenician navigation in the west, navigation on the Red Sea towards Yemen, traffic between Palestine and Phoenicia on the one side and Syria and Anatolia on the other) which is not only not confirmed in any way by archaeology[19] or texts but which has been discredited by most recent investigations. It in fact transpires that the commercial expansion of the Syrian and Hittite cities (those which are said to have ordered chariots and horses from Solomon) took place only in the ninth and eighth centuries BC.[20]

So at the end of our analysis we must accept that both a critical examination of the biblical text and the use of external data radically modify the picture that the Old Testament presents of the tenth century BC with its more detailed 'sources', which are also of a later date. David never killed Goliath, never knew Hiram of Tyre, never fought against the Idumaeans, Ammonites, Amalekites and Aramaeans and did not create an empire. If we are to believe the biblical text he fought only the Philistines and the Moabites and managed to establish himself as a ruler in Jerusalem after fighting against Saul, a king in whose service he previously was (the same thing had happened some centuries before with Idrimi of Alalakh). His son Solomon, who succeeded in preserving his father's small state, built a palace for himself with a small temple for the dynastic god as an annexe (the dimensions given by the biblical text, fifty metres by twenty-five, are exaggerated, as is shown by a comparison with the Syro-Palestinian temples of the time); but he did not marry any daughter of Pharaoh, did not enrich himself with international trade and was also in all probability forced to suffer the military expedition of Pharaoh Sheshonk. This is the most that can be conceded to the history of the biblical text (the least is to consider it a complete invention) from the point of view of a record of 'what actually happened'; all the rest is part of the story of Hebrew ideology.

If we leave aside the biblical traditions, the picture presented by tenth-century Palestine is all the dimmer, especially in comparison with the previous (twelfth and eleventh centuries) and the subsequent (ninth century) periods. Insignificant archaeological remains can certainly be related to this century; inscriptions are almost completely absent (though they were previously quite numerous); one has the impression of being at a time of crisis after the liveliness, even turbulence, connected with the settlement of the 'sea peoples' throughout the region. The tenth century was just as much a period of settlement for the Philistines, who little by little had abandoned the most distinctive features of their culture to assume those of the local culture, Phoenician, as it was for the new semitic population, among them Israelite groups, who had settled in the area following the convulsions of various kinds which marked the end of the Late Bronze age. The fact that only in the tenth century BC was there a real spread of the use of iron[21] forms an admirable chronological reference point for certain situations recorded in some passages of the Old Testament: the lack of iron weapons on the part of the Israelites, stressed in the Song of Deborah (Judges 5),[22] and the monopoly of iron and its working among the Philistines in the time of Saul (I Sam.13.19-21)[23] confirm the general situation in the tenth century and the improbability of a strong Hebrew state in that period.[24]

Chapter 3

Stories of the Kings

We saw in the previous chapter how fragile was the historical framework on which the history of the events relating to the period of the united monarchy has been constructed: this is a fragility which becomes evident from careful reading of the biblical text itself just as much from a comparison with external situations. As we come down in time the record of events necessarily becomes more precise and we often find confirmation in extra-biblical documentation; however, this does not mean either that all the statements of the so-called historical books are correct or that certain situations are not the result of a particular historical view (one might think of the homonomies which conceal the temporary union of the two kingdoms or of the preoccupation with bringing out the legitimacy of Davidic descent). The substantial validity of the biblical narrative, but also its remarkable imprecision, are brought out by texts which refer to Hebrew individuals more or less incidentally; however, in connection with these texts note should be taken of the remarkable atittude of biblical scholars, who systematically tend to undervalue, if not completely to ignore, information that conflicts with the biblical narrative. Some examples will be sufficient illustration of all these statements.

Mesha's victory

There is just one non-Hebrew document from Syria-Palestine which speaks explicitly of the Hebrews: this is the famous stele of king Mesha, discovered in 1868 in Transjordan. In substance, the inscription says that Moab was oppressed by Israel for forty years, in the time of Omri and one of his sons who is not named; in the middle of the reign of the latter, who ascended the throne when Mesha was already ruling, the

Moabite king succeeded in throwing off the Israelite yoke; later he was able to see the end of the dynasty of Omri. This information generally confirms the biblical account in II Kings 3 which speaks of a war won by Mesha against the Israelites, but clashes with the chronology and the dynastic succession given by the Old Testament: according to this, in fact, Omri and his son Ahab reign in total only thirty-four years, so that the years of Omri (twelve) plus half those of his son (twenty-two) produce a figure of twenty-three, little more than half those stated by Mesha; moreover, the biblical text puts Mesha's revolt after the death of Ahab, at the beginning of the reign of Joram.

These not irrelevant discrepancies have been noted, but not much account has been taken of them. E.Renan, for example, paraphrased the biblical narrative limiting himself to putting in a note any reference to one or other of the epigraphical passages; moreover these are misleading references, since they give the reader the impression that they confirm the statements made by the author, whereas in fact they do anything but that.[1] In short, Renan does not seem to be aware that the inscription clashes with the biblical text. Let us take some other historians at random. Having presented the terms of the question, Giuseppe Ricciotti states: 'The most reasonable thing to do is to keep to this last piece of information given so clearly by the Bible [i.e. that Mesha rebelled after the death of Ahab] and to interpret in an approximate way what the stele says both about forty years, which has already been noted as a typical figure, and about "half his days".'[2] And so it would be 'most reasonable' to argue that Mesha, who sees his enemy reign just as many years after having been conquered as he had reigned previously, would have fought against a king who was already dead; nor can it be said that Mesha was ill informed about this powerful neighbour: Ricciotti also accepts that Mesha was aware of the achievements of Jehu. A different method is that followed by Martin Noth. In his *History of Israel* the German historian resolutely declares: 'The Mesha inscription mentions the name of king Omri, who had "oppressed Moab for a long time" (l.5) and ...reckons "the reign of Omri and half the reign of his sons" at "forty years" (l.8). This is clearly very much a round figure. But it implies that Mesha's victorious campaign came at the very end of the dynasty of Omri.'[3] Into these hasty lines Noth has succeeded in cramming various errors which certainly do no credit to his name: the textual quotation of line 8 of the inscription is erroneous, because the Moabite text does not speak of the 'reign of Omri' but of Omri who had occupied the land of Madaba and had kept it 'to his days' (*ymh*); as for the 'sons' (instead of 'son'), this is only a hypothesis, contradicted by the Moabite text, advanced by some exegetes to make less strident the clash between Moabite epigraphy and the biblical text and presented by Noth as fact: the number 'forty' is not 'very much' rounded up because in the terms implied by Mesha it comprises the thirty years of the reign of his father Chemoshyat and the beginning of his own reign. In short, Noth has not made use of an extra-biblical text but has limited himself to turning it into a *midraš in usum Delphini*. The South African scholar A.H.van Zyl, to whom we are indebted for a systematic historical treatment of the Moabites,[4] obviously attached more importance to the Mesha document and had more trust in it than the historians of Israel. He seeks to reconcile the two texts, stating that the Moabite revolt could have begun during the reign of Ahab (as Mesha says) but only spread after the death of the Hebrew king (as the Bible says). As for the 'forty years', the figure will be an approximation, seeking to indicate a generation, from the middle of the reign of Omri to the middle of the reign of Ahab: the argument would be intrinsically valid, but since van Zyl, too, accepts the biblical chronology without discussion we arrive at the absurdity of a 'generation' reduced to just seventeen years.

There is no point in producing other examples of the treatment reserved for the one non-Hebrew text which contains references to figures and facts narrated by the Bible; all behave in the same way, according unbounded trust to the biblical text and regarding the text of king Mesha as an almost negligible mass of gross approximations written by someone who did not know what he was doing.[5] It is not worth commenting on this historiographical attitude which is common to both famous and less famous names. Let us attempt, rather, to look at things in a really historical way.

There is basic agreement between the biblical account and the Moabite text: after a long period of subjection, the Moabites under the leadership of Mesha succeeded in shaking off the yoke of Israel. The terseness of the epigraphy, especially as regards the period of Hebrew domination, and the particularized biblical narrative, especially as regards the final defeat of the Israelites, are fully justified by the diversity of the literary genres of the two texts and even more by the fact that each of the two opposed parties sought to present the facts in the most convenient way for itself. There is, however, the great obstacle of the chronology. The main thing to be inferred from the Mesha text is that Omri had a long reign. The 'forty years' of oppression is certainly a symbolic figure, equivalent to 'a generation', but that means that while they can be less than forty they can also be more: probably no less than thirty but perhaps even fifty. Now, whether Omri subjugated Moab at the beginning of his reign or later, whether Chemoshyat was subjugated quickly or not (who can rule out the possibility that Chemoshyat, who was certainly a usurper, was not put on the throne by Omri, as a vassal ruler loyal to him?), the fact remains that Mesha, who wrote after 840 BC and began to reign when Omri was still alive, projected the majority of the 'forty years' on to the period when Omri was reigning. That means that, even if it is not said that Omri had conquered Moab just after ascending the throne, we must allow a reign of about forty years for Omri. This fact certainly conflicts with the twelve years that the Bible attributes to the king of Israel, but agrees with another piece of information: the political power attained by Omri was such that he wanted a new capital, Samaria, and the Assyrian rulers often called the kingdom of Israel the 'house of Omri', assigning to this house rulers who, as we know from the Bible and the Mesha stele itself, did not belong to his dynasty. Now conditions in the ancient Near East were such that only a long reign made it possible for a ruler to acquire political power, especially if he began from a position of inferiority, as the usurper Omri must have done. So if we allow, as seems inevitable, that Omri had a notably long reign, the mention of just one son before the dynasty came to an end at the hand of Jehu is fully plausible in chronological terms. Unfortunately Mesha does not give us the name of this son, perhaps as a sign of his contempt; however, it seems quite probable that he was Ahab.

Now we come to the biblical text. After the brief reign of Omri this gives the names of three rulers who succeeded to the throne: Omri's son Ahab, who reigned twenty-two years, and the latter's two sons Ahaziah and Joram, who reigned two and twelve years respectively. This is the information provided by the chronological framework of the book of Kings; however, if we go on to read the various narrative parts, we can make some interesting discoveries. The reign of Ahaziah is schematically treated in I Kings 22.52-54; the next chapter (II Kings 1), in which the death of the king is narrated and the prophet Elijah is the protagonist, consists of a narrative in which the ruler of Samaria remains anonymous and is given the name Ahaziah only by the redactor. The haziness of the figure of Ahaziah is confirmed by another detail: the account of Mesha's revolt at the beginning of II Kings 3 is presented in such a way as to give the impression that Ahab was immediately succeeded by Jehoram: 'But when Ahab died, the king of Moab rebelled against the king of Israel. So King Jehoram marched out of Samaria at the time and mustered all Israel' (II Kings 3.5-6). However, it is interesting to note that in the following part of the account the king of Israel here remains just as anonymous as he was in the Ahaziah episode. It is no less interesting to read the account of Jehu's conspiracy; the anonymous prophet anoints Jehu and among other things says to him 'Strike down the house of Ahab your master' (II Kings 9.7), and it is the sons of Ahab, not those of Jehoram, who are to be killed as 'the king's sons' (II Kings 10); the same is said of Jezebel, Ahab's wife (II Kings 9): no one mentions the true queen, Jehoram's wife. The whole narrative, in its most dramatic parts, reads as if Jehu were rebelling against Ahab and not against Jehoram. To these considerations of a literary kind on the haziness of the figures of Ahaziah and Jehoram is to be added another of even greater weight: these two rulers have exactly the same names as two kings of Judah who reigned in exactly the same years but in the reverse order and one of whom, Joram, is also said to have been the son-in-law of Ahab. As is well known, for this period of Hebrew history the biblical text presents an inextricable tangle of dates, names and facts, so that we are forced to conclude that the tradition has undergone substantial revision before reaching its present form. The Mesha inscription, with its information, gives us the possibility of restoring some order: if we give Omri a reign of about forty years (or a little more) and one successor, Ahab, the biblical chronology remains essentially unaltered, we eliminate two rulers, Ahaziah and Joram of Israel, to whom the biblical text does not succeed in giving any convincing substance, and finally we can understand better certain situations narrated in the books of Kings. In this way the provision of an external piece of information which at first sight seems to contradict the present biblical text in fact allows us to recover an earlier phase of the text itself, that before the chronological framework produced by the 'Deuteronomistic redactor'.

According to the book of Kings, between about 930 BC (the death of Solomon) and 586 BC (the capture of Jerusalem by Nebuchadnezzar), nineteen kings and one queen, Athaliah, reigned in Jerusalem. Athaliah was a usurper who for some years occupied the throne in place of the legitimate ruler. Of these twenty figures some are quite well known for various reasons (Rehoboam, Jehoshaphat, Athaliah, Hezekiah, Josiah, Jehoiachin and Zedekiah); others are important only for biblical specialists. It is certain that notwithstanding the narrative, which is often dramatic and lively, the biblical text is markedly devoid of 'historical' information, whereas it never omits a judgment, expressed in stereotyped form, on the behaviour of all the rulers, depending on their tolerance of the syncretistic religious practices of the people; from this point of view the kings of Jerusalem can be divided into eight good ones (Asa, Jehoshaphat, Joash, Amaziah, Azariah, Jotham, Hezekiah and Josiah) and eleven bad ones. No less important for the biblical author is the idea of the continuity of Davidic descent because 'Yahweh his God left David a lamp in Jerusalem', as the writer states with fine imagery; even if we must say that the legitimacy of the succession does not always seem convincing. The story of the little Joash, removed on the death of his aunt and hidden in the temple for six years, certainly comes from some of the narrative models in circulation in the ancient Near East in connection with usurpers who wanted to legitimize their position;[6] nor does the legitimacy of the pious Josiah seem crystal clear: put on the throne by a bloody conspiracy which eliminated a 'father' who is said to have begotten him at sixteen; even more doubtful is the position of the good Hezekiah, who would have been born when his father was just eleven. In reality the book of Kings only rarely provides anything more than a simple dynastic succession, a succession the validity of which has in many cases been confirmed by extra-biblical material. At all events, quite a few problems remain open, and the following pages are devoted to them.

Azariah's misfortunes

Among the very scanty epigraphic Hebrew documentation on historical persons or events there are two seals belonging to two different officials of the same ruler, Uzziah (*'zyw*): the types of nomenclature (ending in -*yw*) and the representations on the seal leave no doubt as to the north-Israelite origin of these items.[7] So we have clear evidence of the existence of an Uzziah king of Israel, who by the mere fact of being documented by two different seals proves to be a far from secondary figure. But the Bible does not know any king of Israel by the name of Uzziah. And for this reason the epigraphers and the historians of Israel are careful to hide the problem, forgetting the existence of the two seals. But since the problem exists, let us try to resolve it. The name of Uzziah was not entirely unknown to Hebrew historians, since the author of Chronicles gives this name to the king whom the book of Kings called Azariah. Now this Azariah-Uzziah reigned, it is said, for fifty-two years and seems to have done great things, almost all kept silent about by the Bible. II Kings 15.1-7 asserts that Azariah reigned in Jerusalem for fifty-two years and that he died of leprosy: that is all; this is somewhat strange not least because Azariah was a pious king who 'did what was right in the eyes of Yahweh'. The information that Azariah recaptured the port of Elath on the Red Sea appears in II Kings 14.22, put in an appendix to the biography of his father Amaziah. The information in II Chronicles 26 about this king, called by another name, Uzziah, is fuller, but given the nature of that work we have to suspect its authenticity; moreover this is information about the internal organization of the state, with the exception of the detail of the conquest of Philistine cities.[8] The international importance that this Hebrew ruler enjoyed for at least a while was noted in the annals of the Assyrian king Tiglath-pileser III, who states that in 738 BC he conquered a coalition of North Syrian city-states which was headed by none other than Azariah of Judah.[9]

The double name of the Hebrew ruler seems rather strange, nor is the difficulty removed by the usual argument that the names Azariah and Uzziah have substantially the same meaning: by this criterion the whole of semitic nomenclature could be reduced to a few entries. The north Israelite seals suggest that Uzziah must have been the name of Azariah, ruler of Jerusalem, as king of the north, in a period in which the king had unified the two kingdoms under his dominion: this is quite plausible when one remembers that Azariah was powerful enough to head a coalition of the whole of Syria, including Phoenicia, against the Assyrians. There remains the mystery of the silence of the biblical sources about this great ruler.

One significant piece of information is the statement, accompanied by quite a detailed narrative, that Azariah contracted leprosy (II Kings 15.5): the worst form of uncleanness according to Hebrew law, all the more relevant in this case in that Azariah had been 'anointed', i.e. in a sense consecrated, as king of Judah. Doubly impure, Azariah was automatically segregated from society (and according to the Bible he spent his last years in a 'separate house').[10] This story of his illness, which clashes with the information from Assyrian sources about the ruler's political and military activity, seems to have been invented to justify the silence of the historical source on Azariah, whose figure became as it were a tabu (it is curious that Chronicles, which calls the king Uzziah, gives him as an antagonist a high priest called Azariah). At all events, an attentive historian cannot fail to investigate certain details;

so let us look at the historical context of the time of Azariah, i.e. at the second twenty-five years of the eighth century BC.

This is the time of the most intense commercial trading on an international level, trading in which Tyre was the great protagonist;[11] and Tyre was ruled by a sovereign called Hiram. The ruler in Damascus was Rezin (the Assyrian sources call him Rakhianu; this is the same name phonetically in Hebrew and Aramaic respectively) who is said to have caused a good deal of trouble to Azariah's successor. In the desert of Northern Arabia (i.e. within Syria) Sabaeans and queens of Arabia made raids and traded; Egypt was still in a deep crisis, but on the eve of a political revival. When against this background we come upon the activities of our Azariah, i.e. his political interest in northern Syria and the building of a port on the Red Sea, we have all the ingredients for writing the history of... Solomon. So it becomes possible to put forward a hypothesis, which is hard only because the Bible must always be right: the Bible does not say anything about Azariah because at one stage what had been said about him was attributed to Solomon, whose fame had to be enhanced.

This hypothesis takes on even greater substance if we go on to look at the situation of the kings of Tyre, from among whom emerge Hiram the friend of Solomon and Hiram the contemporary of Azariah. Flavius Josephus (*Contra Apionem* I, 113-125, 156-8) tells us a great deal about the kings of Tyre, whom he lists in succession from Hiram (the contemporary of Solomon) to Pygmalion, i.e. in absolute (conventional) chronological terms from 969 to 774 BC. Then Josephus speaks of Eloulaios who reigned thirty-six years and who can be fixed by Assyrian synchronisms as reigning between 746 and 701 BC. In the chronology of Josephus there is therefore a gap of thirty-eight years, which can fortunately be filled with information from Assyria and Phoenicia. Tiglath-pileser III (745-727) received tribute first from Hiram and then from Mitinna of Tyre: the two rulers must therefore have been the immediate predecessors of Eloulaios. Since this latter was already ruling in 736 and Hiram was still alive in 743 we have to accept that the reign of Mitinna was relatively short: four or five years. The Hiram contemporaneous with Tiglath-pileser, whom Josephus does not know of, is also mentioned in a Phoenician inscription from Cyprus[12] which records the vow of one of his governors. And now some strange coincidences recur: between the end of the reign of Pygmalion (774 BC) and the beginning of the brief reign of Mitinna (*c.* 741-740) there is still an interval of thirty-three to thirty-four years during which Hiram, called

Hiram II by modern historians, reigned; is it a coincidence that the so-called Hiram I (the contemporary of Solomon) reigned, according to Josephus, precisely thirty-four years? Josephus's Hiram I put down a revolt by the Itykaioi, usually understood to be the inhabitants of Citium on the island of Cyprus; the Cyprus inscription noted above comes from a 'governor' (*skn*) of *qrthdšt* ('Carthage', 'new city'), i.e. a colonial administrative centre, who recognizes as his ruler king Hiram II: another coincidence?

It is almost impossible to attain certainty in the historical field unless one has rich and varied documentation. We have to be content with a few pieces of information and a few pointers: these all lead us to suppose that in all probability a fairly later biblical redactor beautified Solomon with the plumes of Azariah, who moreover was made to die a leper. The same suspicion of treating the sources with excessive freedom also rests on Flavius Josephus, who probably adapted information from traditional Tyrian historiography to the historical framework outlined by the Bible. But Azariah's troubles were not yet over.

At the end of every comment on the kings of Judah the redactor of Kings makes a note of the burial of the ruler, usually employing the formula 'he slept with his fathers [i.e. died] and was buried with his fathers in the city of David'. This phrase is repeated regularly from David to Ahaz; it is omitted for Hezekiah (but some Greek manuscripts of LXX and Chronicles restore it in various ways) and replaced by various statements, depending on the person concerned, for the kings from Manasseh onwards. The stereotyped nature of the formula, underlined by its application to David himself, and the way in which it is used only for the earliest rulers, betrays the ignorance of the redactor as to the real resting places of remains of the various kings; his desire to give information about their tombs, clearly dictated by ideological motives, was frustrated by the fact that, having been born and having lived in exile, he could not have any direct knowledge of either Jerusalem or of the royal necropolis that probably existed there. The use of the customary formula for Azariah as well reveals that the redactor of Kings was not in a position to make any precise statement about the tomb of this ruler; nothing prevents us from supposing that he was buried in Samaria or in another place in the northern kingdom. The author of Chronicles acted with a degree of freedom over this kind of note: for the last sovereigns he either simplifies or eliminates all the information provided by Kings; for the earlier ones he has a more consistent approach. For the most part he follows the formula of Kings, but he omits it for David and changes it in other instances for religious motives: the wicked behaviour of Jehoram, Joash and Ahaz means that they are buried in the city of David but 'not in the tombs of the kings' (II Chron. 21.21; 24.25; 28.27): of the impious Ahaziah it is said only that he was buried, thanks to the merits of his father (22.9); in connection with Hezekiah the author of Chronicles supplies the formula which was lacking in Kings, but with a small modification: the king was buried 'in the ascent of the tombs of the sons of David' (32.33).

As far as Azariah/Uzziah is concerned, Chronicles provides another of its variants: the king was buried 'in the burial field which belonged to the kings, for they said, "He is a leper"' (II Chron. 26.23). This is a purely formal variant, since it is obvious that the other kings who had died previously must have been buried in a 'field'; it is equally true that Flavius Josephus, who in this one case feels the need to specify the tomb of a king, paraphrases the text of Chronicles in his own way by saying that the ruler was 'buried alone in his own garden' (*Antiquities* 9,227).

The conclusion that we can draw from an analysis of the texts relating to the burial of Azariah/Uzziah is therefore that no one knew exactly where and how the king was buried, but that later Judaism (Chronicles and Josephus) raised the problem of the burial of a particularly impure king, giving it various solutions (royal necropolis, private garden) without any material foundation.

If one remembers this situation, the existence of an inscription like the one produced rather more than fifty years ago which spoke of the translation of the bones of king Uzziah seems at least disconcerting.[13] According to this epigraphic text, from a date oscillating between the second half of the first century BC and the first half of the first century AD, the bones of the Hebrew king are said to have been collected and transferred to somewhere different from their original resting place: the Aramaic text in fact says: 'To this place have been transferred the bones of Uzziah King of Judah. Let no one open it.' Since the provenance of the inscription is unknown, we do not know where the bones of the leprous king were transferred to; at all events one could suppose that this must be in the region of Jerusalem, given that the epigraph was produced there. As I said earlier, this inscription seems disconcerting because it would confirm the historical reality of a fact (the burial of Azariah/Uzziah in a place different from that in which the other kings were buried) which analysis of the text shows to be merely the result of a late literary re-elaboration with an ideological basis. The attempt of a scholar to identify the royal necropolis of Jerusalem on the basis of this inscription has proved fruitless.[14] On the other hand, that the bones of an individual who died of leprosy and was buried underground ('in the field', says Chronicles) could have been preserved for at least seven centuries has caused no little perplexity: Azariah/Uzziah died around 733 BC, whereas the inscription is from the 'Herodian period' (between 50 BC and AD 75).

To these general considerations which cast some doubt on the authenticity of the Uzziah inscription must be added the strange circumstances of its 'discovery'. According to its first editor, E.L.Sukenik, the inscription was found by him in a collection of antiques which were in the Russian church on the Mount of Olives. This collection is said to have been put there by Archimandrite Antony, who was in Jerusalem from 1865 to his death in 1894; but no documentation or catalogue has been found of this: it is said that the Archimandrite's cards were sent to Russia;[15] the catalogue would have been destroyed during the First World War.[16] The way in which Sukenik talks of this phantom collection is also strange: 'I am grateful to the present Board of the Mission for their kind permission to examine and eventually to publish inscriptions from their collection'; reading these words one gets the impression that the Russian Mission had various inscriptions which were studied by Sukenik, who eventually published them – something quite different from the fact that in the work in which these words appear only one inscription was actually published. It should be noted that these words of thanks are missing from the original Hebrew version of the article, of which the English article is an abbreviated version. Moreover we do not know in what year the inscription was 'found': in the Hebrew article, which appeared in 1931, Sukenik does not give a date; in the English one he speaks of '9 February' without indicating the year: since the article was published towards the end of 1931, with this year indicated on the journal, we are to suppose that this was 9 February 1931; moreover, publishing his own article in 1931, W.F.Albright affirmed that the discovery of the inscription had taken place in the 'past year', i.e. in 1930.

Alongside these considerations of as it were an external kind, there are various elements intrinsic to the inscription itself which cause us to have marked reservations. These relate to the framework of the inscription, the fact that Azariah is called by the name Uzziah (which was perhaps that under which he reigned over Israel), the characteristics of the Aramaic language used in the inscription and finally its palaeography. For a detailed analysis of such aspects I refer the reader to my study[17] and here give only the conclusions: the form of the framework round the inscription is not justified; the simultaneous presence of linguistic forms belonging to different periods and the attestation of anomalous linguistic forms are suspect; the inscription, which purports to come from a monument, uses a non-monumental script with anomalous forms.

In conclusion, we have good reasons to maintain that the Uzziah inscription (as it is usually called), so frequently reproduced in books, is a modern forgery produced in Sukenik's circles.[18] The poor Azariah has thus been hoaxed twice.

Hezekiah's siege

During the siege of Jerusalem by the Assyrian army commanded by Sennacherib, in the time of king Hezekiah (we are in 701 BC), an Israelite delegation met some senior Assyrian officials under the walls of the city; the spokesmen of the latter, the great cup-bearer (*rab-šaqeh*), addressed the Israelites in Hebrew; on being invited to speak in Aramaic so that the people standing on the walls would not be able to follow the discussions which were going on, he began to shout in Hebrew precisely so that the people could understand him. All the scholars have always regarded this story as fully valid evidence of the linguistic situation in Jerusalem at the end of the eighth century BC: whereas Hebrew was understood by all, Aramaic was known only to a very restricted group, that of the court. To limit myself to a few of the more recent names, let me mention J.Barr,[19] C.Rabin,[20] and especially E.Ullendorff in this connection. This last, who has devoted a work specifically to a discussion of the knowledge of languages in the Old Testament,[21] attaches particular importance to this statement, which he defines as being 'pregnant with far-reaching implications': these would be that 'the Assyrian officers' command of Hebrew must have been excellent', that 'Rabshakeh may have been specially selected for his mission on account of his exceptional knowledge of Hebrew', and finally that 'Hebrew and Aramaic were not mutually intelligible'. The implications are not particularly far-reaching, apart from the arbitrary transformation of the title of *rab-šaqeh* into a proper name (an attempt to forestall an objection to the historicity of the story, which makes a senior Assyrian official know Hebrew) (moreover Ullendorf has to press on to produce his second argument, the language used by Samson and Delilah in conditions of intimacy).

My position over this biblical episode is not as trusting as that of my colleagues. There are a number of reasons for this mistrust of the historicity of the narrative. First of all it is appropriate to recall that the episode of the conversations between Israelites and Assyrians comes within the story of Sennacherib's expedition against the west, an expedition which resulted in a disaster for the Assyrian army, because it was decimated by the angel of Yahweh (II Kings 19.35). Now by chance the same episode of the unfortunate Assyrian military enterprise is also recorded in legendary form in an Egyptian tradition collected by Herodotus (2,141): according to him, the army of *Sanacharibos* was put out of action by rats who during the night devoured all the leather of the Assyrian army, making their equipment unserviceable so that the Assyrian soldiers were easy prey for an Egyptian army composed exclusively of merchants and artisans. A comparison of the biblical narrative with that of Herodotus demonstrates in the first place the legendary character of both of them (the only truth here is the Assyrian expedition of 701) and also the secondary character of the biblical account. As P.Xella has demonstrated in his study,[22] the singular expression 'eat faeces and drink urine' which occurs in the Hebrew text that we are examining is not meant to indicate the difficulties which the people of Jerusalem would encounter in case of siege, as is usually stated, but is intended to denote the death that awaited the besieged. The literary origin of this phrase has been discovered in Egypt, in the Book of the Dead; here it is the literary matrix of a story which must have arisen in Egypt and from there passed on to Palestine.

Moreover it is impossible to maintain the virtual contemporaneity of the biblical narrative in its present form with the events narrated, as is usually done. Sennacherib's expedition took place in 701 BC, but the Old Testament also speaks of the death of the Assyrian king, which took place in 681, and gives the Egyptian general Tirhakah the title Pharaoh, which in reality he did not assume until around 688 BC. Moreover the use of the form *rab-šaqeh* reveals a direct knowledge of Mesopotamian titles that could have been acquired previously, but which also leads one to suspect more direct contact with Mesopotamian linguistic forms. All the more so, since the 185,000 soldiers killed by the angel of Yahweh are too reminiscent of the 180,000 who according to the Mesopotamian legend are said to have been killed by Naram-Sin to be an invented number.

However, the improbabilities of the biblical text do not end here. The gifted and eloquent *rab-šaqeh* appears fully aware of the fact that a religious reform had been set in motion by Hezekiah in Jerusalem, but strangely he refers to the removal of the altars and high places (II Kings 18.22) which Hezekiah had in fact left in place; it was Josiah who removed them, about a century later. And again, what was the Aramaic that the Assyrians should have spoken and the Israelite officials would have understood? And what about Hezekiah, who reads Sennacherib's letter (19.14), which was evidently written in Aramaic, directly? It is obvious that the whole episode presupposes a linguistic situation in which Aramaic had become an international language, known to the educated class throughout the Near East; but what we call 'imperial' Aramaic seems somewhat anachronistic in 701 BC, when the Jerusalem court must have been more familiar with Phoenician than with Aramaic.

The inevitable conclusion to which all these observations lead us is that the story of the siege of Jerusalem has only the siege as a historical core and has been put down in writing, at least in its present form (which, moreover, is the only one that we know; the duplicate in Isaiah is no different), at least a century after the facts narrated. But it is not so much the problem of the dating of the story which is interesting (even if, as we now see, a good deal of light has been shed on this problem) as rather the underlying linguistic problem. What is important to note in this context is that in an episode attributed to the time of Hezekiah we find the only evidence of the interest of the Old Testament in the linguistic problem of comprehensibility. The biblical text has numerous episodes of encounter and dialogue between people who obviously spoke different languages (from that between Samson and Delilah to Solomon's meeting with the Queen of Sheba, from the patriarchs who have no difficulty in talking with the Egyptians to Moses who succeeds in making himself understood by the daughters of Reuel the Midianite, and so on), but the question of how these could understand one another is never raised. However, the story of *rab-šaqeh* does bring this problem to the fore; so it is evident that a new factor has entered between the stories of patriarchs, judges and ancient kings and that of Hezekiah, which has brought out the importance of spoken language.

It is possible to understand this new factor from the text itself. In the first place it presupposes a contrast between Hebrew and Aramaic: this contrast is, moreover, anachronistic for Jerusalem at the end of the eighth century BC when the languages neighbouring on Hebrew were Phoenician, Moabite and Edomite but not Aramaic. When did Hebrew come directly up against Aramaic? Only after 586 BC, when the Hebrews who had remained at home came into contact with the Babylonian administration (which like the Assyrian administration used Aramaic as the *lingua franca* outside Mesopotamia) and those deported to Babylon found themselves in a largely Aramaic-speaking environment: in the sixth century BC Aramaic was perhaps already spoken in Mesopotamia more than Akkadian.

Another significant indication of the real linguistic situation reflected in the episode of II Kings 18 is the term used to denote the Hebrew language: *yehudit*. This designation, which recurs only once more, in the post-exilic period, was certainly not used in the monarchical period to denote the language of the Israelites of the two Hebrew kingdoms; evidently it arose only after the fall of Samaria. Since, however, it seems improbable that the Israelites in Jerusalem would change the name of their own language after the fall of the northern kingdom, everything leads us to suppose that the name *yehudit* arose in connection with the prominence given to 'Judah', the only legitimate 'remnant' of Israel. In other words, the linguistic data presented by our text lead us to put its redaction in the exilic period.

This result fits in perfectly with the deductions of an ideological kind that we can make from the episode that we have examined. The emergence of an interest in spoken language is conceivable only in a situation in which spoken language, in this case Hebrew, has come to assume an essential importance for characterization, for ethnic identity, in particular over against those who speak Aramaic. This situation, which appears for the first time throughout the ancient Near East, can be noted during the Babylonian exile, when those deported from Jerusalem react to the attempt at ethnic and cultural absorption, creating for the first time in history what we now call 'linguistic nationalism'. In this perspective some aspects of the events narrated become clearly under-standable: the awareness of linguistic diversity and the prestige attached to one's own language by making a senior Assyrian official speak it fluently (it is as if nowadays a pure Yankee American minister were to speak Basque...).

Josiah's sons

We now come down to the last decades of the reign of Josiah. Josiah died at the age of thirty-nine, after reigning for thirty-one years (a somewhat precocious king: a ruler at eight, a father at fourteen, a grandfather at thirty-two). He was succeeded on the throne by his son Jehoahaz (II Kings 23.30-34): however, he only ruled for three months, because Pharaoh Necho deported him to Egypt and put Jehoiakim, another son of Josiah, on the throne. There would not be anything special about the sad fate of Jehoahaz, who died in exile in Egypt, were it not for his name. This Jehoahaz does not in fact appear among the sons of Josiah in the genealogy edited by the Chronicler (I Chron.3.15): instead of him we find a Johanan who is otherwise unknown. Given the remarkable orthographic similarity between the two names in Hebrew (*yw'ḥz-ywḥnn*) it is generally stated that the Johanan of the Chronicler is merely an erroneous version of Jehoahaz; that could easily be accepted did not Chronicles itself say that Johanan was the firstborn of Josiah, whereas according to the chronology of the book of Kings, repeated faithfully by the Chronicler (II Chron.36.2-5), he was younger than Jehoiakim, who was the second son.

In the text parallel to the last two chapters of Chronicles which forms the first chapter of I Esdras we find a remarkable variant: the son who ascended the throne immediately after Josiah is not called either Jehoahaz or Johanan but Jehoiachin;[23] since he, too, is deposed by the Pharaoh, deported to Egypt and replaced by his brother Jehoiakim, there is no doubt about the identity of the person of whom the author of I Esdras meant to speak. But the story of Jehoahaz-Johanan-Jehoiachin is not yet finished. According to the book of Jeremiah, the son who succeded Josiah on the throne and was deported (it is not said where) was called Shallum (22.10-12). In the face of this situation, which reveals great confusion in the Hebrew tradition, any attempt at an explanation seems inadequate; even if we accepted with some scholars that Jehoahaz was the name taken by Shallum on ascending the throne, there remains the mystery of Johanan and Jehoiachin (even if this last, documented by a text which was not recognized as canonical by the Jews, is left out of account). What is certain is that after Josiah the situation of the Hebrew monarchy must have been extremely confused and was therefore recorded in a very approximate way by those who wanted to hand down a recollection of it.

After Jehoahaz-Shallum-Jehoiachin the Jewish tradition is agreed in making his brother Jehoiakim reign; his true name is said to have been Eliakim, which was then changed to Jehoiakim by the Pharaoh who put him on the throne (II Kings 23.34-37). The information about this king is somewhat vague; he is said to have reigned for eleven years and to have paid homage to Nebuchadnezzar, though he was a creature of the Pharaoh; but then he rebelled and fought against the Babylonians and his neighbours who were allied to them; however, he managed to die in his bed. That is what we read in the book of Kings; according to

II Chron.36.5-7, however, Jehoiakim was deported to Babylon by Nebuchadnezzar, though not before having got back his brother Zarhi (Zarios) from Egypt; this last detail, which increases the offspring of Josiah by one (not known to the Chronicler) is provided by I Esdras 1.36, which is essentially the same as the account that we find in Chronicles; finally, Josephus, on his own initiative historicizing the prophecy of Jeremiah 22.19, makes Jehoiakim die in Jerusalem at the hands of Nebuchadnezzar (*Antiquities* 10.97).

We find ourselves on more solid ground with Jehoiachin, son of Jehoiakim, who reigned for three months and was then deported to Babylon by Nebuchadnezzar (II Kings 24.8-15); the solid ground is provided by Babylonian texts which speak either of a siege laid against Jerusalem by Nebuchadnezzar in 598 BC[24] following which the king of Jerusalem (whose name is not given) was taken to Babylon, or of the presence in Babylon of a 'Iauchin' (*yaukinu*) king of Judah.[25] Given this external information we can drop the variants of the names of this ruler which are attested by various Jewish books (Jehoiakim in I Ezra and Josephus, Coniah and Jeconiah together with Jehoiachin in Jeremiah), variants which can partly be explained at least on a linguistic basis. What we should note, rather, is that Jehoiachin's imprisonment cannot have been too uncomfortable: according to Babylonian custom[26] the hostage kings (whoever they might have been) lived at the royal court, and it is difficult to think of a real prison when both the Babylonian and the biblical texts (I Chron.3.17) make Jehoiachin the father of various sons, evidently fathered in exile. Among these, Jehoiachin (the same name as the father), explicitly mentioned in a cuneiform tablet but unknown to the Chronicler, deserves mention.

The greatest problems relating to the last kings of Judah are not, however, those posed by the uncertainties of nomenclature revealed by the Hebrew literary tradition but others produced by the extra-biblical documentation. We have seen how some Babylonian texts substantially confirm the events of 598 BC and the deportation of Jehoiachin; the interesting thing is that these very texts regularly give Jehoiachin the title 'king of Judah'. This means that for Nebuchadnezzar the sole ruler of Jerusalem remained Jehoiachin, regardless of the fact that he lived in Babylon. But in that case is it still possible to speak of Zedekiah as a 'king'? Was he not rather a governor?

Some scholars have wanted to see confirmation of this situation in a seal of which various impressions have been found and which reads 'Eliakim minister of Jehoiachin' (*'lyqm n'rywkn*):[27] since it is improbable that the seal was used only in the three months that the biblical text assigns to the reign of Jehoiachin in Jerusalem, it has been supposed that it was in use in the years in which Zedekiah 'reigned' in Jerusalem and that it therefore testifies to the continuation of the official reign of Jehoiachin. Zedekiah would then have been only a kind of regent, supervised (it appears, somewhat ineffectively) by Gedeliah; another valuable piece of epigraphic evidence[28] has in fact shown that the governor appointed by Nebuchadnezzar over Judah after the destruction of Jerusalem (II Kings 25.22) was already 'superintendent of the palace' (*'šr 'l hbyt*) in the time of Zedekiah. This systematization of the epigraphical material would allow a reconstruction of the final phase of the kingdom of Judah that accords with the biblical data, with the exception of the royal dignity of Zedekiah, which he did not in fact have. But are we certain that the Jehoiachin of the Hebrew seal was the king exiled in Babylon?

The state of the Hebrew tradition, which we saw above, does not allow us to be too optimistic about the possibility of reconstructing events on the basis of the biblical narrative. And a fact should be noted here which, if it is not a case of simple homonymy, could change the pattern of the dynastic succession after Josiah. The figure who on the seal claims to be the minister of Jehoiachin is called Eliakim: the very name that Jehoiakim bore before ascending the throne (II Kings 23.34). Could this person, whom nothing prevents us from also seeing as a son of Josiah, not be the future Jehoiakim? In that case, of the varied and conflicting Hebrew traditions that provided by I Esdras would seem to be confirmed, having Josiah succeeded first by Jehoiachin and then by Jehoiakim (it is obvious that this first Jehoiachin would be distinguished from the second who was to be deported by Nebuchadnezzar). Of Jehoahaz-Shallum-Jehoiachin, epigraphy would give preference to Jehoiachin; but this is not to exclude the possibility that the others were royal personages, if not kings (like the Zarhi who has been noted), who were confused with the sovereigns proper by a tradition which was no longer in a position over the distance of a number of years even to hand down an exact name (the onomastic agreement between the Hebrew seal and the Babylonian texts over against the whole of the literary tradition is significant).

What I have said is in no way meant to be a solution, but merely to suggest new possibilities for a solution to problems which at present remain insoluble. The events of the history of the house of Omri and that of Josiah show how approximate the historical memory of the biblical writers is, even when it relates to late periods (and very close to the author, according to the theory, which I do not share, that the Deuteronomic historian lived in the exile). By contrast, the case of Azariah-Uzziah reveals the confidence with which the traditions handed down could be adapted to new political or ideological situations. The final conclusion is that without the use of external documentation it is impossible to identify where the biblical narrative is sound and where it is not; in other words, without adequate extra-biblical sources it is impossible to write the history of Israel.

Chapter 4

The Origin and Development of Yahwism

The Old Testament as a whole gives a fairly precise picture of Hebrew religion in its origins and its relationships with that practised in the country of Canaan or, to be more precise, with that of Phoenicia. Yahweh, the only God, reveals himself to Abraham, to Jacob, and finally, in a grand manner, to Moses: he makes a covenant with his people by means of which they pledge themselves to a monotheistic faith. The covenant is continually betrayed by the Hebrew people from the very moment that it is concluded, as is shown by the famous episode of Moses breaking the tablets of the law (Exodus 32) and then all the way down to the time of the Judges, of Solomon, and throughout the duration of the kingdom of Israel and that of Judah. In the face of these continual betrayals, actions which the inflexible Yahweh duly repays by visiting his faithless people with an uninterrupted series of misadventures culminating in the destruction of Jerusalem in 586 BC, the voice of the prophets is raised, but obviously is not listened to. Israel is settled in Palestine, i.e. in the promised land, having been made to conquer it miraculously by God, and having already professed faith in the one God Yahweh. But in contact with Phoenician polytheism and especially its licentious sexual practices, it allows itself to be convinced, if not to abandon its original faith, certainly to accompany it with behaviour which is hardly compatible with it. This gives rise to a deplorable religious syncretism which pious rulers like Hezekiah and Josiah try to oppose, seeking to restore the cult to its original Mosaic purity.

According to the historical view put forward by the Old Testament, then, the relationship that has come to be created between Hebrew religion and that of Phoenicia is that of an alien body (Yahwistic monotheism) which by force (by the will of God) has penetrated an alien texture (the culture of Canaan), is at first partially assimilated, but then (with the return from the Babylonian exile) proves completely victorious.

In principle, considering the infinite variety of historical processes, there is nothing against the feasibility of the kind of sequence that the Bible presents for the historical development of Hebrew religion. It is not absurd to suppose that the Israelite tribes which crossed the Jordan with Joshua believed firmly in Yahweh their one God, just as it is not absurd to suppose that this faith, though somewhat abstract, became somewhat blurred in proximity to the tempting hierodules of Astarte. However, we cannot but turn our attention to other historical situations with problems partially analogous to those created by the Israelite conquest, and we cannot fail to note that things usually went in a rather different way. The Germani made a victorious entrance into the Roman empire, but their paganism disappeared very quickly when confronted with the Christianity of those they conquered. The fortunes of the Arabs, who succeeded in imposing their religion with their armies, were different; nor was religion the only thing they imposed: with Islam a large part of the ancient world also accepted, or was subjected to, a new language, a new conception of society and the state, in short a new cultural system. If we remain within the semitic-speaking world, quite a close historical model to that provided by the Arabs is the one presented by Phoenician colonization in the West; various populations of the Mediterranean who came into contact with the Phoenicians (like the Libyans and the Sards) adopted their religion, language and culture while inserting elements of their own. Vice versa, other instances are closer to that of the Germani in the Roman empire: at the beginning of the second millennium BC the Amorites who conquered Mesopotamia were completely assimilated by the pre-existing culture, even in their religion. A partial analogy is the history of the Aramaeans in Mesopotamia and Syria between the end of the second and the beginnig of the first millennium BC: these maintained their own linguistic autonomy, whereas on the religious and cultural level in general they gave way to a syncretism in which the elements taken over from local cultures clearly prevailed over the original ones. The reference to the Amorites and the Aramaeans becomes particularly significant in that these populations had in common with the Israelites (or at least with one of their components) an initial social structure of a semi-nomadic kind.

In conclusion, we must accept that ancient history, and especially that of the semitic peoples, does not offer any model that could compare with the historical and religious process that the Old Testament outlines for Israel. This historical experience says that when two types of religion came abruptly into contact following military conquests, one of the two had to yield to the other; apart from an initial period of uncertainty, it never happened that the religion of the victors was kept only by them: either it was imposed on the conquered or it was the latter who caused the victors to be assimilated to them. But although historical comparisons do not provide any support for the development of Hebrew religion which is outlined in the Bible and by many Jewish scholars, we would not be authorized to put such a development in question – it would be all the more interesting because of its uniqueness – if, outside the existence of external data which tell against it, the Old Testament itself did not give rise to the first doubts about the actual validity of what it affirms.

We begin our analysis with what in a certain sense is the central point of Hebrew religion, the Decalogue.[1] The philological problems raised by this document are considerable: it in fact appears in three different versions in the biblical text (Ex.20.1-17; Ex.34.14-26; Deut.5.6-21) while a fourth variant appears in one of the earliest biblical manuscripts, the Nash Papyrus, which can be dated to about the beginning of the Christian era. The fact that the text of the Decalogue, inserted into what must be an earlier document, i.e. the version of Exodus 20, has what are clearly later additions, has led to the argument that the form of this document which is least tampered with, and therefore the earliest, is the one in Deuteronomy; this means that we do not have the Decalogue in a redaction earlier than the second half of the seventh century BC as the earliest date. But leaving aside this kind of problem and accepting, as is usually the case, that the substance, if not the letter, of the Mosaic Decalogue has a long oral tradition, we must note a remarkable feature of it: promulgated in the midst of the desert to a people who, apart from slavery in Egypt, had so far known only a semi-nomadic life, the Decalogue of Moses in all its versions presupposes an agricultural society, people with stable ties to the land. The obvious conclusion is that the earliest Hebrew religion was practised by an agricultural population, so this religion can only have arisen in Palestine itself, at a time after the conquest and after the complete abandonment of the customs of semi-nomadic life. However, that also means that this type of religion must not have been very different from that of the other agricultural populations which lived in the same region.

This conclusion is confirmed and made more precise by the content of the Decalogue itself: the initial affirmation of the uniqueness of the god Yahweh and the subsequent prohibition, repeated insistently, against constructing divine images and worshipping them, could have been understandable in the time of the patriarchs, with whom the revelation of monotheism began; however, they seem superfluous and even harmful because they suggest the possibility of deviations in the time of Moses which, in the perspective outlined by the Bible, was the time when, if ever, Yahwistic monotheism was fully affirmed and Yahweh had manifested all his power in liberating his people from the slavery imposed by the Pharaoh. The initial part of the Decalogue, however, becomes completely relevant if seen in the perspective of a religious reform which originated in Palestine and which with its monotheistic message tended towards a conscious and total revolt against the Phoenician religion which had largely been followed up to that time. Moses with his message did not reveal a religion to people who should already have known it, but created a new one in contrast to that professed hitherto.

Let us now go on to examine the extra-biblical evidence. Notwithstanding its sporadic and apparently secondary character, the epigraphic evidence is a basic point of discussion for our topic, because it is the only original evidence relating directly to the worship of Yahweh. It should be said straight away that the epigraphic evidence, and more generally the written extra-biblical sources, do not confirm the picture that the Old Testament presents of the rise and establishment of the cult of Yahweh in the form that we usually denote with the term Yahwism. This explains the attitude of mistrust, if not direct rejection, shown by almost all scholars towards the epigraphic or literary data outside the Bible. Down to the present day, for reasons that can easily be imagined, the Jewish tradition has exercised such a theological or even psychological pressure that it has conditioned even historical research, which only very recently, thanks also to key discoveries, has begun to release itself from the fetters in which it had been bound during our century by famous scholars, for whom an unacknowledged confessional interest now appears to have predominated over a concern for scientific objectivity.

In this connection let us look at the treatment received by some onomastic evidence which the Old Testament itself provides favour of the existence of the cult of Yahweh outside the Israelite sphere. The Joshua in whose field the ark drawn by Philistine cows ended up (I Sam.6.14,18) was a Canaanite from Beth-shemesh: but it has not been difficult to attribute to him a more or less close Israelite descent. Then (II Sam.8.10) we meet a certain Joram, son of the king of Hamath: but self-styled philologists emend the text to Hadoram (a name which contains the Aramaic divine name Hadad) following the example of the pious Chronicler, who had already taken his own steps (I Chron.18.10) to eliminate an inconvenient piece of evidence. Then as for Jochebed, Moses' mother (Ex.6.20; Num.26.59), no better expedient has been found than to affirm, without producing any evident justification, that in this name the presence of the Hebrew divine name is quite uncertain. This assertion is all the more remarkable in that it is made by no less a scholar than Noth, who, in the pages which he devotes to the presence of the divine name Yahweh in Hebrew nomenclature,[2] in fact proves more of a theologian than a linguist: this is demonstrated clearly by the final words of his investigation, in which, having summarily liquidated the Amorite onomastica and having also turned Yawbidi, the Aramaean king of Hamath known to us from the Annals of Sargon II, into an Israelite, he calmly went on to say: 'Thus in no case is the name Yahweh to be encountered outside and independently of Israel; so the tradition of the book of Exodus could be right, namely that the divine name Yahweh arose for the first time in Israel, or better, for the first time with the people of Israel, and therefore in some way goes back to the work of Moses.'

If this has been the fate of the biblical evidence it will not be difficult to imagine that reserved for the extra-biblical evidence that the discoveries of texts have produced. Leaving aside the mention of Yahweh in the stele of Mesha, because of the corruptness of the context, we have already noted Yawbidi of Hamath. Then there are the Amorite onomastica of Mari and of some other Syrian cities which can be dated around the eighteenth century BC which offer various attestations of names compounded with *yaḥwi/yawi* and *ya*: since this last element is taken as a hypocoristic suffix, it has long been quite certain that the nature of the word is verbal, and it is thus safeguarded from dangerous onomastic comparisons: from Noth to W.F.Albright and to the latter's docile pupil H.B.Huffmon.[3] It has been the merit of A.Finet, first in a study dedicated to king Yawi-ila and then in a specific article,[4] to have demonstrated convincingly the formal identity between *yaḥwi/yawi* and the name of the Hebrew god. When a fragmentary text from Ugarit belonging to the mythological Baal cycle produced a verse in which the god El said: 'The name of my son is Yaw' (VI AB, IV, 13-14), many scholars hastened to correct the text to remove the mention of Yaw; when the arbitariness of this procedure was pointed out they found different ways to deny the evidence: one was to see *yw* as the usual verbal form, interpreted in different ways; one was to suggest a phonetic variant of Yam, the Ugaritic god of the sea: very few scholars follow Abbé H.Cazelles[5] in accepting the existence of the god Yaw at Ugarit, even though he is a god who, moreover, continues to be attested in the area even in the next millennium, as Porphyry testifies (in Eusebius, *Praeparatio evangelica* 1,9, 21) when he asserts that the god Ιευω was worshipped at Berytus.

The reluctance to accept the presence of Yahweh outside Israel is unexpectedly transformed into enthusiasm in the face of the information provided by the Ebla texts. The premature and rash announcement that in some texts the theophoric names containing *ya* have this last element preceded by the divine determinative *dingir*[6] has provoked in some scholars a kind of triumphalistic exaltation under the banner 'Yahweh = Hebrews'. And so we can see an attempt at the Hebraization of Syria in the third millennium BC with poor Abraham unexpectedly moved back 700 years towards prehistory.

If we want to draw any conclusion from the extra-biblical evidence relating to Yahweh we can state that the texts show a divine figure worshipped in the region of Syria and Palestine from the beginning of the second millennium BC on, both by sedentary people and by nomads: a divine figure connected with the local pantheon but in no way pre-eminent; a divine figure, in short, the form of whose name fluctuates remarkably: Yah, Yaw, Yahweh. With this information, the historian immediately faces a problem: how, when and where did this pre-Israelite god come to be accepted as the national Hebrew god? It is quite impossible today to give an answer to even one of these questions; given the present state of the evidence and of our knowledge of the earliest Hebrew history, any kind of suggestion would have no greater validity than the mythical foundation created by the Hebrew tradition around the figure of Moses. What is certain is that traditional Yahwism has lost its starting point: Yahweh existed before the Hebrew people existed and was worshipped in the land of Canaan when the Hebrew tribes were still practising the cult of their 'fathers'.

One indication, albeit tenuous, of the origin of the god Yahweh has been provided by a Hebrew inscription written on the wall of a tomb at Khirbet Beit Lei. In one of the religious invocations the formula *yh yhwh* appears: these words not only confirm the Hebrew text of Isa. 12.2 and 26.4, which hitherto has not been understood, but seem to me to make it possible to suggest an explanation of the divine name itself. The word *yah* in Isaiah and the epigraphy of Khirbet Beit Lei can hardly be other than the form Yah which the divine name takes in certain onomastic compounds. Since, moreover, it is absurd to think that *yah* could be a proper name when it is found in front of Yahweh, the only possible alternative is to suggest that *yah* was originally a generic term, which later came to denote a specific deity: we would thus have a phenomenon which is similar to Il-El, a generic term for 'god' and the proper name of a deity at a temple. The substantial semantic identity of *yah* with *il* is also demonstrated by the interchange of the two names in a name borne by one individual, as happens in the Assyrian texts with the name of Yawbidi, mentioned above, who is also called Ilubidi. The attestation in Isaiah and at Khirbet Beit Lei would therefore demonstrate the persistence in Hebrew of the use of *yah* simply to denote 'god'.[7]

The observation that earliest Hebrew religion has its roots in Palestine itself, or at any rate in the area of Syria, and that it was practised by an agricultural society, leads us to another consideration. All religions of an agrarian type are characterized by polytheism and a developed mythology, and by a series of practices which often have a sexual basis. For these last, it is enough to recall the frequent rebukes made throughout the Old Testament to the poor Israelites, who are always accused of 'prostituting themselves' (this is the significant verb used in these cases) to alien deities, for making sure the rites typical of agrarian religions were performed. It is difficult to speak of a Hebrew mythology in the traditional sense, since the whole of the Old Testament is a testimony to the work of demythologization carried out by some Hebrew religious circles who have transferred the work of the deity from nature to history. Nevertheless, in the poetic texts it is still possible to rediscover quite explicit allusions to myths relating to Yahweh: the most recurrent one is that of the struggle against a sea monster, sometimes called Rahab and sometimes Leviathan (cf. Psalms 74; 89; Isa.27; 51; Job 40-41): this myth certainly could not have arisen in the desert. Moreover there are echoes of Phoenician myths here and there: the cosmogony that Tyre developed in relation to the god Elqunirs ('the creator of the land') recurs in an adaptation from the Phoenician in Ps.104,[8] while in the account relating to the struggle over primogeniture between Esau and Jacob (Gen.27) it is possible to single out some analogies with the myth about the origins of Tyre, schematically narrated by Philo of Byblos.[9] And only our almost total ignorance of Phoenician mythology prevents us increasing the incidence of contacts between it and the biblical narratives. Moreover, the way in which Yahweh is sometimes presented in poetic compositions shows how the god of Israel came to be virtually identified with the Phoenician Baal: if one thinks of the song of Deborah (Judges 5) or Ps.29, with mythological allusions which can only relate to the Phoenician mythology reflected in the Ugaritic texts.

There remains, finally, the discussion of monotheism. Today it is quite generally accepted that in the period before the exile the faith professed by Israel was a henotheism rather than a monotheism in the full sense of the word: the worship that the Hebrews offered exclusively to their own God Yahweh did not exclude the existence of other deities among other peoples, even if in the case of ideological conflict these proved markedly inferior to the God of Israel (the episode of Elijah on Mount Carmel is famous). Moreover Yahweh was identified with El, the supreme god of the Canaanite pantheon, thanks also to the possibilities offered by language: in many semitic languages in fact the word *el* (and similar words) is simultaneously both the name of a specific deity and the generic term for 'god'. That at least to begin with the Hebrews also had quite a numerous pantheon is suggested, once again, by the poetic texts when they speak of 'sons of god' who form a corona round Yahweh: nowadays, as in late Judaism, it is natural to understand this expression as 'angels'; but when the angels had not yet been invented the effect of these words on the reader must have been different.[10]

In almost every locality in Palestine in which excavations have been made, terracotta figurines have been found, either in bas-relief or as a complete shape, representing a nude woman or just a female head with somewhat elaborate hairstyle. These figurines, which can be assigned to the first centuries of the first millennium BC, certainly represent a female deity associated with fertility, and even if it is not possible to give her a precise name ('Astarte plaques' is a purely conventional name) there is no doubt that here we have representations of a goddess widely worshipped by the Israelites. To this evidence, which has been known for some time and which leads us to postulate the existence of a female deity in the ancient Hebrew pantheon, recent excavations have added quite significant material: in the locality of Kuntillet 'Ajrud, between the Negeb and Sinai, a sanctuary from the ninth-eighth century BC has provided Hebrew inscriptions (still largely unpublished) with the texts of prayers addressed to Yahweh (*yhw* and *yhwh*), but the text of one prayer was accompanied by two representations, albeit rough ones, of the god Bes, while in another Yahweh was invoked along with his consort Ashera.[11] In the Old Testament the term *ašerah* denotes an unspecified object connected with the cult of Astarte, whereas in the mythological texts of Ugarit and in the pre-Islamic Arab world it is the proper name of a goddess; at Ugarit Asherat is the spouse of El, the head of the pantheon. The new epigraphic evidence provides proof that Ashera was a goddess who was also venerated among the Israelites and that this goddess was closely connected with Yahweh.[12] This testimony relating to the existence of a consort of the god of Israel at the end of the ninth century BC confers decisive importance on another piece of epigraphic evidence, often ignored because it is regarded as an expression of late syncretism: I mean the Jewish Elephantine papyri and other texts relating to the Jewish colony in Egypt in the fifth century BC; Yahu (*Yhw*) was worshipped by the Judaeans along with Egyptian deities (ostracon Clermont-Ganneau no.70) and had a consort, the goddesss Anat-Yahu (Cowley Papyrus 44). So when Jeremiah (ch.44) rebukes his compatriots in Egypt for following the cult of the 'queen of heaven' and local deities, he is quite simply speaking the truth. At this point it becomes difficult to deny that real polytheism for a long time existed alongside the worship which the Hebrews offered to their national god Yahweh.

What then is to be the conclusion of this discussion? A critical reading of the Old Testament, the epigraphic and archaeological[12a] information, leaves no doubt of the fact that, contrary to what is explicitly stated in the Bible, the religion of the Israelites was originally substantially analogous to that professed by the other populations of the same geographical area. The pre-eminence of the national god Yahweh (who, as we have seen, moreover pre-existed the formation of the Hebrew people) was a form of henotheism no different from that attested among the other populations who lived alongside the Israelites: Yahweh was the national god of the Israelites just as Chemosh was that of the Moabites, Milkom of the Ammonites, Hadad of the Aramaeans and Melkart of the Tyrians. With these populations, and especially with the Tyrians and Phoenicians of the other Canaanite cities, Israel initially shared polytheism and a certain mythological heritage, and in addition offered worship to a goddess of fertility who was considered the consort of the national god.

Against this religious situation, which made the Israelites completely similar to their neighbours, there arose the preaching of some prophetic circles which championed a religious reform based on the purely moral cult of one God. This was a reform which had as its premise the complete religious identity between Israel and Canaan and which had the aim of making Israel something exceptional, unique, among all the other peoples, putting them in a direct and exclusive relationship with God. As I said earlier, the religious message placed in the mouth of Moses was not something new which came from outside Palestine to change the religious face of the country of Canaan, but a reaction which originated in Palestine itself against a type of religion observed by the whole population, the Israelite part of it no less than the Phoenician or the Moabite. In this way the relationship between Yahwistic Hebrew religion and Phoenician religion no longer takes the form of two different entities unexpectedly coming into contact, as in the historical examples I noted at the beginning, but is the result of an internal evolution, albeit through conflict, within the sphere of the same reality. This means that the historical process which led to the formation of Hebrew monotheism as a reaction to Phoenician polytheism was not so different from that which gave life to Christian universalism as opposed to Hebrew nationalism.

Confronted with the marked discrepancy between the result of historical analysis and what the Bible says about the origins of Yahwism, it is natural to ask why the latter painted a picture which was so far from reality. A first reply, of a general kind, in a way shows the naivety of the question: it obviously presupposes that the Old Testament, or at least its narrative parts, offers a reasonably faithful account of certain events, that it is a history book. In reality the Old Testament is not the more or less objective history of a people and its religious fortunes, but only the final result and at the same time the basic ideal of a religious reform. In it everything is markedly ideologized and bent to the sole purpose of showing the truth of a particular religious vision – a vision which presents the history of the Hebrew people as a theatre for the work of God, thus creating a new type of mythology. Since this is the 'sacred' nature of this book, it is evident that we cannot ask of the Bible an account which is 'faithful to events'; all it gives is an interpretation of them.

If we then go on to look at things rather more closely, we find that the situation is complex: pre-exilic Hebrew writings substantially agree in offering glimpses of the 'real religion' of Israel (with fleeting allusions which are none the less explicit ones): polytheism, the adoption of Phoenician cults, sacral prostitution and the cult of Tammuz even in the temple of Jerusalem, and so on. This picture of religion, which is certainly not very edifying, is one that is being increasingly confirmed by discoveries: on this point at least, the Bible was right! On the other hand, the Old Testament shows a long and powerful force opposed to to this situation and aimed at giving the Israelites something different in religious terms: an ethical monotheism which in effect comes to be realized fully during the exile. It is quite natural that, having become the aim of a small minority (the few exiles of Judah who were not assimilated to their Babylonian environment), this should have sought to present itself as a legitimate representation of all Israel; and therefore that it should have given life to a reconstruction of the past which was ideologically consonant with the actual situation: a small group deprived of political power and always facing the risk of ethnic assimilation. The whole history of Israel and indeed of the world is seen in a perspective which is meant to highlight the priestly caste of a small group of deportees who want to maintain their ethnic identity: the prophetic preaching over many centuries, which had been made in quite different conditions, was taken over and collected only to the degree that it was useful for the ideological 'priestly' positions. Who can say how many Hebrew prophetic writings were lost because they did not fit in with the ideas of the priests of Jerusalem? (One might think of the fate of all the 'apocryphal' literature, which was in part saved by the Christians and the Essenes of Qumran.)

So what the Old Testament gives us is a history of the religious evolution of Israel from the point of view of the priestly class of Jerusalem in the post-exilic period: a history with irritatingly nationalist connotations, characterized by an increasingly marked exclusivism.

If we compare the picture that we have been able to outline with that painted by the Old Testament, we shall note that there are three essential points of difference: the Old Testament projects the religious message on to a somewhat remote time, at the very origins of the Hebrew people; moreover it locates this event on Sinai, i.e. outside Palestine, and denies all connections between Yahwism and Phoenician religion, with which the relationship is shown to be one only of antagonism; finally, by making Yahweh relate exclusively to the Hebrew people it eliminates the link which on the religious level was able to unite, albeit partially, the Hebrews with other semitic populations who worshipped the same god.[13]

The first point can be justified fairly easily. It was the first time in history, but certainly not the last, when a religious reform was presented as a return to the purity of first origins, origins which, however, each person understood in his own way. It is certainly more effective propaganda to say that a certain thing must be done because our ancestors used to do it than to invite people to do something new, especially when, as in this case, the society is markedly traditional and largely illiterate. The back-dating of events seems to have been a constant practice in the Hebrew circles who carried out the religious reform; the episode narrated in II Kings 22 in connection with the rediscovery of the book which prompted Josiah to carry out his religious reform in 621 BC is a significant one. Modern scholars, even those who do not think it was a pious fraud, accept that this book was substantially the book of Deuteronomy which we have now, which would make it the only book of the Pentateuch that can be dated with some exactitude. That some kind of religious reform was carried out at the time of Josiah, or at any rate in the seventh century BC, is demonstrated by the fact that from this point on, Hebrew epigraphy presents a very rich Yahwistic nomenclature.[14] But that this reform coincided with the ideas expressed in Deuteronomy and in particular with the centralization of the cult at Jerusalem remains quite doubtful. The mention of a 'temple of Yahweh' in one of the Hebrew ostraca discovered at Arad, in the Negev, a temple clearly related to the locality (perhaps Tell Ira) from which the ostracon had been sent, shows that the centralization of the cult had not been achieved by the end of the kingdom of Judah and provides a not insignificant argument to those (though of course there are not many of them) who argue that Deuteronomy is to be dated to the exilic or post-exilic period.

If we remember the positive outcome of the struggle between Yahwism and Phoenician religion, it is difficult to give an adequate explanation of the motive that moved the redactors of the Old Testament to give an extra-Palestinian origin to a type of religion which came into being in the land of Canaan. Today, in our eyes, the creation of Yahwism within Phoenician polytheism seems much more of an achievement, much more exceptional than the importation of it from Sinai which is claimed. So it is evident that the way in which those who brought about this religious revolution thought must have been different. In seeking to identify them we should consider the phenomenon as a whole as it is presented in the Old Testament.

The message of Moses, including its religious content, is inextricably inserted into a historical context which is that of the conquest (a miraculous conquest) of the promised land. The Hebrews bring into Palestine not so much a new religion as a new people, namely themselves. This is the ideological vision put forward by the Bible. It is a vision that is only partially true, because we know, as the authors of the Old Testament knew, that not all the Israelites came from outside, with Joshua. The Hebrews knew as well as we do that 'Hebrews' were the outlaws who lived on the margins of society in an ambiguous position, and that these 'Hebrews' (the Babylonians called them *khabiru*) were particularly numerous in the areas and periods of greatest political and social disturbance – like those which favoured the settlement of some Israelite tribes in Palestine.[15] 'Hebrews' were those who lived hidden away in caverns and gave a hand to Jonathan son of Saul in his foray against the Philistine camp (I Sam.14.11). The arrival in Palestine of a new people who believe in Yahweh thus seems anachronistic if referred to the protohistory of Israel, whereas it fits perfectly into another historical situation, the return to Jerusalem of a group of exiles from Babylon. It is on this arrival in Palestine at the end of the sixth century BC that the historical narrative of the origins of the Hebrew people is constructed, and at this moment and in this way that Yahwism was founded, projecting on to a period that we calculate to be around 1200 BC the situation existing in the second year of Darius. The hostility on the part of those who returned and their desire to be separate from the 'people of the land' (those who were spared deportation), transferred to the time of their origins, give rise to a remarkable historical conception: autochthony, which for other peoples of ancient civilization was a point of honour, was felt to be a cause for shame. The legend of the conquest under Joshua contrasts significantly with the words of Thucydides, 'only Attica, which from time immemorial, because of the aridity of the soil, remained immune from all invasions, was always inhabited by the same people' (1.2), and with the haste with which Livy (1.2) makes his Trojans become Latins.

This same need to distinguish themselves from the rest of the world, and in particular from certain neighbours, is the cause of the failure to recognize the fact that other people also worshipped the god who was, at least in origin, also the god of the Hebrews. Today we are not in a position to assess how far the Hebrews were aware of the diffusion of the cult of their god among other people: however, the good geographical knowledge and ethnological reflections in Gen.10; 25 suggest that they must have had some idea of this. Whether intended or not, the exclusiveness of the relationship between Yahweh and the people of Israel remains quite significant.

It is the duty of the historian to take note of the concern of the Hebrews to regard themselves as being different from the other peoples, a concern of which the Old Testament is the ideological projection and of which the behaviour of a large part of Judaism, ancient and modern, is the reflection in practical life. But it must not be forgotten that this attitude is the consequence of a relatively late religious view, even if it is supported by so authoritative a text as the Bible.[16] In the period before the exile things were very different, and this needs to be investigated without prejudice. I shall limit myself to a single example. One of the fundamental rites of Judaism is circumcision, the origin of which is narrated in Genesis 17. According to this text, which is quite late, circumcision is imposed by God on Abraham as a tangible sign of the covenant concluded between them. The pious reader of this passage, Jew or Christian, will obviously be led to believe that circumcision was a rite particular and exclusive to the Hebrews, for whom it was also an external sign of their faith in Yahweh. The historian, more shrewd, even if equally pious, will see things rather differently, remembering that circumcision was widespread among the Egyptians and also among the Phoenicians, as Herodotus (2,104) as well as Philo of Byblos testifies. We cannot but think that this rite is a good example of the survival of Phoenician religion.

Chapter 5

From the Anointer to the Anointed: the 'Messiah'

According to the biblical texts, all the Hebrew kings of the south were 'anointed' and some of those from the north, like Jehu, beginning with Saul; this is not said explicitly of all of them but it is difficult to doubt that in the thought of the authors of the sacred text all the kings of Judah were anointed. Unction was not, however, the exclusive prerogative of the king: the prophets were also anointed. In this connection a passage which reports the words that Yahweh spoke to the prophet Elijah is significant: 'Yahweh said to him: "Go, return on your way to the wilderness of Damascus; and when you arrive, you shall anoint Hazael to be king over Syria; and Jehu, the son of Nimshi, you shall anoint to be king over Israel; and Elisha the son of Shaphat of Abelmeholah you shall anoint to be prophet in your place"' (I Kings 19.15-16). It follows clearly from this passage that being anointed by a prophet in fact amounted to being designated king or prophet with full rights, i.e. someone in a position to 'anoint' in his turn. The kingdom for which one is destined is irrelevant: Hazael will be king of Damascus, Jehu of Israel; neither Elijah nor Elisha anointed any king of Judah. So before the exile, being anointed amounted to being king, i.e. acquiring certain privileges – not only political and economic but also religious – which were not given to anyone else.

Well on in the post-exilic period, in texts attributed to the Priestly writer, we find a completely different conception of anointing: the one who is anointed, 'consecrated' in an exclusively religious sense, is the priest (cf. Ps.84.9), and the oil of consecration is reserved to the sacred objects: 'Yahweh said to Moses: Take the finest spices: of liquid myrrh five hundred shekels, and of sweet-smelling cinnamon half as much,

Davies, P.R.   rev. Giovanni

<u>J Th S</u> n.s. 41 (1990) 124-29.

History and Ideology in the United Israel.

(London: SCM, 1988.)

that is, two hundred and fifty, and of aromatic cane two hundred and fifty, and of cassia five hundred, according to the shekel of the sanctuary, and of olive oil a hin; and you shall make of these a sacred anointing oil blended as by the perfumer; a holy anointing oil it shall be. And you shall anoint with it the tent of meeting and the ark of the testimony, and the table and all its utensils, and the lampstand and its utensils, and the altar of incense, and the altar of burnt offering with all its utensils; and the laver and its base; you shall consecrate them, that they may be most holy; whatever touches them will become holy. And you shall anoint Aaron and his sons, and consecrate them, that they may serve me as priests. And you shall say to the people of Israel, "This shall be my holy anointing oil throughout your generations. It shall not be poured upon the bodies of ordinary men, and you shall make another like it in composition; it is holy, and it shall be holy to you. Whoever compounds any like it or whoever puts any of it on an outsider shall be cut off from his people'" (Ex.30.22-33). The implementation of these prescriptions is narrated succinctly in Lev.8.10-12. As can be seen from the detailed prescription, this priestly oil is a long way from the oil from the prophets' flask, which moreover could hardly have dispensed the precious Yemenite fragrances which only began to be developed after the eighth century BC. The Priestly conception of anointing, which a fairly late text (I Sam.2.35-36) projects on to the time of Samuel (just as the prophecy of Nathan projects the conception of Davidic descent on to the time of David), is very interesting if analysed in connection with prophetic and royal anointing. Whereas in this latter case, as we shall see better in due course, the anointing materially sanctions a designation already made or a quality already possessed, the Priestly anointing itself confers a particular quality, we might say *ex opere operato*, with an expression not as remote from this context as it might seem at first sight. In other words, the king is anointed (designated 'messiah') because he is king; the priest becomes priest by virtue of being anointed (made 'messiah'). The relationship between the two anointings is that of an inversion of cause and effect, which shows the profound difference which came about in the idea of anointing from the time of the exile on. What we must clarify at this point is the original significance of anointing; in later Judaism the priests were anointed to confer a sacral character on them; but why were kings and prophets anointed before the exile?

The Hebrew root *mšḥ* (whence *mašiaḥ*, 'messiah', 'anointed') appears in other semitic languages like Aramaic and Arabic; its meaning is 'anoint', but in a sense that has nothing to do with religion: the specific sense of the root is that of 'rubbing', evidently with an oily substance; we might say 'massage'. This word, used in a purely secular sense, can also be found in a Jewish text (written in Aramaic) dated to 403 BC, one of the Elephantine papyri.[1] Anointing with oil in the world of the ancient Near East meant in the first place expressing a state of joy (rather like our wearing perfume, but that on the whole is limited to women, while at that time anointing with perfumed oil was particularly a male practice). Another meaning of anointing was the quite obvious one of purification: to anoint (obviously after washing) meant to cleanse oneself, and thus also to purify oneself in a liturgical sense. Another character that anointing had was in Mesopotamia, where the action served to seal the clauses of a legal transaction, for example a sale; we also find this significance at Ugarit, in the second millennium BC, where for example anointing is attested as the ratification of the liberation of a sacred prostitute. It can readily be conceded that not only do all these significances of anointing attested for ancient Asia Minor have no connection with Hebrew anointing; they do not have any sacral dimension at all.[2]

To find an analogy within certain limits to Hebrew anointing we must turn to Egypt: here anointing was practised to indicate the investiture of an official by the Pharaoh. To be anointed meant entering the service of the Pharaoh in the state apparatus; foreign princesses were anointed when they were chosen as brides of the Egyptian king.

What is lacking completely in the ancient Near East, even if every now and then (even recently) there are attempts with specious arguments (but without factual data) to make the phenomenon less consistent, is the rite of anointing as royal investiture.[3] The Egyptian rulers were not anointed (as we saw, they had their dependents anointed); the Mesopotamian rulers were not anointed. The only evidence to be discussed is that of a Hittite text from which it emerges that a substitute for the king was anointed who was destined to die in the king's place in particular circumstances; now leaving aside any relevance that possible Hittite anointing could have for Hebrew custom, one has to note that the anointing of the royal substitute could not in any way be regarded as tantamount to royal unction, because of the evident difference in situations.[4] So since there is no explicit evidence in this connection, we can say that the Hittites, too, like the Egyptians, the Babylonians and the other peoples of the Near East, did not anoint their kings. But at this point we must ask: in that case, what then was the anointing of the Israelite kings?

The answer to this question is given by an attentive reading of the biblical text itself, approached without the preconceived idea of royal 'consecration'. When Samuel goes in search of David to 'anoint' him he goes to Bethlehem; Jesse and his seven sons stand in front of him and Samuel then asks Yahweh: 'Surely Yahweh's consecrated one is before him?' (I Sam.16.6). Note that the 'consecrated' one ('messiah', 'anointed'), i.e. David, was not present at that moment; but he is called 'anointed' even before he is known, and therefore anointed, by Samuel. The exact translation of the term would in any case be: 'designated', 'chosen beforehand'. In the Davidic succession narrative we see that Absalom and then Adonijah are considered to be kings and behave as kings (the way in which Absalom takes possession of David's harem is significant, cf. II Sam.16.21-22), but without being anointed; the anointing of Solomon himself is spoken of in a rather strange way: first it is said that it was the priest Zadok who anointed the new king (I Kings 1.39), but after a few lines (v.45) it is said that Solomon was anointed by Zadok and the prophet Nathan; the peripheral character of the reference to anointing, to say no more than that, arouses the suspicion that these are additions to the original text, which probably did not speak of an anointing of Solomon at all. One thing is certain, and that is that the 'messiah' Cyrus, designated with this name by Deutero-Isaiah (Isa.45.1), was not anointed. On the other hand it seems strange that we have three anointings for David: one by Samuel (I Sam.16.13); one by the men of Judah (II Sam.2.4) and finally one by the men of Israel (II Sam.5.3). If only the first was sacralizing, in that a prophet performed it, what is the significance of the other two? And how could an assembly of citizens anoint, i.e. confer a supposedly sacred character on, a king?

In its bias, secondary character and indeed contradictions, the biblical evidence has a coherent logic only on the hypothesis that the anointing of a ruler had the same significance as that of anointing in Egypt: the anointing simply indicated a 'designation' without any sacral character. Thus the meaning of pre-exilic anointing becomes perfectly clear: in an ideological perspective of an Egyptian kind, like the one we have indicated, the fact of being able to anoint someone meant asserting the power of the anointer over the anointed. Just as it was for the Pharaoh to anoint, i.e. to nominate, his dependents, so the fact of being able to subject a king to anointing by a prophet was meant to assert the superiority of the prophet, as a man of God, over the king himself. So here we come to the nub of the problem: the anointing of Israelite kings is the expression (in all probability an exclusively literary expression) of the struggle carried on by prophetism against the monarchy, an attempt to declare the inferiority of the king to the prophet[5] – and later (see Zadok) to the priest and even to the whole popular assembly.

The political and religious position of the prophets in their opposition to the monarchy and the emphasis of the historical books (inspired by prophets) on the fact that it was for prophets to designate the kings themselves by anointing them, can be explained from the royal ideology of the ancient Near East, an ideology which was, of course, partly shared by the Hebrews. The king had no need to be consecrated for the simple reason that he was already sacred *per se*, simply by the fact of being king: the activity of the king, as we saw from the texts of the ancient Near East and the Old Testament itself, was essentially that of a priest; he was the one who performed the most important sacrifices and ceremonies. The clergy under the ruler, who must have been quite numerous, were necessary for the ordinary administration of the cult, for the lesser needs of the population. But the essential relationship between the deity and the people was maintained by the king in his own person. The king was so little 'anointed' that it was for him to anoint, i.e. to make more vital, the deity himself: in a Ugaritic ritual text we read that once a year the king made a libation of oil (i.e. an anointing) for Baal;[6] and what else was the anointing that Jacob did to the pillar on which he had slept (Gen.28.18)? It is against this historical background that the biblical narratives relating to the kings and their anointing must be set; this anointing probably never actually took place except perhaps in the case of a ruler very close to prophetic circles and was in any case understood exclusively in terms of designation, not of 'consecration'.

So in pre-exilic Israel (and perhaps also in the rest of the land of Canaan) there were two types of anointing, one which sanctified and one which designated, both the prerogative of the king: one in his most strictly religious functions, the other in his political functions. With the transplanting of the educated classes of Judah to Babylon this situation must have changed radically for objective reasons: because there was no longer a king, and because, as we have seen, the Babylonians had a completely different conception of anointing from the Egyptian one which was also adopted by the Israelites, and especially because among the exiles the most authoritative voice, and the one most listened to, was that of the prophets, who were hostile to the king.

From the exile onwards the figure of the king who anoints, which basically corresponded to a magical conception of the world, disappears; with it the functions of being the link between God and people exercised by the king also disappear: now God deals directly with the people. We read in a continuation of Deutero-Isaiah: 'Ho, every one who thirsts, come to the waters, and he who has no money, come, buy and eat! Come, buy wine and milk without money and without price... Incline your ear, and come to me; hear, that your soul may live; and I will make you an everlasting covenant, my steadfast, sure love for David. Behold, I make him a witness to the peoples, a leader and commander for the peoples' (Isa.55.1,3-4). These words are quite clear: God wants to bind all the people with the covenant which had previously had been bound up with the house of David. At the same moment, however, the 'anointed' king, the 'messiah' king appears: Cyrus (Isa.45.1), Zerubbabel (Zech.6.12, even if the title 'messiah' is not used explicitly). This anointing combines in itself the two previous functions, simultaneously designates and sanctifies, because it is carried out directly by God; the prophetic function has triumphed. When later the high priest prepared the oil of anointing, he was repeating on a smaller scale an action reserved for God.

At this point it would seem that the king was definitively eliminated from 'messianic' ideology, since his place had been taken first by the people and later by the one who claimed to represent them, the high priest. However, the event had a sequel which it is worth narrating.

It is known from more or less embarrassed allusions by various biblical writers[7] that Darius attempted to put a descendant of the ancient ruling house, Zerubbabel, on the throne of Jerusalem (certainly in a vassal position, like the kings of Phoenician cities). This was thwarted, we do not know in what way, by the priestly class, and in particular by Joshua son of Jozedek. What could have become a small monarchical state became instead a modest hierocratic enclave which at a certain point, in the third century BC, remained excluded from even the most lively economic activity.[8] It seems natural that at this point the dream should begin of a better future, with a greater, richer, more important Jerusalem than that which had been reduced by the rule of priests; out of this sense of frustration was born the messianic expectation, the expectation of a descendant of that king whom the history writer had already presented as the founder of an empire.

'There shall come forth a shoot from the stump of Jesse, and a branch shall grow out of his roots. And the Spirit of Yahweh shall rest upon him, the spirit of wisdom and understanding, the spirit of counsel and might, the spirit of knowledge and the fear of the Lord' (Isa.11.1-3); 'Behold, the days are coming, says the Lord, when I will raise up for David a righteous Branch, and he shall reign as king and deal wisely, and shall execute justice and righteousness in the land. In his days Judah will be saved, and Israel will dwell securely. And this is the name by which he will be called, "Yahweh our righteousness'" (Jer. 23.5-6). In the sphere of history writing the hopes become evident in the prophecy which Nathan makes to David: 'Thus says the Lord of hosts, I took you from the pasture, from following the sheep, that you should be prince over my people Israel... When your days are fulfilled and you lie down with your fathers I will raise up your offspring after you, who shall come forth from your body, and I will establish his kingdom. And your house and your kingdom shall be made sure for ever before me; your throne shall be established for ever' (II Sam.7.8,12,16).

The emphasis in the Old Testament writings on the continuity of the dynasty of David needs to be explained. From our point of view, if God wanted to redeem his people it would have been enough for him to have raised up a new king, obviously in favourable conditions. But our point of view does not take account of the ideological demands of ancient Near Eastern culture. The conception of the monarchy attested in the area of Syria and Palestine at least from the end of the second millennium BC was based on the preferential relationship of the sovereign with the god of his own dynasty, a god who might not even be the most important of the pantheon, but who had secured the accession to the throne of the founder of the dynasty; it was he who in one sense guaranteed the continuity of the reigning house. This conception was also shared by the Hebrews: Yahweh had procured the throne for David, taking it away from Saul, and assured him a long dynastic descent; the fact that Solomon built the temple of Yahweh next to his own palace confirms that in the context of the monarchy Yahweh represented the dynastic god. But though the Hebrews shared the ideology of the monarchy with other people, they had a peculiarity which put them in a special position. Their monotheism, fully developed and operating in the post-exilic period in which the Davidic ideology was worked out, implied a marked restriction which the other monarchies escaped. In a polytheistic environment, a usurper who formed the beginning of a new dynasty had no difficulty in finding a dynastic god different from that of the previous dynasty; because the Hebrews recognized only one god they could only choose Yahweh. So what does this mean for the problem of the dynastic sequence of the Hebrew kings?

Our reply to this question is clearly very much conditioned by the historical information that we have at our disposal; and since this is provided exclusively by the Old Testament, in fact we have only the point of view of the Deuteronomistic historian, who reflects the position of Judah, which was very polemical towards Israel. In the northern kingdom, where the cult of Yahweh was just as rooted as it was in the south, there were various dynasties; how these resolved the problem of the alliance with the dynastic god we do not know. In the kingdom of Judah it is very probable that Yahweh was the dynastic god of various dynasties (remember what was said in Chapter 3), except that the case of Saul, who was first chosen and then abandoned in favour of David, shows that the covenant contracted by Yahweh need not be eternal and could be subject to a change of mind. With the refinement of religious sensibility episodes of this kind could no longer be accepted. Yahweh could not go back on a promise that he had made; hence the necessity for the one Davidic dynasty which the Deuteronomistic historian stresses so much.

The transformation of Maccabaean rule into a real monarchical dynasty, that of the Hasmonaeans, seemed for a short time to match the expectations of the Jewish people, but very soon their discontent returned. In Ps.Sol. 17 we can read: 'Lord, you chose David to be king over Israel, and swore to him about his descendants for ever, that his kingdom should not fail before you. But because of our sins, sinners rose up against us... With pomp they set up a monarchy because of their arrogance; they despoiled the throne of David with arrogant shouting... See, Lord, and raise up for them their king, the son of David, to rule over your servant Israel in the time known to you, O God.'[9] This text, which comes from shortly after the middle of the first century BC, displays an intolerance towards the ruling house which recalls the opposition of the pre-exilic prophets to the monarchy. The priestly monarchy, lauded by the so-called royal psalms (which generally can be dated to this period, even if they have references to the Davidic period, which guaranteed their entry into the canon), with its abuses and its crimes, certainly could not meet the political and religious aspirations of the Jewish people. Subjection to Rome, with the degree of Hellenization which that involved, was certainly appreciated by many, and it is easy to suppose that the expectation of a decidedly earthly messiah, who was therefore attributed to the house of David, was quite widespread, especially in popular circles. Here 'popular' is virtually equivalent to Pharisaic, i.e the educated class which by basing itself on the people in fact determined their ideological tendencies.

The heightening of messianic expectation in late Judaism thus contributed to the conception of the Davidic messiah on the part of the

Pharisees and a large part of the Hebrew people. But now we know that in this period Israel recognized two 'anointed', the king and the priest. So it is not surprising that in such an environment, and primarily in the priestly environment, the messiah was expected in priestly rather than royal garb. The Testaments of the Twelve Patriarchs and various Qumran writings (of Zadokite, i.e. priestly, origin) speak of two messiahs, a royal one born from the tribe of Judah and a priestly one, specifically from the tribe of Levi: and it is almost superfluous to add that the latter here seems more dominant than the former.[10]

This is also the ideological background against which, at a certain point, the figure of Jesus is delineated. The essential way in which the New Testament writers characterize the figure of Jesus of Nazareth is to say that he is the Messiah, i.e. the Christ: this is so much his nature that already in the letters of Paul the expression 'Christ Jesus' (without the article) is extremely frequent; often we just have 'Christ' by itself. So Jesus is first of all a messiah, indeed *the* Messiah *par excellence*. We need do no more than recall just one instance, the confession of Peter recorded by the Synoptic Gospels: 'And who do you say that I am? Peter replied: You are the Messiah' (Mark 8.29). Luke and Matthew have less schematic expressions, 'the Messiah of God' (Luke 9.20) and 'the Messiah, son of the living God' (Matt.16.16). For the contemporaries of Jesus that would mean being the messiah whom the writings of the New Testament clearly show: the messiah was a descendant of King David, and therefore of royal blood, destined to ascend the throne of the legitimate dynasty, that of Jerusalem. While the genealogies of Matt.1.1-17; Luke 3.23-28 document, though each in its own way, the fact that Joseph is of Davidic stock, thus providing the 'legal' premises for the designation of Jesus as Messiah, Luke 1.30-33 is quite explicit: addressing Mary, the angel says to her: 'You will bear a son and you shall call his name Jesus. He will be great, and will be called the Son of the Most High; and the Lord God will give to him the throne of his father David, and he will reign over the house of Jacob for ever and of his kingdom there will be no end.' So the Messiah will be a king of Davidic stock.

An observation which can be made at this point is that though he was defined as Messiah, i.e. anointed, Jesus was not 'anointed' by anyone. On the theological level this detail has been well brought out by the author of the Letter to the Hebrews, who, addressing someone obviously familiar with the Jewish tradition, could not pass over the essential point: 'But of the Son he says, "Thy throne, O God, is for ever and ever, the righteous sceptre is the sceptre of thy kingdom. Thou hast loved righteousness and hated lawlessness, therefore God, thy God, has anointed thee with the oil of gladness beyond thy comrades'" (1.8-9). And it is certainly no coincidence that these words are a direct quotation of Ps.45, one of the royal psalms. The special character of the royal nature of the Messiah, anointed directly by God without a human intermediary, is immediately evident here. However, it can be recalled that the lack of any material anointing in the case of Jesus was felt in one popular circle, perhaps a late one, as a kind of slur which had to be remedied with a legend. In the Apocryphal Gospel of St John, composed after 800 and handed down in an Arabic and an Ethiopic version (known as Miracles of Jesus), there is a story, already known to St Ephrem Syrus in the fourth century AD, that the perfumed oil which Mary Magdalene put on the feet of Jesus was none other than the oil of Moses used for the consecration of Israelite kings, priests and prophets, which had remained hidden for centuries. So in this way Jesus will have been also materially anointed with the oil of the kings of Israel.[11]

Thus Jesus appears as the royal messiah of the house of David expected by the Jews, but at the same time as a messiah of a new kind, ruler of a spiritual and eternal realm. Here, too, he closes one chapter of religious history and opens another.

Chapter 6

Abraham among the Chaldaeans

As they appear in the biblical text, the narrative cycles relating to the patriarchs Abraham, Isaac and Jacob seem extremely complex in terms of literary redaction. The subdivisions of the individual narratives or parts of them between the traditional 'sources' J, E and P is quite inadequate, and does not take account of what strikes any reader of the Hebrew text, namely the continual changes of names, vocabulary and style which have to be attributed to more than a few and distinct ancient 'sources': one senses the superposition of many different hands, and especially many different ideas, which can be fitted much more easily into the later manifestations of Hebrew thought than into what the ancient ideologies must have been. Be this as it may, it is not my intention to dwell on these problems; here I shall limit myself to referring to de Vaux's history for an analysis of these traditions within the sphere of the biblical text,[1] to Thompson's basic study for the problem of their historicity,[2] and to the most recent report by Bonora for an up-to-date panoramic survey of the relevant bibliography.[3] My aim here is to consider Abraham.

Some years ago the traditions about Abraham were the object of an extensive study by Van Seters,[4] which appeared soon after the more general study by Thompson, with which it agrees – and this is very significant – in what might be called its negative part; however, Thompson wrote a severe review of it,[5] not for its results but for its methodology: the great weakness of Van Seters, and not just in the book on Abraham,[6] is in fact that he cannot extract himself from that same traditional methodology with a Germanic stamp which he so bitterly criticizes. The way in which Van Seters succeeds in dating the whole Abraham cycle to the middle of the first millennium BC is exactly the same way in which others arrive at the eighteenth century BC, with the further disadvantage of being remarkably superficial; the consequence is that a number of good observations remain isolated and are not, as with Thompson, part of an organic approach which is methodologically new and convincing.

A series of different themes come together in the narrative cycle relating to Abraham: the emigration from Mesopotamia to Palestine via Syria, the promise of numerous descendants and of a land, relations with Lot, the miraculous birth and near-sacrifice of Isaac, the end of Sodom and Gomorrah, the problems caused by Sarah's beauty, and so on. To give any kind of dating to these themes and to identify the developments which led to the constitution of the cycle in its present form is not an easy task, and as far as the latter aspect is concerned is virtually impossible, because of the lack of any sound studies in this direction. However, there are two points in the Abraham narrative on which it is worth dwelling because they combine to give a fairly precise date, not to the relevant passages of the biblical text (which is what German biblical scholars would suggest)[7] but to the moment at which certain narrative themes arose.

The most obvious point to single out, which has moreover already been noted by both Thompson and and Van Seters,[8] is the reference to Ur of the Chaldaeans and to Harran. Such a precise geographical location has certainly not been provided by chance, nor is the mention of the Chaldaeans casual: talk in this connection of anachronism or even a late addition to a text which is regarded as being earlier does no good service either to biblical exegesis or to historical research, because in both cases it puts particular preconceived hypotheses before the objective data of the text, and before it is emended, that text has the right to be understood in its total ideological and literary character. The mention of Ur of the Chaldaeans seems anachronistic in respect of Abraham only to someone who considers the patriarchal narratives to be a kind of annalistic account which is to be referred to the second millennium BC – but this is only an idea of certain biblical scholars which is opposed first of all by the biblical text itself. The mention of Chaldaeans, of Ur, of Harran, and the choice of the name Terah for Abraham's father (a name which, as has already been noted, recalls that of a place in Syria not far from Harran) had a quite precise aim: to give Abraham a geographical and chronological base which pointed to Mesopotamia and Syria in the time of Nabonidus. This Babylonian ruler is well known for having been a fervent adherent of the cult of the moon god Sin, who had his most important sanctuaries specifically in Ur and at Harran; it is probable that Nabonidus' preference for Sin over Marduk indicates the influence of the aged queen mother who had been a priestess of Sin, and perhaps also reflects the ethnic origins of the Chaldaean ruler, which lie quite close to those of the Arabians and Southern Arabians; at all events, it is certain that there were good political reasons, such as the quest for the support and even the control of Arab populations and an attempt to reduce the power of the Babylonian clergy of Marduk.[9] In the past scholars have wanted to see the reference to the lunar cult as a reflection of the supposedly mythological character of Abraham;[10] to these references should be added the name Terah, which with the corresponding Syrian toponym is explained as 'ibex',[11] the sacred animal of the moon god in Arab circles. But mythology does not come into it; the reason (which the scholars cited above have not asked about) for the presence of references to Nabonidus and his politics in the narrative of Abraham is to be sought in the desire of the Jews in Babylon to create an original link between themselves, as exiles, and the king they obeyed. By having Abraham born in Ur the Jews proclaimed themselves autochthonous, albeit only at a distant time, to the land in which they found themselves a conquered people, and by linking Abraham first with Ur and then with Harran they had a way of reminding Nabonidus of the places most dear to him. This was an elegant way of declaring themselves 'fellow-countrymen' of Nabonidus, precisely the same practice as the Phoenicians rather later who, during the period of Achaemenidean domination, circulated the claim, recorded by Herodotus (7.89), that they came from the 'Eritrean sea': this is not the Red Sea, as many scholars have wrongly supposed, but the Persian Gulf, over which the original land of the Persians looked.[12]

This *captatio benevolentiae* on the part of the Jews towards the Chaldaean dynasty is not an isolated fact. The oracles of Ezekiel against Tyre and Egypt (chs.26-32) can be read from different perspectives, but there is no doubt that one way of looking at them is to see them as providing unconditional support for the imperialistic policy of Nebuchadnezzar, with praise of the exploits of the Babylonian ruler. These exploits are presented as an example of the power of Yahweh and of his revenge, but we cannot understand what revenge this is, seeing that Tyre and Egypt were the traditional allies of the Hebrew states. Thus the imperialism of Nebuchadnezzar, even if it had been directed against Jerusalem, was interpreted in a theological key, but if someone had read the verses of Ezekiel to the Babylonian king he would certainly have been pleased.[13] On the other hand, we must not forget the good treatment which Awel-Marduk accorded his prisoner King Jehoiachin (II Kings 25.27ff.); the fact that some centuries later Nabonidus appears as protagonist of a Jewish literary work (attested only by the Aramaic fragment of the 'Prayer of Nabonidus') confirms the close tie which bound the Jews to the Chaldaean dynasty, if only in an ambiguous love-hate relationship. This is a relationship on which much light is shed by the observation that throughout the period of the Chaldaean dynasty, before and after Nebuchadnezzar destroyed Jerusalem, the great Jewish bank of Egibi-Aqibah flourished in Babylon.[14]

If the narrative theme of the migration of Abraham easily finds its origin in Babylon at the time of Nabonidus, the theme of the promise is also capable of being determined chronologically. That this is a relatively late theme was already brought out some decades ago[15] (even if this is not usually taken account of, since virtually all biblical scholars today adopt the position of the once-abhorred Wellhausen, with his Yahwist in the ninth century BC): it has, however, been the merit of Van Seters[16] to have understood that the blessing and the promise to Abraham represent a transfer to the people generally of what were once the prerogatives of royalty, according to the ideology developed by Deutero-Isaiah. Leaving aside the 'Priestly' insertions which appear in the present text, it appears quite clearly that the relationship which is instituted between God and Abraham has nothing to do with the 'covenant', which in fact is always imposed by the stronger on the weaker of the two parties. God promises Abrahaam numerous descendants, without laying down any conditions; he gives him the blessing which is the gift of fertility, of which in the ideology of the ancient Near East the king was the guarantor. We find this ideological change, which we can truly call revolutionary, applied in Gen.15, but it is enunciated theoretically elsewhere: 'I will make you an everlasting covenant, my steadfast, sure love for David' (Isa.55.3): 'Behold, I am against the shepherds; and I will require my sheep at their hand, and put a stop to their feeding the sheep... I myself will search for my sheep' (Ezek.34.9,10). In these writings from Babylonian Judaism the denunciation and the repudiation of the monarchy are expressed without middle terms; now all the people has become sovereign, to put it in modern terms, in the strict sense of the word. It is certainly no coincidence that in these same texts we find an explicit recollection of Abraham as founder of the people (Isa. 51.2; Ezek.33.24). The moment in which this new conception is affirmed can be identified with remarkable closeness; it obviously presupposes the end of the monarchy but also the end of the ideological clash between the adherents of the new ideas and those who had remained faithful to the monarchical ideology and to the Davidic dynasty, for example the followers of Zerubbabel. Now the first part of Deutero-Isaiah (chs.40-48) reflects precisely the political ideology of Darius,[17] while the second presents itself as a further development of the 'Book of Consolation'. We therefore find ourselves around 500 BC.

In short, we have recovered two chronological points of reference within the Abraham cycle, the beginning and end of the sixth century BC, in a decidedly Mesopotamian context. By having Abraham born in Mesopotamia the Jews acted in precisely the same way as the Romans, who at a certain moment thought it opportune to call themselves descendants of the Trojan hero Aeneas.

However, the time has now come for us to analyse the most specifically historical aspect of the patriarchal narratives. The first point to make is that the whole operation of projecting certain events (the migration from Ur, the promise) back on origins was possible to the degree that there must have been traditions (for the moment it does not matter whether they were written or oral) according to which the Jews, or at least those Jews who were in Babylon, recalled that they had a founder of their people, Abraham. That means that certain traditions about Abraham, like those about Sodom and Gomorrah or about the status of Abraham as *ger* of the Philistines (Gen.21.34), must have been earlier than the exile, during which others were created and were added to the former ones; the hypothesis that all the traditions relating to Abraham are no earlier than the exile, which Van Seters seems to hold, seems improbable, because if they had all been invented in Babylonia they would have been different (and shortly we shall see why). At this point we must consider another point about the patriarchal narrative cycles. It is a generally accepted fact that the figure of Isaac is somewhat flimsy and that the narratives which have him as protagonist are justified only in relation to Abraham, when they are not late repetitions. This means that essentially there are only two real patriarchs with their respective narrative cycles, Abraham and Jacob. It is also well known that while Abraham moves in a decidedly southern area, Jacob presents a more complex situation. What is generally surprising about this is that the Hebrews liked to call themselves 'sons of Jacob' but were even fonder of calling themselves 'sons of Israel', and we know absolutely nothing about this Israel, the eponymous ancestor of the northern kingdom – in other words, the Bible is completely silent about this figure, who was only identified with Jacob at a late stage and almost incidentally.[18]

For a rather clearer view in this situation we must fix our attention on Jacob, taking as our guide an acute mind like that of the late Fr de Vaux. Four strands can be recognized in the Jacob cycle: one typically southern, connected with Esau/Edom; one from the Transjordan, connected with Laban; one from central Palestine (Shechem and Bethel), and finally a secondary one of the combined Jacob-Israel.[19] All this shows that the traditions about Jacob were complex, whereas their localization in various areas of Palestine suggests probable shifts of tribal groups between the south and the north, as well as obviously in Transjordan; but it also reveals that the present form of the cycle must have been determined in the south,[20] where in part it takes place. In other words, the northern traditions about Jacob are as unknown as those about Israel, if these ever existed; at any rate, the double localization of Jacob in the south and in the north, along with the Transjordanian setting, explains how he came to be accepted as the eponymous ancestor of all Israel, as father of the twelve eponymous ancestors of the twelve tribes. So in the south, too, Jacob was the true tribal head of the Hebrew people. In that case, what is Abraham?

The biblical narrative as we now have it makes Abraham the grandfather of Jacob and therefore in fact the true tribal head, since God made the promise to him. After what I have said in this connection, however, it is difficult to doubt that this systematization of relationships between the two patriarchs goes back to a relatively late period; all the more so since the original independence of the Jacob cycle from that of Abraham is generally accepted. To understand the historiographical operation that the biblical author carried out we have to explain the motives which led him to the present systematization.

Given that to begin with the traditions about Abraham were completely independent from those about Jacob, theoretically several solutions were possible: one of the two traditions could be completely abandoned, as happened with that of Israel; or if there was a desire to maintain both, it was possible to combine them in various ways, putting Jacob before Abraham, for example, or making him a collateral kinsman of Jacob. There must have been an internal logic for the traditions to have been fixed in the form with which we are familiar, and that is what we shall now try to discover. The fact that Jacob and not Abraham was considered the direct ancestor of the twelve tribes means that this tradition must have been so rooted among the southern Hebrews as well that it proved impossible to modify. However, that the pre-eminence was given to Abraham means that the person who systematized the cycle or at any rate who fixed the direction of the future systematization felt a particular bond with this figure: Abraham's sphere of activity in southern Palestine fits perfectly with the southern origin of the exiles who lived in Babylon at the time of Nebuchadnezzar. It was the Jews of the kingdom of Judah who put Abraham first and above Jacob; nor is it necessary to suppose that this happened during the exile; with the fall of Samaria Jerusalem presented itself as the political and cultural heir of its more powerful northern sister. The historical process which began at the time of Hezekiah would undergo a phase of intensive acceleration during the exilic period, which certainly would not end with 539 BC. The result was that at that time a completely new view of the history of the Jewish people was establihsed, the main features of which could be summed up in three points: the exiles from Judah affirmed their right to represent all Israel, making their ancestor Abraham the direct ancestor of Jacob and the repository of the divine promise; the institution of the monarchy was repudiated and the sacral figure of the king with his direct relationship with the deity was replaced by the people as a whole, who in this way automatically became a sacred people; and the distant origins of the Jewish people were put in southern Mesopotamia.

This is the distant past which the Jewish people, or rather that part of it which survived the whirlwind of historical events, created at a certain moment of its existence. It is, if you like, a mythical and legendary past, curiously similar to that which Rome created for itself not much later: an origin abroad which put it in direct contact with the cultural (and in the case of the Jews also the political) centre of the time, and providing a close contact with the divine world: Venus mother of Aeneas and Mars father of Romulus perform the same function in a different ideological context as Yahweh who makes his promise to Abraham. The Hebrew people is sacred because it has taken on royal sacrality and has the mission of testifying to the will of God (Isa.43.10-13); the Roman people is sacred because it has in it divine blood and has a mission to *'regere imperio populos'* (*Aeneid* 6,851). These are the premises of that juxtaposition between the two cities, the *caelestis* and the *terrena*, that St Augustine will make by opposing Israel to Rome.

So far we have attempted to reconstruct the sphere and the ideology in which some of the themes of the Abraham cycle came into being: now it remains to see how these themes were narrated, i.e. what kind of historiography was practised.

In the accounts relating to the patriarchs as they are now, leaving aside the origin of their components, we can claim that there is a kind of

narrative which is articulated in various ways but is centred from time
to time on an individual. To use a term which is by no means new in this
case, we can say that here we have *logoi*; from the narrative point of view
the stories of Abraham, Isaac and Jacob are not substantially different
from those which Herodotus wrote about Gigas, Croesus or Tomiris,
the queen of the Massageti. This comparison seems obvious and almost
banal, but it is so only in appearance. Its importance emerges when we
note that outside the Jewish and Greek world there are no prose
narratives of this kind. In Mesopotamia there are stories of figures like
Sargon and Naram-Sin, but these are extremely brief narratives and
moreover are written in verse. As for Egypt, a literature of this kind
never existed, since the narratives about the Pharaohs with romance-
like features were an integral part of the royal inscriptions, and romances
like that of Sinuhe cannot be considered *logoi*. After the observations
made by Van Seters,[21] it is difficult to consider the Königsnovelle, a
term brought into fashion in 1938 by A.Herrmann, as other than a
mystification: another of the fables invented by German culture in the
first half of this century.

    If we take the *logoi* of Herodotus as a starting point, it is easy to see
that the Old Testament offers other and even more relevant parallels in
addition to the patriarchal narratives: one thinks of stories about Saul,
David, Solomon, Jehu and Athaliah. These Hebrew *logoi* have a further
element in common with those of Herodotus, namely that they are
stories about rulers. But at this point a fact of great interest becomes
clear: leaving aside the literary genre, the ancient world knew of
written stories only in connection with rulers, about Egyptian Pharaohs,
Akkadian kings now legendary, famous rulers of Palestine, Lydia or
Persia. Only the Hebrew patriarchs had the honour of having *logoi* about
them without being kings – but this is true only up to a certain point,
because we have already seen that the patriarchs are the eponymous
ancestors of a people which was its own king. The adoption of a literary
type which was exclusive to the kings to narrate the history of the
patriarchs thus represented the inevitable historiographical reflection of
the new ideology according to which the patriarchs, and Abraham in
particular, had taken the place of the king: Abraham-people dealt directly
with God, Abraham-people was spoken of as a king. Over and above
this ideological element, at any rate attention should be paid to the new
course embarked on by Hebrew historiography over against that of the
rest of the Near East; albeit from a theocratic perspective, the biblical

writer resembles Herodotus in also narrating events which do not involve rulers.

The inevitable result of this discussion is that it is quite difficult to think in terms of *written* traditions relating to the patriarchs at a period earlier than the end of the sixth century BC. But I have also already said that these written traditions would not have been possible had there not been other oral traditions before them. It is worth making clear that this does not mean that I agree with that criticism which presupposes the conservation over long periods of time of oral traditions which remain unaltered and which are finally set down intact in writing. To suppose that the non-exilic and non-Priestly passages in the Abraham cycle faithfully reproduce pre-exilic traditions would be like claiming that Virgil limited himself to putting into hexameters a story exactly corresponding to his Aeneid which had already existed for a thousand years. The only thing that we may take to be reasonably certain is that in southern Palestine before the exile there were oral narratives centred on some figures who were considered the ancestors of one or more tribal groups.

At this point we must go back to our question: if Jacob was remembered as being the ancestor of all the tribes, what was Abraham? However did this figure exist who, before being linked with the Jacob cycle, does not seem to have had any direct relationship with any Hebrew tribe? The only possible answer to this question seems to me to be that we should see Abraham as the ancestor of a minor ethnic group which was subsequently incorporated into one of the southern tribes. The hypothesis put forward some years ago by M.Liverani, according to which the name Abraham is to be understood as 'father of Raham', a tribe mentioned in an inscription of Sethos I, to be dated around 1300 BC and coming from Beth Shean,[22] fits the bill perfectly.

So Jacob and Abraham were two eponymous figures of southern Palestine, just as Israel must have been an eponymous figure of the north – though we have no direct traditions about him. Now we must note that the existence of eponymous figures for populations is not attested among any other people of the ancient Near East outside Israel: neither the Sumerians nor the Babylonians nor the Assyrians nor the Phoenicians nor any others have left anything of this kind. However, we do find analogous figures elsewhere: let us recall in the first place the family of Hellenus with its sons Aeolus, Dorus and Xutus, and the sons of this last, Ion and Achaeus; then there are Pelasgus, Teucrus and, in the Hellenized West, Romus-Romulus. It is in Greek historiography that we find narratives of the origins of the people through genealogies and the fortunes of the eponymous figure; therefore the earliest Greek historiographical works were written under the title of 'genealogies' (like those of Acusilaus, in the sixth century BC, Hecataeus, who wrote towards the beginning of the fifth century, and Pherecydes, from the first half of the fifth century), [23] evident models of the *toledot* of 'Priestly' historiography.

Such a close similarity between the historiography of a Greek kind and Hebrew historiography with the use of the eponymous figure cannot be coincidental, any more than is the almost simultaneous appearance of Greek *logoi* with Jewish *logoi* at the end of the sixth century BC. The explanation of this latter point is relatively easy. Jews and Greeks began to write history for different but essentially analogous reasons, i.e. to assert a new vision of the world which markedly contrasted with the one that had gone before – it must not be forgotten that we are precisely in the so-called 'axial age'. The Jews wrote, as we have seen, to back up their repudiation of the royal ideology and to affirm the ideal supremacy of the Judaism of Babylon: this is the birth of Judaism. The Greeks, having first been influenced by oral *logoi* of Asiatic origin,[24] very much like romances, wrote under the pressure of the religious and social demands spread by Orphism[25] to oppose mythological historiography in the name of a new historical awareness: 'The *logoi* of the Hellenes are many and ridiculous', says the famous fragment of Hecataeus.

The common use of eponymous figures by Greeks and Jews calls for a different discussion; here it is necessary to postulate a more direct and specific historical contact than the general and profound change in mentality experienced throughout the ancient world in the sixth century BC. That is all the more the case since this is a cultural affinity which shows itself well before the sixth century BC. Since we have to exclude any direct contact between Greeks and Jews, an intermediary seems indispensable, one which was in a position to transmit to the Jews a certain way of thinking of the past, customary among Greco-Anatolian people but unknown to the Semites. Many years ago an analogous problem, on a much wider scale, was noted by C.H.Gordon, who resolved it by projecting the data of the first millennium BC on to the period of the Late Bronze age and making Ugarit the intermediary between Canaan and the Aegean, to use his own expression.[26] The solution proposed by Gordon is illuminating, but does not take account of the profound cultural crisis which lasted three to four centuries, in which both the Greek and the Near Eastern world became involved; the points of contact, especially at a literary level, are decidedly later than the thirteenth century BC and therefore call for a later intermediary. It seems to me that this can be identified in the Philistines, direct heirs of Aegean and Anatolian culture, notwithstanding the rapid process by which this became assimilated to that of Canaan, and remained in close contact with the Greek world thanks to the intense commercial activity brought about through seafaring.[27]

This is not the first time that I have been led to speak of the Philistines as a possible source of inspiration for cultural elements among the Israelites of the southern kingdom;[28] even if that might sound somewhat unusual, it would not be inappropriate to recall that the Old Testament itself provides some pointers in this direction. Abraham was a 'guest' of the Philistines; David was a mercenary for them and when he became independent he enlisted them as his own chosen troops. Not to mention the 'Song of Deborah' which, in my view, is a hymn exalting the victory of Yahweh over the great Philistine god.[29] If this hypothesis is correct, the southern kingdom began to take on features of its own over against the north, being completely within the sphere of Phoenician culture: through Philistine culture, Judah was also able to absorb Aegean cultural motives, thanks to which we have been able to see Abraham, guest of Tjeker, in a light not too dissimilar from that of the Teucrian '*pater Anchises*'.

Chapter 7

A Prophet and the King of Kings

One of the most significant moments in the history of Jewish religious thought was that of the encounter between Cyrus and 'Deutero-Isaiah', between the greatest of the Persian kings and the greatest of the Israelite prophets. It was this encounter which marked the transition from Yahweh Sabaoth as 'God of the armed bands' to being 'God of the universe' and which laid down the premises for that type of universal religion which was later realized by Christianity. So it is worth our while analysing this encounter.

To have an idea of what a Hebrew prophet living in Babylon in the last decades of the sixth century BC would have been like, we must try to understand what a prophet was. The Hebrew prophets were men who for two hundred years had vigorously fought against a certain type of religion, but almost always in vain. When the kingdom of Judah was still an insignificant entity the prophet Amos left Tekoa, a village south of Jerusalem, to go and preach at Bethel; a few decades later, in his place we find Hosea, a prophet native to the north; on the fall of Samaria in 722 BC the interest of the prophets shifted to Jerusalem, which had now become the 'remnant' of Israel; here, in the last decades of the eighth century, Isaiah carried out his mission; a century later it would be the turn of Jeremiah.

There were three tones to the prophetic message: rebuke, an invitation to repent and the threat of tremendous punishments. The threats were clear, and indeed were realized; rather less clear were the purposes and the aims of these terrifying preachers. The most serious of the rebukes that the prophets directed at the people was that they were idolatrous, that they were 'prostituting themselves', as the prophets loved to say, and making themselves idols; but if it was foolish to worship pieces of metal or wood, it was not very intelligent even to offer sacrifices to

Yahweh. The prophets issued some calls to pursue moral behaviour inspired by justice, but their interventions in matters of foreign policy were more numerous: the kings were utterly mistaken and immoral if they chose to ally themselves with Egypt or recognized Babylonian supremacy. In this remarkable mixture of religion, ethics and politics, all the people were judged guilty, but the prophets deliberately stressed the responsibility of the ruling class, and primarily the priests, here.

What is striking in the prophetic message is that the long and detailed list of what should not be done is not matched by any specific indication of what should be done. It is quite evident that this message must have contained various entreaties and requests, but it is not always easy to identify these either because of our profound ignorance of the real historical environment in which the prophetic preaching was delivered (an environment which new discoveries and new studies are showing to be quite different from that described by the biblical texts) or because of the unilateral and subjective interpretation that Jews and Christians have made of the words of the prophets. According to the texts that we have, the struggle was directed against a polytheistic religion of an agrarian kind, characteristic of all the sedentary populations of the ancient Near East.

Sacral prostitution was condemned not because it was prostitution (the ancient Hebrews were in fact very broad-minded in sexual matters) but because it was sacral; the sacrifice of children was condemned not for humanitarian reasons but because the children were being sacrificed for a perverted purpose; even the sacrifices offered to Yahweh were damnable because they reflected a certain kind of relationship with the deity. The prophets fought against fertility religion, but in the name of what? Certainly the need was felt for a moral renewal – and it is no coincidence that the Israelite prophets are an essential element in the 'axial period' – but the prophetic ideal is that of the nomadic life of the desert, the worship of Yahweh Sabaoth, the god of the warrior bands. This is the reconstruction which the texts allow, full of gaps and in the last resort not very convincing. And now we are beginning to have a specific reason for not being convinced.

Recent excavations, begun in 1975 and still largely unpublished (and perhaps largely destined to remain so) have revealed at Kuntillet 'Ajrud, between the Negeb and Sinai, a sanctuary which can be dated to about 800 BC. Hebrew and Phoenician inscriptions discovered in it allow us to affirm that it was administered by a group of prophets[1] and that Yahweh was worshipped in it: not by himself, however, but with his consort Asherah, the great Canaanite goddess and wife of El, who was fought against and vilified (her proper name was reduced to being a generic name) in the historical books of the Old Testament. In the sanctuary rough but significant representations have been found of the Egyptian god Bes, of the tree of life, and so on: this is a repertory unequivocally connected with fertility.

It is probable that neither Amos nor Isaiah were habitual visitors to Kuntillet 'Ajrud, but the quite unexpected discovery of this sanctuary causes us to revise profoundly the ideas that we had about Israelite prophecy. The innumerable additions and transformations which, as biblical scholars are well aware, are characteristic of all the prophetic texts of the Old Testament, are not the only kind of interference with the texts; to this we need similarly to add omissions of everything that conflicted with the new interpretations of these texts that were proposed. The strange silence of the prophets on their actual purpose is most simply explained by these omissions.

As for the political aspect of the prophetic preaching, a better understanding of the ancient texts relating to the royal ideology in Syria and Palestine allows us to put the problem in its real terms. Though moving almost always within the sphere of the royal palace, the prophets had a markedly anti-monarchical attitude: the king was in fact the pivot of the religious ideology which the prophets fought against, in that it was his personal relationship with the deity that guaranteed the well-being of the people. The 'national' deities were in fact dynastic deities bound exclusively to the person and the house of the king; it is not for nothing that the first temple in Jerusalem was attached to Solomon's palace, almost as a private chapel; it was the king who every year renewed his covenant with his god, so that the people could have fertility and peace. Fighting against the king meant fighting against the religion which he represented; and since, for obvious reasons of opportunity (or opportunism), the king could not be attacked directly, attacks were made on his foreign or economic policy, in this way concealing the real aim of the criticisms.[2] It is no coincidence that the attack on the monarchy took place in Israel at the very period when there was a crisis over it in other areas of the eastern Mediterranean, as is evident from an acute study by Cristiano Grottanelli.[3] So religion and politics were closely connected, in the crisis of the 'axial era' as well.

Allow me to make a brief digression at this point. For some millennia the peoples of the ancient Near East had practised a religion the aim of which was primarily to provide them with daily bread, something which was not always easy at that time. So how, almost unexpectedly, did the need arise to eliminate such a religion? To keep within the sphere of Israel, it should be observed that there was nothing to eat in the desert, the ideal place for the prophets, and manna did not fall every day. But the prophets not only ate but, as the legends of Elijah and Elisha show, also gave food to others: they must have got food for themselves in some way or other. Now in recent years three prophetic sanctuaries have been discovered, all from the eighth-seventh century BC: in addition to that of Yahweh in Kuntillet 'Ajrud already mentioned, one has come to light at Deir 'Alla in Transjordan, with a text relating to Balaam, the well-known prophet with the ass, and another at Sarepta, in Phoenicia, perhaps dedicated to Shadrapa, a god of healing. Note the positioning of these three sanctuaries: Sarepta is on the Phoenician coast between Tyre and Sidon; Deir 'Alla on the road which led from Damascus to Samaria; Kuntillet 'Ajrud on the caravan route which led from southern Palestine to Elath, the port on the Red Sea. Three sanctuaries, situated in three sites of great commercial importance, emerged along with the prophets at the very period which saw the greatest commercial expansion in the ancient Near East. Since as a result of the trading it became possible to eat even when the rains did not fall, an agrarian religion became useless, and the kings begin to count less than the merchants.[4]

Now at last we come to 'Deutero-Isaiah', a prophet who lived in exile in Babylon, spokesman of a god who was bound by a covenant to the ruling house of a small people. This god had carried out his threat to punish the people and the king for their faults: and now the people, far from its native land, were experiencing the punishment without knowing exactly what their fathers had done wrong: 'Why do you say, O Jacob, and speak, O Israel, "My way is hid from the Lord, and my right is disregarded by my God"?' (40.27).

It was now almost fifty years since the time of the generation which had still heard, in Jerusalem, the rebukes and the threats of Jeremiah; those born in the exile were beginning to feel themselves victims unjustly punished for a crime which others had committed: this is the first manifestation of an attitude clearly expressed by Joel (4 [EVV 3].19) when he speaks of Judah as 'innocent blood'. There was probably still some hope of rescue; someone certainly recalled and even began to reinterpret, in order to find a motive for consolation, the verses of the prophet Nahum (of course from 2.4 onwards) which celebrated the destruction of hated Nineveh: but if the end of the Assyrian empire had cheered those who were still in Palestine, it could not have been much of a comfort to the descendants of the Hebrews who had been deported more than a century previously.

Yahweh's revenge had come too late, and we do not find a Deutero-Amos or a Deutero-Hosea. However, Cyrus appeared in time to find a Deutero-Isaiah, who could see with his own eyes the end of the hated Chaldaean dynasty. Nor was that all: an educated person in the sixth century BC was well aware how many empires and how many dynasties had passed and for how little a man, even a king, counted on earth; so that the disappearance of another dynasty was not in itself an enormous matter. The new fact, hitherto unheard of, was that the new king wanted to do justice to those who had been the victims of his predecessor, especially in the religious field: having been restored triumphantly to their places, the gods vilified by the Chaldaean king were reintegrated into their function as protectors of their respective peoples; Yahweh and his priests, too, could return to Jerusalem,

So Yahweh had conquered, had kept his word of redemption after the expiation of guilt; and he had conquered by means of a barbarian king even whose name no one knew. With Cyrus, Yahweh showed to his people that he was not only the God of the house of David but the God who could use any king on earth for his own ends. This was the revelation which overwhelmed 'Deutero-Isaiah', who understood that his God was no longer the lord of a few ill-armed bedouins but the lord of the greatest empire in the world.

This change in the conception of the deity is presented in the Old Testament in a very evocative way. First of all we see the scene among the disconsolate exiles: 'By the waters of Babylon, there we sat down and wept, when we remembered Zion. On the willows there we hung up our lyres. For there our captors required of us songs, and our tormentors, mirth, saying "Sing us one of the songs of Zion!" How shall we sing the Lord's song in a strange land?' (Ps.137.1-4). Then the announcement of liberation: 'Comfort, comfort my people, says your God. Speak tenderly to Jerusalem, and cry to her that her warfare is ended, that her inquity is pardoned, that she has received from the Lord's hand double for all her sins' (Isa.40.1-2).

So the liberator is presented: 'Thus says Yahweh to his anointed, to Cyrus, whose right hand I have grasped, to subdue nations before him and ungird the loins of kings, to open doors before him that gates may not be closed: "I will go before you and level the mountains, I will break in pieces the doors of bronze and cut asunder the bars of iron, I will give you the treasures of darkness and the hoards in secret places, that you may know that it is I, the Lord, the God of Israel, who call you by your name"' (Isa.45.1-3).

And finally the long awaited news: 'who says of Cyrus, "He is my shepherd, and he shall fulfil all my purpose"; saying of Jerusalem, "She shall be built," and of the temple, "Your foundations shall be laid"' (Isa.44.28). The picture painted before our eyes is a vivid one, really beautiful – too beautiful to be true.

The imagery of the Israelites who went to lament on the banks of the rivers, under the malign eye of their warders, evokes our piety; but we can be consoled by the thought that they did not all go to weep. The members and the descendants of the royal house lived at the expense of the Babylonian court and always had a place kept for them at the royal table. Some Jews certainly worked in the offices of the rich Jewish Egibi family, who some time previously had set up a bank,[5] anticipating the Murashu. Various others studied Babylonian language, literature and culture, and assimilated them deeply, then transferred them into their works in Hebrew: this was a group whose living conditions were not so unpleasant that they were prevented from keeping, cultivating and developing the old culture, the old language and the old religious traditions.

'Deutero-Isaiah' also belonged to this group of scholars. Let us read some of his words: 'Thus says the God Yahweh, who created the heavens and stretched them out, who spread forth the earth and what comes from it, who gives breath to the people upon it and spirit to those who walk in it. "I am Yahweh, I have called you in righteousness, I have taken you by the hand and kept you; I have given you as a covenant to the people, a light to the nations, to open the eyes that are blind, to bring out the prisoners from the dungeon, from the prison those who sit in darkness"' (42.5-7). In these verses Yahweh is addressing Cyrus, communicating to him that he has been chosen as a king who must make a covenant with the people (according to the royal ideology that we have already seen) so that justice may be done. Now note these other words: 'The lord has made me live, he has drawn me from the well, he has called me forth from destruction... he has taken me by the hand... Where the earth is spread forth and the skies are stretched out... those whose clay [= men] Aruru has formed, endowed with life, set on the way, mortal, who do not exist, give praise to Marduk.'[6]

It is easy to see the very close affinity in expression between these two statements, which use precisely the same imagery: the heaven and the earth which are spread out, the men who live and walk on the earth, the god who takes by the hand and who frees from the dark depths of the earth (the prison, the well). Even if it is not identical, the context of the two compositions is very much the same: on the one hand it is Yahweh who presents the king chosen by him as the one who brings liberation and does justice; on the other hand it is Marduk, who, after putting one of his faithful righteous to the proof, rewards him by exalting him in Esagila, the temple of Marduk in Babylon. Since it is difficult to deny that 'Deutero-Isaiah' will have known the Babylonian poem called 'The Righteous Sufferer' (the model for the biblical Job), from which this passage is taken, we must note the good literary education of the prophet.

But the discussion does not end here. The Hebrew writer also reveals manifest thematic affinities, which have been noted for some time, with another Babylonian text only part of which has been preserved: the Cyrus inscription;[7] here, too, we find themes that we have already come across, like the deity who calls the king to make him perform works of justice, to liberate the oppressed from the yoke, to bring back the inhabitants of the country from death to life. This last is particularly interesting because it picks up to the letter the basic theme of the Babylonian poem I have already mentioned. For a precise evaluation of the relationship between these three works (a wisdom text, a prophetic text and a political text), it is necessary to know precisely what the Cyrus inscription was. With its last part missing, the fact that towards the end it speaks of the rebuilding of the sanctuaries of Mesopotamia and Iran and of the return of the inhabitants of these regions to their homes has generally suggested that despite the profound difference in its character, this text would represent as it were the 'original' of the edict of Cyrus recorded at the beginning of the book of Ezra; indeed, the Babylonian text has been read only in the light of the biblical text, though the one who is exalted in it is the Babylonian Marduk and not 'Yahweh God of heaven'. This umpteenth imposition of a bibliocentric view on the documentation of the ancient Near East became very evident a few years ago when some more of the inscription was found (though not all of it)[8] and it was thus learned that the inscription is a foundation text which faithfully follows the ideological positions of the Assyrian Assurbanipal (he is specifically mentioned), who also restored the Babylonian cults. As has rightly been noted,[9] Cyrus's policy was simply a continuation of the lines marked out by the previous rulers of Babylon: the 'heretical' positions of Nabonidus, moreover, provided a specific foundation for the 'restoration' promoted by the Achaemenidean ruler. In short, there was a Babylonian literary text which should be considered a classic,[10] providing ideas both for Achaemenidean political literature which followed the furrows of the most classical Babylonian tradition, and for the political and religious message of an Israelite prophet.[11] That an Achaemenidean ruler should be lauded in the sphere of the Hebrew diaspora (or perhaps only in part of it) and that this exaltation is also brought about through the literary echo of a Babylonian text used for the same ends by the Achaemenidean chancellery demonstrates the perfect ideological and political alignment which Deutero-Isaiah shows with the policy initiated by Cyrus.

On the basis of these literary considerations we can see in a new light the famous policy of religious tolerance pursued by the Achaemenideans. In reality this tolerance was part of the normal policy of all the Mesopotamian rulers with aspirations to an empire, and could seem a novelty only in the light of the recent experience undergone with Nabonidus, who for political reasons wanted to impose the cult of the moon god. There is not a trace in the Cyrus text of what is supposed to be Iranian universalism, realized in the name of Ahura Mazda, and of which the biblical text of Ezra could be regarded as a faithful historical record.

Let us take a closer look at things. Cyrus thanks Marduk and, in a subordinate way, Nabu; there is not a word of Ahura Mazda; the fact that in the only other inscription, also in Babylonian, which Cyrus has left he proclaims himself 'builder [i.e. restorer] of the Esagila and the Ezida', the two main temples of Marduk and Nabu, in Babylon and Barsippa respectively, must have meant something; and it is also significant to note that Cyrus did not write in Persian. Again: it is true that Cyrus had announced the restoration of the cults that Nabonidus had suppressed, but that applied only to the cities of Mesopotamia and those beyond the Tigris. To read the text of Cyrus in the light of Ezra 1, as is usually done, is not only unacceptable historical methodology but also wrong, given that in 539 the cities of Syria and Phoenicia had not yet made a act of submission to the Achaemenidean sovereign. If at the time of writing his foundation inscription Cyrus had already been able to count on the Syro-Phoenician cities, he would certainly not have failed to record the fact. Moreover, the violent attack that 'Deutero-Isaiah' mounts on Marduk and Nabu (46.1-2) seems hardly compatible with the way in which Cyrus exalts these particular deities.

This means that the Persian policy of tolerance, even towards the Jews, was not connected with Cyrus's religious position and that if it began in 539 BC, i.e. with his conquest of Babylon, it continued to manifest itself also at a later date. In other words, we should not take literally the biblical statement (II Chron.36-22 = Ezra 1.1) that everything took place 'in the first year of the reign of Cyrus'; that was only the beginning.[12] In addition to what is now said about the religion of Cyrus, other facts should be noted: in two passages (43.3 and 45.14) 'Deutero-Isaiah' clearly alludes to the conquest of Egypt, Cush and Saba; since I do not have much of a belief in prophets who forecast the political future exactly, let us note that these words relate to a date after 525 BC, the year in which Cambyses conquered Egypt. And another feature: the insistence with which 'Deutero-Isaiah' presents Yahweh as creator of the world has rightly been stressed,[13] and Morton Smith, who has already been cited, has made an detailed comparative analysis of the Hebrew text alongside Yasna 44 of the Avesta. Now it should be noted that if the creation of the world is one of the fundamental aspects of Persian conceptions relating to Ahura Mazda, the fact remains that it only becomes an essential element of the royal ideology with Darius.

Ms C.Herrenschmidt has done us the service of demonstrating the progressive definition and precision of an ideology which gives the monarchy of Darius the religious foundation of a universal monarchy: the king of all the world as a mirror – the image is that of Ms Herrenschmidt – of the God who is creator of the world.[14] This is precisely the ideological approach that we rediscover in 'Deutero-Isaiah': the juxtaposition of the greatness of God and the greatness of Cyrus is developed in the Hebrew work as a counterpoint (40.12-31 greatness of God, 41.1-5 greatness of Cyrus; 41.25-42.7 greatness of God, 44.27-45.8 greatness of Cyrus).

In conclusion, a series of themes the content and ideology of which are present in 'Deutero-Isaiah', forces us to bring down the dating of this work (or at least of certain parts of it) to the time of Darius. The conquest of Babylon by the latter in 521 BC with the consequent destruction of the walls of the city justify the song that 'Deutero-Isaiah' raises over the fall of the city (ch.47); the end of the last Chaldaean pretenders, who evidently revived the traditional Babylonian deities even in their names, explains how Darius abandoned Marduk for Ahura Mazda and how 'Deutero-Isaiah' could hymn the fall of Marduk and Nabu. The Hebrew prophet aligned himself with Achaemenidean policy, but in the perspective held by Darius, not in the still philo-Bablyonian perspective of Cyrus. This explains why the latest and most confused Hebrew recollections, repeated from one writer to another, from Haggai to Zechariah and then to Ezra, should agree on one point: that is that despite the celebrated decree of Cyrus, the rebuilding of the temple took place in the reign of Darius.

There is quite a widespread feeling, even if it is not always expressed, that there was a kind of preferential relationship between the Persians and the Jews: the fact that it is possible to cite biblical pasages in confirmation and to integrate Achaemenidean texts seems to offer concrete support to this attitude, which instinctively makes a connection between Yahwistic and Zoroastrian monotheism. It is certainly not my intention to enter into a discussion of Persian religion; however, it is impossible not to note that on the documentary level the religion of the Achaemenideans is still presented as being polytheistic;[15] and I ask myself how they would have reacted if they had seen in 'the God of heaven', the expression with which the Jews introduced their Yahweh to foreigners, not their own Ahura Mazda but another deity who claimed to be the one true God.

In reality, a preferential relationship did exist; not, however, with the Jews alone but with all the north-western Semites, and in particular with the Phoenicians. According to Herodotus (3.91) the area of Syria and Palestine was the fifth satrapy, but it is never mentioned in the various lists which the Persian kings left of the provinces of their empire;[16] in its place we find the term 'Arabia', the ambiguity of which it is difficult to miss. That we should see this omission as an indication of a certain regard towards people who spoke Aramaic and Phoenician is confirmed by other facts: the explicit testimony of Herodotus, who in various places stresses the particular attachment of the Phoenicians to the Persian court (5.108; 6.6, 33, 104; 7.98; 8.68), after having explicitly noted (3.19) that the Phoenicians 'were given to the Persians of their own free will'. It is no coincidence that in the lost tragedy of Phrynicus written after the battle of Salamis the chorus is represented by the 'Phoenicians', who provide the title for the tragedy (perhaps because of the massacre of the Phoenicians ordered by Xerxes; cf. Herodotus 8.90-91). Then we should note a well-known Phoenician inscription (KAI 14) in which Eshmunazor king of Sidon says that he has received Dor and Jaffa from the 'lord of the kings' (*adun milkim*) in return for the undertakings he has performed. Finally, it is significant that in conquering Egypt Cambyses destroyed various Egyptian temples but spared that of the Jews at Elephantine (Cowley, 30).

To sum up, 'Deutero-Isaiah', and in particular chs.40-48, which to some degree are a literary unity and are also known as the 'Book of Consolation',[17] appears here as the perfect expression of a historical moment of great cultural importance. The faithful spokesman of the religious policy begun by Cyrus and continued by Darius, all of whose ideological themes he takes up and develops, 'Deutero-Isaiah' at the same time promotes a religious vision which grafted on to traditional Yahwism, bound up with Jewish particularism, the universalist aspiration and the ethical and metaphysical vision of Zoroastrianism. The stress on the typically Iranian motive of the 'first and the last',[18] the deity who is outside time and who knows all, reveals the profound conviction of the Jewish writer that Yahweh had much to gain by taking on the characteristics of Ahura Mazda. And thus once again – but now for the last time – a prophet performed his mission of bearing a new religious vision and at the same time of mediating it between the political power and the mass of subjects. And once again it remained unheard.

The accord between the Achaemenideans and the Jewish intelligentsia did not last long; in all probability the politics of Xerxes put an end to it. What consequences this rupture had on a practical level is difficult to say, even if the existence of a tradition (we do not know how well founded it is) about the interruption of the work on the rebuilding of the temple in Jerusalem, an interruption which the biblical tradition now puts in the time between Xerxes and Artaxerxes but which if it really happened would have to be attributed to Xerxes, is significant. What is certain, and of greater interest to us, is that on the ideological and religious level the decline in this accord brought the end of the universalist vision – if not throughout the Jewish sphere, certainly in that reflected by the Old Testament texts.

If we read the poetic part of Isaiah 14.4b-23, a text generally attributed to 'Deutero-Isaiah' despite its current position, it is not too difficult to recognize the Achaemenidean Xerxes in the king of Babylon who is ironically called 'the resplendent son of the dawn'.[19] The violent song of joy on the death of the tyrant contains quite transparent allusions (transparent, at least, to anyone who does not look in this sentence for suspected direct derivations from Ugaritic poetry) to the history of this ruler: the end of religious tolerance, the destruction of cities (one might think of Babylon and Barsippa), the ruin of his own country with the death of his own subjects (one might think of the expedition to Greece) and his violent death. There is yet another argument in favour of this identification: the stress in the Hebrew poem on the contrast between the wretched death of the king, going down to Sheol a shade among the shades, and the claim that he made when alive that he was as god, exalting himself to heaven, can be explained as a polemical reference to the ideological position that Xerxes takes in his inscriptions. Gherardo Gnoli has paraphrased this position as follows: 'I want to be completely happy in both existences (though I am well aware that to be a faithful follower of Arta in this world cannot give happiness) and therefore pray Ahura Mazda to grant me not only to be *artavan* in the future life but also to be happy in this earthly life.'[20]

So with Xerxes the Jews detached themselves from the Achaemenidean monarchy. 'Deutero-Isaiah' had in part overcome the ancient conception of the relationship between God and king by making God choose, for Israel, the king of another people; the continuator of 'Deutero-Isaiah' goes further, abolishes the king, and inaugurates a direct covenant between God and the people without intermediaries: 'I will establish with you an eternal covenant, the privileges granted to David' (Isa.55.3). In this way, towards the beginning of the fifth century there arose that 'theology of the promise' which the biblical writers projected into the pre-exilic period, since they did not take account of what actually happened. The king was no longer of use; Cyrus may have been able to retain the prestigious title of 'messiah' and 'servant of Yahweh' (Isa.42.19), but from now on Israel itself would be the 'servant', whether in glory (49.1-6) or in degradation (50.4-9; 52.13-53.12). The detachment of Babylonian Judaism from the Achaemenidean monarchy also brought with it a progressive attenuation of the sense of universalism in Yahwistic religion. This ideal, so alive in 'Deutero-Isaiah' ('Turn to me and be saved, all the ends of the earth! For I am God, and there is no other', 45.22), still continues in his successor, even if it is reduced to having a nationalistic sense ('I will give you as a light to the nations, that my salvation may reach to the end of the earth', 49.6b) and in Trito-Isaiah (56.3-7); then it gets less. All the interest of Ezekiel is in the vision of the future temple (and we must ask if this is not some psychological projection of the imagery of the Babylonian Esagila) and the liturgy relating to it. Haggai also thinks of the temple, with words which have little universalism about them: 'I will shake all nations, so that the treasures of all nations shall come in, and I will fill this house with splendour, Says Yahweh Sabaoth' (Hag.2.7-8). As is evident, the parenthesis formed by 'Deutero-Isaiah' is definitely closed and we have returned to the situation of before the exile, if not to the situation that preceded the prophetic message, which repudiated the cult.

Nor were developments different in the circles distinct from the prophetic sphere. The historical vision of the so-called Yahwist, whose literary activity presupposes the assimilation of late Babylonian literature[21] and is therefore dated to the post-exilic period, is markedly anti-universalistic. The progressive focussing on the final objective so that it becomes fixed on the Hebrew people alone carries with it a series of exclusions which are shown by successive curses on the part of God: after Adam and Eve are driven out of Eden, Cain and his family are cursed; then all humanity is destroyed with the exception of Noah; but of his three sons, Ham is cursed along with his decendants; Abraham chases out one of his sons, Ishmael; Esau is destined to be the slave of Jacob his brother, and at the point of death Jacob again finds strength to curse two of his sons, Simeon and Levi. With these precedents, to prohibit mixed marriages was the least that Ezra could have done. Many things today would be different had Xerxes had a more tolerant policy.

Even if it lost its universalistic aspiration, Jewish religion at least retained some of the specific motives of Zoroastrianism, like the importance of the divine light,[22] in which we find Yahweh arrayed in some psalms,[23] and the presence of the same light in the creation of the world according to the Priestly writer[24] – even if it should be noted that in the first chapter of Genesis this light, the first work of God, does not have any function. In this same account we find another echo of Persian conceptions, that of the goodness of creation.[25] Recollections of royal Achaemenidean ideology can be found later in some of the so-called 'royal psalms', like 2, on the divine adoption of the sovereign;[26] 101, on the justice implemented by the king; and 110, where the king is said to be 'begotten by the dawn'.[27]

In all the cases that we have noted the Iranian motives are, all things considered, marginal; this is more a literary legacy than real ideological adherence, and in any case that elaboration is missing which reveals the vitality of an idea. The same thing could be said of other Jewish works which have remained outside the canon, like the recollection of the creative work of God in the first of the 'Hymns of Thanksgiving' found at Qumran, or the exaltation of wisdom as the emanation of the light of God in a passage (7.25) from the book of the same name. However, there was a strand in Judaism in which the awareness of being the 'holy people' chosen beforehand by God did not take the pre-eminent position that we find in almost all the Old Testament; and it is certainly no coincidence that this strand was kept out of the canonical collection. In this Judaism, which seems marginal in the perspective constructed by the rabbis, themes were alive and discussed which related not only to the Jews but to all human beings, we might say universal themes, among them pre-eminently the problem of evil. It is difficult to say, even if it were worth the trouble to discover, how much is Iranian and how much Babylonian in the various aspects of this much-debated problem; it is certain that it would not be conceivable without the one or the other.

Ezekiel 14.14 notes three just men of former times; Noah, Daniel and Job.[28] The Old Testament has kept the book of Job and that of Daniel, but not that of Noah; however, by chance parts of the book of Noah have been transmitted by works which then came together in Enoch. With these three books are bound up the most fertile developments of Judaism from the point of view of conceptual elaboration; in them there is reflection on the themes of evil and of history.

In the Book of Noah, Babylonian Judaism gave an explanation in a mythological vein of the origin of evil seen as the consequence of the union of angels with human beings. The theme was then taken up in other works like the Book of Watchmen and the Book of Giants appropriated by Mani. Without dwelling on the themes of these writings, we can at any rate note that the solution envisaged is along the lines of Zoroastrianism; as Paolo Sacchi has written in connection with the Book of Watchmen: 'history is the place of encounter between good and evil, where good will certainly triumph, but where evil has all the freedom of action'; 'therefore the meaning of history becomes the meaning of the life of each individual in his own eyes and those of God.'[29] This sense of history as the scene of the struggle of metaphysical powers is the greatest spiritual conquest of Zoroastrianism. It is opposed, certainly not by chance, by the purely individual approach of Job, the book of another of the three ancient sages which reflects the traditional Jewish position while at the same time denouncing its inadequacy, with the obvious result that it does not find any solution to the problem of evil. However, Daniel, the book named after the third wise man, returned to history, albeit in its own way.

That the answer to the problem of evil is to be found in the history of humanity was the great insight of Iranian thought. Through apocalyptic literature of Iranian and Babylonian inspiration and with direct use of the text of 'Deutero-Isaiah', the most mature Christian thought, that of John, links up with this. As though after a long subterranean course, certain tendencies of Iranian religious speculation reappear, partially transformed, in either Iranian or Christian texts. The world that Ahura Mazda had created 'for the joy of humanity' has proved a source of pain, involving the creator himself. Christ, 'the first and the last', the Word, was made flesh to conquer death. But *Yasht* 19.58 says that even 'Ahura Mazda must suffer distress in the creation of contrary creatures' and

Ohrmazd creates himself as the seventh of the Amesha Spenta and as the seventh element of creation *geteh* (heaven, water, earth, plants, animals, man, Ohrmazd).[30] At the end of his eschatological expectations the seer on Patmos sees 'heaven opened, and behold, a white horse! He who sat upon it is called Faithful and True, and in righteousness he judges and makes war. His eyes are like a flame of fire, and on his head are many diadems; and he has a name inscribed which no one knows but himself. He is clad in a robe dipped in blood, and the name by which he is called is "Logos of God" ';[31] but this Christian theophany has significant points of contact with the Iranian theophany of Ohrmazd, the Form of Fire, who 'will appear by night in the atmosphere in the form of a man riding a fiery horse'.[32]

Chapter 8

Moses' Anger

The Israelites encamped at the foot of Sinai had become used to the frequent absences of Moses, summoned by Yahweh to the summit of the mountain to receive instructions. This time, however, his absence was more than usually protracted: the leader was away for forty days and forty nights. The people, who were beginning to fear being left without a head, then turned to Aaron, Moses' brother, asking him to fashion a god to be their guide. Aaron made no objections, asked the women to give him their golden jewellery, melted it down and made a golden calf, which was hailed as the god who had brought Israel out of Egypt. Then Aaron built an altar and announced for the following day 'a feast in honour of Yahweh', a feast which usually took place with sacrifices, followed by a banquet (at which the flesh of the sacrificial victims was eaten) and festal merrymaking. At this point the anger of Yahweh exploded: he wanted to destroy all the people apart from Moses; however, Moses succeded in placating the divine wrath and hastened down the mountain to put things right. Seeing the people singing and dancing, Moses threw to the ground the tablets which had been inscribed directly by God and they broke into fragments; then he destroyed the golden calf, ground it to dust and threw this into water which the people was forced to drink. Moses then asked Aaron for an explanation, but did not rebuke him; in the meantime, however, the people had gone wild, indulging in an orgy. Then Moses called the Levites and ordered them to kill the sinners tent by tent: brothers, friends and neighbours: 'on that day there fell three thousand of the people'. Then Moses spoke to the people, rebuked them, but also told them that he would intercede for them with Yahweh; the intercession was only partially successful, because God limited himself to postponing the punishment.

This is the story which one can read in Exodus 32; it is a story which presents a number of disconcerting aspects and evident contradictions which have forced exegetes to posit a series of successive additions to what must have been the original nucleus of the story.[1] On the purely narrative level, i.e. leaving aside the dialogue, this nucleus omitted only the episode of the massacre perpetrated by the Levites; it is commonly assigned to the so-called Elohist (a narrative source which is dated around the ninth-eighth century BC).[2] Since a series of recent arguments have cast serious doubt on dating the so-called Yahwist to the tenth-ninth century BC and even on his very existence,[3] with the 'Elohist' we would have the earliest narrative strand of the Pentateuch, at least according to the opinion of some biblical scholars. In beginning to develop our reflections from this original basis of the tradition we would therefore have a way of going through several stages in the history of Hebrew religious thought.

The central theme of the story is Moses' anger. Why was he so angry with his people? Because they had built a solid image of his god Yahweh in the form of a 'calf'. There is no doubt that here we find a clear assertion of the principle of religious aniconism; but there is also no doubt that if anyone in the world should not have been angry at the making of the golden calf it was Moses. For while the people were melting the gold to produce the statue, Moses was receiving instructions from Yahweh for building 'two golden cherubim' (Ex.25.18). To understand the whole story we have to go back to the religious conceptions of the ancient Near East, which were less naive than one might imagine. The 'calf' is only a derogatory term used by the biblical author to denote what was in fact a 'bull'; and the bull was the symbol of the storm god, i.e. the most important god of the pantheon: Yahweh, too, is often presented by the Bible as a storm god.[4] The symbol of the deity, the bull, was also the visible support for his presence; several monumental representations show the storm god with his feet on a bull; the representation of a bull meant simultaneously calling to mind the person of the god and indicating the invisible presence above the image which in a sense was a materialization of him.[5] This also applies to Moses' cherubim. The two winged figures, which we are certainly to imagine as sphinxes, put at the sides of the covering of the ark, indicate by their presence that this was in fact a throne, as the monumental representations also show: it was the throne on which Yahweh sat, invisible. 'I have seen Yahweh sitting on his throne,' a prophet said.[6] It would not be out of place to recall in this connection that whereas representations of deities on thrones are widespread everywhere, the representation of an empty

throne,[7] the symbol of the invisible presence of God, is almost exclusively
Mesopotamian. To sum up, then, Moses' cherubim and Aaron's calf
correspond to the same religious conception. But in that case, what was
the cause of Moses' anger?

The real fault of the people in the earliest version of our story is
revealed by the punishment which Moses inflicts on them. The water
in which the dust of the pulverized calf had been dissolved and which
the Israelites were forced to drink cannot fail to recall the bitter water
in which dust had been mixed, used to wash off the curses written on a
leaf and then given to an adulterous woman to drink, according to an
ritual ordeal (Num.6.12-31). Moses acts like a husband who has been
betrayed (Yahweh was a 'jealous' God...), not because the people had
represented Yahweh in the form of a bull but because this symbol of
fertility had unleashed reprehensible sexual orgies, which were also
connected with the cult of Yahweh.

It was only later (and this was a first addition to the original story) that
a redactor directed Moses' anger at other objectives: literally quoting
the phrase uttered by Jeroboam to the Israelites when they detached
themselves from Jerusalem ('Israel, these are your gods who brought
you up out of the land of Egypt', I Kings 12.28) without even bothering
to change the plural of the source to the singular (Jeroboam used the
plural because he had made two 'golden calves', one for Dan and one
for Bethel); the biblical author wanted to locate the sin of the people in
the 'calf' as such, so as to be able to show up the hated Samaritans,
worshippers of the 'golden calf', as 'idolaters'.[8]

But let us go back once more to Moses' anger: burning with anger,
'he threw the tablets out of his hand and broke them at the foot of the
mountain'. But what tablets were these that could break so easily? The
Bible says that they were made of stone; but it also says that they were
inscribed on both sides (and were therefore flat) and that Moses had
been holding them in his hands, so they were not too big. There were
no tablets of this kind in the ancient Near East; there were no fairly small
stone tablets, written on both sides and containing a fairly long text like
that which Moses was preparing to present, namely the Decalogue.
However, if Moses' tablets had been made of terracotta instead of stone,
they would have been two perfect examples of Babylonian tablets:
manageable, flat, inscribed on both sides, covered with very fine writing
and therefore capable of containing a fairly long text, easy to break if
they were thrown to the ground. It is precisely this feature which shows
how the biblical author, though speaking of stone tablets, had in mind

the terracotta tablets used for cuneiform writing. But that means that the whole story was thought up in Babylon, the land of exile; also because it is not only the tablets which are broken. We have already recalled the ideology of the empty thrones, but there is also a literary motive here which goes back to a late date: Moses' allusion to the 'book' in which God lists the living suggests the 'book of the living' of which Isa.4.3; Dan.12.3 and Ps.69.69 speak, all texts of an exilic or post-exilic date (moreover Psalm 69 has marked analogies with Babylonian compositions of the same type).[9]

We cannot abandon the ancient stage of this story without dwelling for a moment on another aspect which is just as strange: Moses, seething with anger, has only a few bland words of reproof for his brother Aaron, who was the one most responsible for the corruption of the Hebrew people, and does not threaten him with any punishment. Leaving aside any consideration of the unequal distribution of punishment, it remains significant that in this story the figure of Aaron, i.e. of the head of the Hebrew priesthood, appears in what is certainly not an edifying role. The attempts made by some exegetes to regard the insertion of Aaron into the episode as secondary are unconvincing; and at any rate the fact remains that Aaron was inserted at one point or another. It is difficult not to see here a degree of polemic against excessively permissive behaviour on the part of the clergy of Jerusalem before the exile (cf. also Ezek. 40-48): these priests had on their conscience the toleration of much worse things than the golden calf. But perhaps the polemic was more subtle and aimed at incriminating someone else who was also present at the scene. As I have said, the story comes from an ambience familiar with Babylon – where the priesthood which had served the monarchy and which saw itself as descended from Zadok, priest at the time of David, had been in exile. Having returned to Jerusalem with Joshua son of Jozedek, this group found the place occupied by another priestly branch, probably originating in Bethel, which proclaimed itself to be descended from Aaron. A clash was inevitable, and to begin with saw the victory of the Zadokite group: Aaron (and his descendants) was indirectly accused of sharing in the 'sin of Jeroboam'. Later the Aaronite group, which also included the Levites,[10] prevailed, and that led to the remedy of inserting the episode of the Levites into the texts to rescue Aaron.

The origin of the Levites is still a matter of discussion (were they a landless tribe or simply a group of people who performed certain duties?). Initially they occupied a subordinate position over against the priests

proper, though belonging to the priestly class; their progressive assertion
of themselves is documented in the biblical texts and is definitively
sanctioned by the book of Chronicles. We can easily understand how in
this late phase of Hebrew history, when they were now the majority
representatives of the clergy, the Levites would have felt the need to
wipe out or at least to tone down a stain which was a blot on them all:
then, even better, they could make themselves the protagonists of the
rescue.

And so we come to the episode which has been inserted into the story
in so clumsy a way that it gives rise to blatant contradictions: the very
Moses who had interceded for the life of his people becomes the
promoter of a massacre, which moreover is carried out with criteria
which are almost impossible to identify, since whereas the golden calf
had been worshipped by all the people (including the Levites), only three
thousand men are killed. And then, if all the Levites were with Moses,
as the text stresses, why did he exhort them to kill their 'brothers' also?
And this is even without taking account of the utter unlikelihood that
the people would give themselves over to an orgy after Moses had already
destroyed the calf and made the Israelites drink the water of penitence.
This is a story most of which is absurd, inserted into the biblical text
exclusively for ideological reasons: to give the Levites revenge on the
priests and at the same time to show them to be faithful custodians of
the cult of Yahweh.

However, with the massacre of the worshippers of the golden calf
there appears for the first time in the biblical account a theme which
bursts out from time to time: that of the violent extirpation of heresy and
of the fierce struggle against the other religions – in other words, the
theme of religious intolerance.[11] On the surface this appears to be one
of the basic characteristics of the Old Testament (Yahweh is a 'jealous'
God), not only at the theoretical level but also at the narrative level.
'Anyone who sacrifices to a god other than Yahweh alone shall be put
to death', runs one of the laws in the so-called 'Book of the Covenant'
(Ex.20.22-23.33), which is regarded as the earliest of the Hebrew codex.
Anyone who practises a cult different from the official one is condemned
to death, just like the sorcerers who practise magic and those who
commit the sin of bestiality: the three capital crimes are lumped together
(Ex.22.17-19; later, in the so-called 'Holiness Code', Lev.17-26, the
death penalty will be threatened for many other categories of crime,
mostly of a religious or sexual nature). On the narrative plane, apart
from the golden calf we can recall the episode of Elijah on Mount

Carmel (I Kings 18) with the 450 prophets of Baal first mocked and then personally slaughtered by the prophet, and that of the massacre of the priests and the worshippers of Baal ordered by Jehu in the temple of Baal at Samaria (II Kings 10). If we took these and other episodes literally we should think of the Hebrew people as being fierce and intolerant on the religious level; that is in marked contrast with the behaviour of other peoples of the ancient Near East, who were always tolerant in religious matters.[12]

The intolerant attitude of the Hebrews has sometimes been justified as a direct consequence of monotheism;[13] where there is only one God, there is no longer room for the others, for if only one God is the true God then all the others have to be false – and thus merit derision and destruction. However, this argument is only partially true; because if we need to recognize that the polytheistic religious conception has to be tolerant, we also have to accept that the first monotheism to assert itself politically, that of the Achaemenidean Darius, was no less tolerant. If there is one God, he is God of all men; they may call him by different names but he always remains the same (there were political reasons for the exceptional behaviour of Xerxes towards Babylon and its temples). It is also true, however, that not all monotheisms have been as tolerant as that of Persia. On the other hand, it is difficult to reconcile the idea of religious intolerance, which is also manifested in attitudes of cruelty, with that of the lofty religious and moral teaching which the Hebrews themselves gave to humanity: the Elijah who covers his face with a mantle when he feels the divine presence in the gentle breeze (I Kings 19.11-13) could not have had his hands stained with the blood of the prophets of Baal. So we are led to ask how true is the image which certain pages of the Old Testament paint of Hebrew religion, in other words what is the actual historicity of the biblical text.

The biblical text itself gives us an answer. For the northern kingdom, the great sin of Jeroboam in which all the kings of Israel shared was not that he tolerated the cult of Baal, because even Jehu, who sought to extirpate the baalism of Samaria, 'did not depart from the sins of Jeroboam' (II Kings 10.29); it was that of erecting a sanctuary of Yahweh at Bethel in competition with the sanctuary at Jerusalem (I Kings 12.28-33; 13.33-34). During the two centuries of its existence the kingdom of Israel practised the cult of Yahweh while tolerating that of Baal, as is evident from the Old Testament and as has been confirmed by epigraphical evidence; in the Samaria ostraca of the eighth century BC, in fact, baalistic theophorous names are attested alongside Yahwistic ones among the personnel of the royal administration. With the exception of Jehu, the Hebrews of the north were therefore tolerant in matters of religious policy.

Things were no different from Samaria in the southern kingdom. Here the biblical text presents an excerpt from the religion practised in Jerusalem and throughout Judaea with the story of Josiah's reform (II Kings 23); among all the details it will be enough to single out the fact that the cult of Baal was actually practised in the temple in Jerusalem! Obviously there have been those who have argued that the text in question contains many exaggerations, since the author wants to bring out the reforming action of Josiah in greater relief, but two arguments can be made against this attempt at an apologia. The first is that if from the Yahwistic point of view held by Josiah, Hebrew religion had not been markedly degenerate, the reform itself would not have made sense. To reduce this reform simply to the centralization of the cult in Jerusalem, as is commonly done, means to refuse to take into account the information provided by the archaeology and epigraphy of Palestine in the seventh century BC. This information (and with it we pass on to the second argument) fully confirms the substance of the biblical account: the great spread of figurines of a nude woman fits well with what is said about Ashera, whom we now know to have been the consort of Yahweh;[14] on the other hand the many theophoric names attested from the second half of the seventh centry BC suggest a religious change analogous to that attributed to Josiah, so we have reason to argue that at least up to Josiah, in the kingdom of Judah too the cult of Yahweh was not as exclusive as certain biblical texts would have us believe. But tolerant Yahwism continued for some time yet, at least in certain circles. At the end of the fifth century BC a group of Jews who felt ties with Jerusalem had a temple in Elephantine in Egypt, where they worshipped Yahweh along with the goddess Anath and other Egyptian deities. It is true, however, that the religious authorities in Jerusalem would not reply to a request from these Jews for help which was addressed to them; this is therefore a sign that at the end of the fifth century something was changing in Jerusalem, and that tolerant Yahwism was coming to an end.

Unlike the Buddhist religious reform of Ashoka, which even put an end to the killing of animals for food, Josiah's reform is presented by the biblical text as carried out by means of the massacre of almost all the priestly class (II Kings 23.5,20; II Chron.34.5). But this is a massacre not unlike that of the worshippers of the golden calf, as is shown by an analysis of the text.

Josiah's reform was not a bloody one: the temple was cleansed and purified by the very priests who, probably until a short time beforehand, had sacrificed to Baal (II Kings 23.4); the clergy of the cultic centres which had been suppressed were brought to Jerusalem and kept there, maintained at state expense; however, they were forbidden to sacrifice (vv.8-9). The text in v.5, where it is said that Josiah 'exterminated' (*hišbit*) all the priests of Judah with the exception of those of Jerusalem, contrasts with this information. That this was 'extermination' and not 'removal' (as the word is often translated) is shown by the Greek version (κατέκαυσεν, 'burnt') and the paraphrase by Flavius Josephus (ἀπέκτεινε, 'killed', *Antiquities*, 10.65) together with the parallel passage II Chron 34.5 (*šarap*, 'burned'). Which of the two traditions is the earlier is not difficult to recognize; since v.5 interrupts the discussion of the purification of the temple of Jerusalem, its intrusive and therefore secondary character is evident. The massacre of the priests of Judah, like that of the priests of Samaria (v.20), was not part of the original story but was added at a later stage.

The brief textual history recalled here is no different from that which led to the insertion of the episode of the Levites into the story of the golden calf. In both cases we have additions to earlier texts which, moreover, are not very old; the presence of the Levites in one case and the agreement in ideology with the book of Chronicles in the other suggests that such additions are to be attributed to the period in which the Levitical class achieved predominance in the Jewish hierocracy, namely in the third century BC. The cruelty and the religious intolerance of the Jewish people are thus in reality a late invention of the priestly environment and do not correspond to any historical reality; the Hebrews were never less tolerant than the other peoples of the ancient Near East.

If that is the truth, we cannot but ask why the Bible would have us believe the opposite. But the answer is easy: the Old Testament is not a history book but a collection of sacred texts which are the basis for a religion and develop a particular religious ideology. Absolute mono-theism is the result of a long process which began in the pre-exilic period but came to completion only in the post-exilic period. Underlining, with laws and episodes referring to the distant past, the exclusiveness of Yahwism, the sacred writer reinforced the faith and zeal of the faithful. When reading that his ancestors condemned to death anyone who sacrificed to other gods and killed those who worshipped Baal or the golden calf, the believer knew very well that this sort of thing no longer happened. But he was induced to think that at least it was right that it should have happened. Tolerance of the sinner, intolerance of the sin.

Chapter 9

The Blood of the Innocent

The expression 'blood of the innocent' (*dam ha-naqi*, in the singular) or rather 'innocent blood' (*dam naqi*), which is more common especially in the Greek version,[1] arises from the sphere of the practice of 'blood vengeance'[2] and therefore appears with a connotation which we could define as being legal. It denotes the individual who has been, or could have been, the victim of a homicide without it being his fault. Two passages of Deuteronomy clarify this concept well. 19.1-13 talks of six cities of refuge in which the right of sanctuary is granted to someone responsible for a culpable homicide (as for example a woodcutter whose axe slips out of his hand and strikes his companion); the institution of the cities with the right of sanctuary are 'lest innocent blood be shed in your land which the Lord your God gives you for an inheritance, and so the guilt of bloodshed be upon you' (v.10). The refuge does not, of course, apply to anyone who has committed a murder deliberately; such a person must rather be delivered over to the 'avenger of blood', so as to 'eliminate[3] the blood of the innocent [i.e. that of the victim] from Israel and all will go well with you' (v.13). 21.1-9 describes with a wealth of detail the ceremonies to be performed to purify from 'innocent' blood the place in whose territory the corpse of a murdered man has been found if the identity of the killer is unknown.[4] Outside these two passages the Old Testament does not provide any other attestations of the expression 'blood of the innocent/innocent blood' in contexts of a legislative kind; this is significantly confirmed by the fact that only in these two Deuteronomic sentences does the Septuagint use the expression αἷμα ἀναίτιον.

The language connected with 'innocent blood' indicates the victim of a homicide, obviously excluding those cases in which the killing of a man was provided for, and demanded by, the law itself. In this sphere the

Greek uses the expression αἷμα ἀθῷον. Thus in Deut.27.25 we read in a series of late curses added to the book: 'cursed be he who takes a bribe to smite to death innocent blood'. In I Sam.19.5, for Jonathan 'innocent blood' would be that of the young David if Saul carried out his plan to kill him, since David 'has not sinned'. However, the expression has a generic sense in the two parallel passages to Jer. 7.6; 22.3, in Jer.22.17 and Prov.6.17; in Jer.26.15 'innocent blood' is that of Jeremiah himself threatened with death by the priests and the prophets, and in Jonah 1.13 the same expression similarly refers to the prophet.

A particular case of 'innocent blood', but still in the semantic sphere of the 'victim of an assassination', is that of the children sacrificed in the rite of *molok*.[5] In all probability there is an allusion to this in II Kings 21.26; 24.4 in connection with the religious crimes of king Manasseh; however, the reference in Ps.106.38 is explicit: 'they poured out innocent blood, the blood of their sons and daughters, whom they sacrificed to the idols of Canaan'; the evidence retains all its value even if, as many argue, this was a gloss added to the original text of the psalm. Even clearer is the reference to the 'blood of the innocents' made by Jer.19.4; the words of the prophet are pronounced at the *tophet* in Jerusalem. There is a last allusion to the sacrifice of children, though limited to the Septuagint text, in Jer.2.34.

One thing which strikes the reader of the biblical passages I have recalled, especially if they are compared with others in which the expression 'innocent blood' does not occur, is the scant moral importance attached to the killing of a person. In the curses of Deuteronomy 27 the assassin in his own right and the hired assassin occupy the last two places, but it cannot be said for certain if these positions mark the culmination of a progression, given that we find in first place idolatry, the most serious of sins in the religious system of the Old Testament; it is therefore evident that for the Hebrews homicide was less serious than offences against one's parents (a relic of tribal structure), shifting boundary marks (a concession to sedentary culture, with the recognition of private property), wronging the blind, the guest, the orphan and the widow, and finally various forms of incest. No less significant is Jer.22.17: 'For you have eyes and heart only for your dishonest gain; for shedding innocent blood, and for practising oppression and violence.' Here homicide is put after the thirst for gain, and if the phrase relating to 'blood of the innocent' must be considered, as I think it should be, an addition to the original text, that does not do away with the fact that if not for Jeremiah, at least for his interpolator, human life must have counted for very little. No less eloquent is the passage in Prov.6.16-19, clearly inspired by Isa.59.2-8: 'There are six things which Yahweh hates, seven which are an abomination to him: haughty eyes, a lying tongue, and hands that shed innocent blood, a heart that devises wicked plans, feet that make haste to run to evil, a false witness who breathes out lies; and a man who sows discord among brothers'; the sequence of sins here follows as it were an anatomical order from high to low (eyes, tongue, hands, feet) and not a scale of values; however, it is impossible not to note the ease with which moral precepts are subordinated to the demands of a literary scheme. Moreover, we might remember the regulation in Ex.21.20-22: a man who kills his own slave by striking him is subject to the law of blood vengeance only if the death is immediate; if the slave survives a day or two, the killer is no longer considered a killer. Finally, the Decalogue itself considers murder less serious than idolatry, the violation of the sabbath and lack of respect towards parents.

The scant moral relevance of homicide and the devaluation of the principle of blood vengeance when the interests of the powerful are involved are well illustrated by some episodes relating to king David. He flares up in contempt for the person who killed Saul (someone who, moreover, had simply carried out an order given by the king himself) and has him killed (II Sam.1), but is careful not to avenge the blood of Abner, of which he solemnly proclaims himself to be innocent (II Sam.3.28); he entrusts this task to Solomon (I Kings 2.5). The explanation of this behaviour, in contrast to the Hebrew law, is to be found in the fact that Joab, Abner's killer, had been the accomplice of David in the killing of Uriah, the unfortunate husband of Bathsheba, a killing of which David was explicitly accused by the prophet Nathan (II Sam.12.9). This is an episode which is so unedifying that the person who extended our Massoretic text, who had now become sensitive, as we shall see in due course, to the problem of 'innocent blood', eliminated this expression from I Kings 2.5, where it referred to the unavenged Abner, and clumsily substituted for it the repetition of *deme milḥamah*, a textual subterfuge revealed by a comparison with the Septuagint, which kept the original αἷμα ἀθῷον.

In the post-exilic period we see a profound innovation in the use of the expression 'innocent blood'; alongside the previous generic sense of 'victim of a homicide' (various texts noted above are from the post-exilic period) a new one developed which in one sense was truly unthinkable. If we read Joel 4[EVV 3].19 (a passage later than the previous chapters of the book) and Ps.94.21 we will discover that at least in certain circles 'innocent blood' comes to be identified with 'righteous' (*ṣaddiq*) and that this new designation is applied to the whole of the Jewish people. Joel says: 'Egypt shall become a desolation and Edom a desolate wilderness, for the violence done to the people of Judah, because they have shed innocent blood in their land'; the syntatical structure of the Hebrew text, obscure and on the verge of incomprehensibility apart from the context, brings out more than the English rendering the parallelism between 'sons of Judah' and 'innocent blood'. In Ps.94 we read, 'They band together against the life of the righteous, and condemn innocent blood'; it is clear to whom these words refer from the initial verse of the psalm, which speaks of the 'wicked' (v.3) who tyrannize 'your people' (v.5), i.e. the people of Yahweh. So the identification of 'innocent blood', 'righteous' and 'people of Israel' is quite explicit.[6]

The semantic development in question is again recorded faithfully in the Greek version, which in the later texts (Prov.6.17; Jonah 1.14; Joel 4.19) no longer has αἷμα ἀθῷον but αἷμα δίκαιον, 'righteous blood', in this way giving a precise rendering of the thought of the Hebrew original. The fact that αἷμα ἀθῷον still occurs in Ps.94.21 (93 in the Septuagint) can easily be explained by the presence in the same verse of the parallel expression ψυχὴν δικαίου, which prevented the use of this last term also with reference to αἷμα. The expression αἷμα ἀθῷον will reappear later (I Macc.1.37), to denote the inhabitants of Jerusalem killed near the temple by Apollonius, the general of Antiochus IV; since these seem to have been unarmed citizens, the victims of a surprise attack, the adjective ἀθῷον is quite relevant.

It is not easy to explain how in the development of Jewish ideology there could have been such an unexpected change from Deuteronomistic thought (according to which all the misadventures of Israel had been largely deserved by the faithless people) to a conception which we could define as being victimistic (the people of Israel unjustly persecuted by their enemies) and requires much further investigation; also because I have the impression that the totality of this phenomenon has never been noted. At any rate it seems to me significant that the expression of this anti-Deuteronomistic vision (not necessarily post-Deuteronomistic) has been inserted into a poetic text, the so-called 'Song of Moses' (Deut. 32.1-43), put after the end of Deuteronomy. In the final verse of this poetic composition we in fact find written: 'he will vindicate the blood of his servants' (v.43).[7] At any rate, whatever may have been the origin of the new conception it could not fail to provoke a quite obvious question: if Israel had betrayed the faithfulness of its God, the punishment (destruction of the state and exile) was just; but if, as people were now beginning to say, Israel had been 'righteous', whose was the blame for the 'innocent blood' that was shed? It was certainly not easy to reply to this question, not least because the historical traditions which had been chosen by the Deuteronomistic history school to form the canvas of its own ideological re-elaboration did not really provide a documentation capable of sustaining the hypothesis of an 'innocence' and 'justice' of the Hebrew people. On the other hand, to identify in some way those responsible for the ruin of Israel, as well as to give a reply to an essential historical question, meant defining the very identity of the true Israel: the post-exilic community, the 'innocent blood', could thus recognize its true enemies.

The great accuser was Jeremiah, or better, to be exact, the writer who at some unspecified time wrote many parts of the present book of Jeremiah in Babylon (the prophet who lived in Jerusalem and was then deported to Egypt certainly could not have used the large number of words of Babylonian origin which are to be found in his book).[8] The accusation was made without mincing words: 'The prophets prophesy falsely and the priests rule at their direction' (5.31);[9] 'from the prophet to the priest everyone deals falsely' (6.13 = 8.10).[10] Ezekiel (or whoever is writing for him) heightens the charge and does so even more explicitly: 'Her priests have done violence to my law and have profaned my holy things; they have made no distinction between the holy and the common, neither have they taught the difference between the unclean and the clean, and they have disregarded my sabbaths, so that I am profaned among them. And her prophets have daubed for them (i.e. the wicked leaders of Jerusalem) with whitewash' (Ezek.22.26,28). The exegetical inconsistency of those who would see in these verses, as in many others, an allusion to 'false prophets' instead of to 'true' ones is shown by the coupling of these prophets with the priests, both united with the 'princes' (v.27) to indicate the whole ruling class of Jerusalem. However, from the point of view of our investigation and its concern to follow the development of the conception of 'innocent blood', the most important passage is Lamentations 4.13: 'This was for the sins of the prophets and the iniquities of her priests, who shed in the midst of her the blood of the righteous'; the rendering αἷμα δίκαιον of the Septuagint guarantees and justifies the use of this passage for our discussion.

The standpoints now noted, in which prophets and priests alternate in first place as those responsible for having provoked the ruin of Israel, form an eloquent counterbalance to the historical vision of the

Deuteronomistic school, which put all the blame on the kings. But the two tendencies, we might say the two 'parties',[11] which found themselves on an equal footing during the brief period of exile and the by no means brief subsequent period in which all Jewish intellectual life was in Babylon, with the emergence of the authority of the new clergy of Jerusalem round about the fourth century BC, were to have different destinies. Whereas there was agreement everywhere with the branding of the hated kings as criminals, the indiscriminate attack on the old priestly class began to give offence to the new priests, which they tried to remedy. Certainly they could not deny the idolatries of Samaria and Jerusalem, favoured by the kings and tolerated by the priests (who moreover had direct responsibility for many liturgical acations); but a distinction began to be made: alongside the wicked priests there were also pious priests who tried to oppose idolatry, but in vain; indeed among them there were finally victims, martyrs, who paid for their fidelity to the Yahwistic ideals with their lives. And in this way there arose, probably out of nothing, the figure of the pious priest Zechariah son of Jehoiada, whom king Joash had killed in the courtyard of the temple (II Chron.24.20-22); see the lament on the faithful servants of God, the priests of Jerusalem, killed by the faithless who had profaned the temple: blood which looked to God for vengeance (Ps.79). Evidently the Psalmist had forgotten what had been said and written about the priesthood of Jerusalem the capital of Judah.

Later, presumably around the second century BC, there emerged someone who joined in the traditional accusations against the kings of Jerusalem and was by no means displeased with those directed against the priestly class, but who could not bear that evil should be spoken against the prophets. The Pharisees were the ones to come to the defence of the prophets, of whose memory they proved to be ardent worshippers; but their task was not easy. The substantial group of writings which took their name from the 'prophets' recorded some good prophets, in general advisers and supporters of the hated kings, spoke of many wicked prophets, whom it now began to call 'false prophets', and handed down the words of various others who for the most part had nothing to do directly with events prior to the exile; almost all seemed to have had the good fortune to have died a natural death, or at any rate not to have shed their own blood for faithfulness to Yahweh. The only exceptions were those prophets who lived at the time of the wicked queen Jezebel whom Obadiah did not manage to rescue (I Kings 18.4) and who therefore fell victim to the persecution of the foreign queen; but as was known, the blood of these prophets (II Kings 9.7) had been abundantly avenged by the bloody Jehu (II Kings 10). In contrast to what had happened when the reaction developed in favour of the priests, it was now too late to insert into the writings which had begun to become canonical statements in which the heroism of such a prophet martyred for his faith shone out. However, it was not too late to do some opportune retouching to already existing texts, and to create a scriptural basis for the 'innocent blood' shed among the prophets, blood which was rightly felt indispensable for rescuing the good name of the old prophetic class which the Deuteronomistic historiography had in fact condemned *en bloc*.[12]

There was a passage in the book of Jeremiah which admirably lent itself to manipulation. The original text (preserved by the Greek version, the Septuagint, which allows us to have some idea of when the text was interfered with) said: 'In vain I have smitten your children, but they did not learn their lesson; a sword devoured your prophets like a ravening lion, but you were not terrified' (2.30). So here is a sentence in which the prophets also appeared victims alongside the people; but they were victims of the vengeance of God himself, who certainly could not be accused of shedding 'innocent blood'. After the slight but skilful Pharisaic manipulation the text became, as we now read it in its Hebrew garb: 'In vain I have smitten your children, they did not learn their lesson; your sword devoured your prophets like a ravening lion'; the deletion of the final line, the change of person in the verb 'learn', and especially the insertion of the pronominal suffix in the word 'sword', radically transformed the significance of the verse. Born from a falsification of the text, the martyr prophets had no difficult in multiplying. We find others in the same chapter of Jeremiah. In v.34 the original (Greek) text said: 'and in his hands is found the blood of innocent lives; and they did not find them in the act of breaking in, but under every oak.' The verse alluded to the sacrifice of children, killed not as thieves caught in the act, but as innocent victims involved in the cult of Astarte (the tree).[13] The Pharisaic hand transformed the text like this: 'Also on your skirts is found the lifeblood of innocent poor; you did not find them breaking in yet in spite of all these things.' Note the word 'poor', *ebyonim*; if it is not just a textual corruption for *nebi'im*, prophets (as some assume), it certainly recalls the latter by assonance; and also note the absurd Massoretic correction which in order to avoid any relationship between the 'prophets' and the 'oaks' has transformed this last word (*elah*) into the impossible demonstrative pronoun (*elleh*).[14]

Despite the lack of any kind of episode in Hebrew history which could have justified this opinion, the idea that in the past the innocent blood of the prophets had been shed spread rapidly and widely, to the degree of becoming a common heritage. Without question a contribution was made to this by the great authority of the Pharisees as interpreters of the Law, including the unwritten law, so that any statement by them became a text.[15] It is no wonder that in the preaching of Jesus of Nazareth we find again the theme of the blood of the prophets having been shed, but here we find a great novelty. In his lively polemic against the leading class in Judaism, Jesus, who also comes to the defence of the prophets, challenges the right of the Pharisees to act as defenders of their memory since they, too, belong to the same ruling class which in the past had killed the prophets: 'Woe to you, scribes and Pharisees, hypocrites! For you build the tombs of the prophets and adorn the monuments of the righteous, saying, "If we had lived in the days of our fathers, we should not have taken part with them in shedding the blood of the prophets." Thus you witness against yourself, that you are sons of those who murdered the prophets. Fill up, then, the measure of your fathers... Therefore I send you prophets and wise men and scribes, some of whom you will kill and crucify, and some you will scourge in your synagogues and persecute from town to town, that upon you may come all the righteous bloodshed on earth, from the blood of innocent Abel to the blood of Zechariah the son of Barachiah, whom you murdered between the temple and the altar' (Matt.23.29-32,34-35). From these words of Jesus it seems evident that he took the Pharisaic position: going by his words the zeal of the Pharisees in showing themselves venerators of the prophets had come to the point of raising and embellishing tombs to prophets whom we know never to have existed! The weak evidence for the Pharisaic position is reflected in Jesus' argument: wishing to give the name of a prophet who had been killed, the only one he could find was the Zechariah I have already mentioned. But he was a priest, not a prophet, hence the need to make him become a prophet, identifying him ('son of Barachiah') with the writing prophet of the same time. A historical error, prompted by the need to cite at least one martyr prophet by name: but this inaccuracy is in all probability not to be imputed either to Jesus or to the evangelist but to those Pharisees who built and decorated tombs for the prophets: a 'tomb of Zechariah' can still be seen in Jerusalem, in the Kidron valley, alongside other tombs (all of the Hellenistic era) attributed to figures of the Old Testament.[16]

The invective of Jesus against the Pharisees which I have just quoted is the culminating point (it is the seventh 'Woe to you') of a violent attack on the Pharisees. Having criticized their mode of action (vv.13-26), Jesus attacks their mode of morality (vv.27-28, 'whited sepulchres', full of bones and putrefaction); declaring them unworthy of venerating the memory of the prophets, Jesus succeeds in destroying the ideological foundation of their being as a social group. In the light of what has been said about the post-exilic development of the conception of 'innocent blood', this formed the central nucleus of the Jewish identity; the Jew who retained innocent blood and who had God himself as the 'avenger of blood' was the one who did not follow idolatry (like his ancestors from the period before the exile) and who took the part of the victim, not that of the persecutors (kings and priests according to the Pharisaic point of view). To say to the Pharisees that they were among those who had persecuted the prophets was tantamount to saying that they were unworthy to be called 'innocent blood', i.e. to belong to the people of God.

But the accusation of Jesus is even more radical. With a truly brilliant dialectical intuition he introduces the name of Abel into his argument. Why? Abel was neither a priest not a prophet: but he was the first innocent blood shed, the prototype victim.[17] And this victim was never avenged: indeed a special impunity was granted to his murderer (cf.Gen.4.15). To recall the case of Abel mentioned in the first pages of the Law in the heated atmosphere of the discussion as to who had the right to belong to the 'innocent blood' was to dismiss all the Old Testament ideology at a stroke. How could anyone claim to speak of 'innocent blood' who made his own Law begin with an unpunished murder? Where was the justice in a religious commmunity where God made himself the guarantor of the assassin instead of the victim, killed simply for having worshipped him? By leaving the blood of the first righteous man unavenged, the old covenant had accepted its own inability to resolve the essential human problem (evil) and in so doing had marked out its own end.

First-century Christian thought developed and took to extremes the consequences which were already implicit in the preaching of Jesus: his killing was a further example of the shedding of αἷμα δίκαιον (Testament of Levi 16.3), but this blood does not remain unavenged like that of Abel (Heb.12.24); the instrument of a new covenant (Hebrews 12.24) finally provoked the divine judgment: 'And in her was found the blood of prophets and of saints, and of all who have been slain on earth.' 'After this I heard what seemed to be the mighty voice of a great multitude in heaven, crying, "Hallelujah! Salvation and glory and power belong to our God, for his judgments are true and just; for he has judged the great harlot who corrupted the earth with her fornication, and he has avenged on her the blood of his servants' (Rev.17.24-19.2). With the death of Christ God has finally accomplished the blood vengeance of all the just men who were awaiting justice (Rev.6.9-10), by condemning the main culprit, Jerusalem.[18] Once again the New Testament offers itself as a conclusion and contrast to the Old.

Chapter 10

The Twelve Tribes

According to the biblical account the twelve tribes of Israel appear for the first time as such when Moses at Sinai orders the first of the two censuses of the people of Israel (Num.1). But along with this first appearance there also comes the first arithmetical strangeness; if we set out to count them, we notice that the twelve tribes are in fact thirteen: Reuben, Simeon, Judah, Issachar, Zebulun, Ephraim, Manasseh, Benjamin, Dan, Asher, Gad, Naphtali and Levi; only the men of the tribe of Levi were not registered. However, this extra tribe cannot have caused much trouble since earlier, at the moment of concluding the covenant, Moses had erected only 'twelve pillars for the twelve tribes of Israel' (Ex.24.4) and the stones, also one per tribe, which were in some way raised on the occasion of the crossing of the Jordan (Josh.4), were also twelve in number. The moment of glory which was also their very *raison d'être* was experienced by the twelve tribes at the time of the conquest of the Promised Land when under the leadership of Joshua they together attacked and conquered the inhabitants of the southern part of Canaan, dividing between them the territory they had conquered by force of arms. After some reversals of fortune the extreme north then extended as far as Dan: going towards the south there followed, beyond the Jordan, part of Manasseh, Gad and Reuben; beyond that, i.e. to the west, and from north to south, there were Naphtali, Asher, Issachar, Zebulun, the other part of Manasseh, Ephraim, Benjamin, Judah and Simeon. If we want to be pedantic, we could note that the twelve tribes, once again apart from Levi, in fact occupied thirteen territories, and therefore the numbers do not fit here either.

The attentive reader of the Bible will not take long to notice that the number twelve is far more important than the actual reality of the Israelite tribes, who are made to descend from the twelve sons of Jacob;[1] to rescue this number the authors of the sacred text had to resort to not always painless expedients. One of the sons of Jacob was Levi; but the tribe of this name not only had no territory of its own but, as we have seen, was not even involved in the census. To restore the right number of twelve territorial tribes the place of Levi was taken by the duplication of Joseph, whose two sons Ephraim and Manasseh were counted in his stead; but in the count this made the tribes thirteen and not twelve. An earlier tradition, however, found another solution: when Moses, at the point of death, blesses the tribes (Deut.33), he pronounces what are obviously twelve benedictions; but this time it is Simeon who is left out; we shall soon see why.

The choice of the number twelve is certainly connected with the months of the year and most probably has its basis in ritual demands related to the worship which took place in the temple: we need only think of the twelve stones, one per tribe, inlaid in the pectoral of the high priest (here the secondary nature of the reference to the tribes should be noted, given that the ritual character of the number twelve recurs in many cultures other than Hebrew). However, there was to be a consequence of a practical kind to the territorial sub-division into twelve parts, like the prefectures attributed to Solomon with the aim of obtaining a monthly rotation for the provisioning of the court; the four districts of the so-called 'royal seals' of the kingdom of Judah which are documented in the second half of the eighth century BC can easily suggest a total of twelve districts for the two Hebrew kingdoms when they were united.[2] It is interesting to note that a similar organization also seems to be in evidence for the Syrian city of Ebla in the third millennium BC.[3] These considerations, which presuppose on the one hand the united kingdom (in any case not earlier than the tenth century BC) and on the other a priestly organization which is too similar to that of the second temple (if one thinks of the stress of the Book of Chronicles on the families and priestly tribes) to be capable of being projected directly on to the priesthood of the pre-exilic temple, not to mention that of the pre-monarchical period, which did not even have a temple at which to officiate, must have been present in the minds of some biblical scholars who have sought to justify the number twelve at a liturgical level but without accepting either the intrinsic sacrality of the number or external circumstances too late to explain a fact that they wanted to be very ancient.

So it is that various German scholars, from H.A.Ewald to M.Noth, who has been the most recent and systematic theorizer in this area,[4] produced the hypothesis that the tribes of Israel, twelve in number, will have constituted a league of a religious and political character around the sanctuary where, from time to time, the ark of the covenant was located: Gilgal, Shechem, Bethel, Shiloh. This amphictyony, as it has been called ('an assembly of those who live around' a sanctuary), will have been formed on analogy with the Greek amphictyonies, of which the most famous are that around the sanctuary of Delphi, and the Etruscan amphictyony. In recent times the theory of the Israelite amphictyony has enjoyed some temporary favour among scholars, even if the existence of such an institution could seem strange in the Semitic sphere which does not have anything similar, and a cultic league around a non-existent sanctuary could seem singular; now, however, this theory seems to have fallen into deserved oblivion.[5]

The specifically ritual value of the number twelve readily leads us to suppose that its origin is to be found in the liturgical sphere and that it took on importance especially among the priesthood of Jerusalem in Achaemenidean times (in the pre-exilic period the most important functions in the religious sphere were performed by the king). We must, however, ask how and when a cultic demand could have had a historical projection of so essential a kind as to identify all the people of Israel under the number twelve. To reply to this question let us first see if the biblical text itself, in its earliest parts, justifies the assertion of the existence of the twelve tribes.

It is an assured finding of biblical criticism that the story of the Mosaic census comes from the hand of a fairly late author (absolute dates range from the fifth to the third century BC); but even that of the conquest of Palestine by the twelve tribes, with a subsequent partition which is handed down in the book of Joshua, does not appear either credible or ancient. This finding follows not only from external evidence, historical and archaeological, which is silent about or even disproves the biblical narrative, but also from the Bible itself, which despite continual revisions and additions has preserved ancient traditions going back to the period before the exile. One of these, which forms the first chapter of the present book of Judges, presents the conquest in a totally different way from Joshua; each tribe acts on its own account and more than once with a negative outcome.

But the first chapter of Judges has another interesting feature for us; it lists the tribes of Israel as: Judah, Simeon, Benjamin, Joseph, Manasseh, Ephraim, Zebulun, Asher, Naphtali and Dan. This gives a total of ten tribes, despite the presence of Joseph alongside Manasseh and Ephraim; Levi, Reuben, Issachar and Gad are missing. Yet another different situation emerges from what is probably the earliest text of the Old Testament, the Song of Deborah (Judg.5). Here there is a celebration of a collective enterprise in which five tribes take part: Ephraim, Benjamin, Machir, Zebulun and Issachar; and in a passage subsequently added to the Song (vv.15-18) there is a recollection of another five tribes who did not take part in the enterprise: Reuben, Gilead, Dan, Asher and Naphtali. Here, too, the total is ten tribes, two of which (Machir and Gilead) have different names from those used later (Manasseh and Gad). Of particular interest is the absence of the southern tribes; Simeon, like Levi, had already ceased to exist (that is why Simeon did not receive the blessing of Moses), and this disappearance is explicitly confirmed by the curse which Jacob puts on these two tribes: 'Simeon and Levi are brothers... cursed be their anger, for it is fierce, and their wrath, for it is cruel! I will divide them in Jacob and scatter them in Israel' (Gen.49.5-7). Judah, on the other hand, did not yet exist at the time of the Song of Deborah, as emerges from the earliest part (vv.20-36) of Judges 1.

The lack of consistency among the twelve tribes seems even more evident with the formation of the two Hebrew states, the northern state of Israel and the southern state of Judah. Traditionally ten tribes are attributed to the former and two to the latter: this is a division affirmed in the biblical text itself, but it has little foundation.

Given that only two tribes remained faithful to the house of David, namely Judah and Benjamin (I Kings 12.21-23), it would seem obvious that the northern kingdom was made up of the other ten. It is worth dwelling for a moment on these ten northern tribes which would have been dispersed following the Assyrian conquest in the eighth century BC and on which there were fantasies throughout the Middle Ages (it is enough to recall the name of Eldad, who in the ninth century declared that he belonged to the lost tribe of Dan), fantasies which still continue today. When Shalmaneser III king of Assyria deported the inhabitants of the kingdom of Israel into the territories of his empire after destroying Samaria (II Kings 17.6), the northern kingdom was made up only of the central nucleus, i.e. the tribes of Ephraim and Manasseh. Not long before Shalmaneser, king Tiglath-pileser III had stripped Samaria of a large part of its territory; according to the biblical text (II Kings 15.29) various cities in the territory of Dan and Asher, Naphtali, Gilead and Galilee, were conquered by the Assyrian king and their inhabitants deported. There is no doubt that this part of northern Palestine on both sides of the Jordan was conquered by the Assyrians and annexed to their empire (Tiglath-pileser created a province in Transjordan, in the territory of Gad, and another west of Jordan, with Megiddo as its capital); it remains to be seen if these lands were truly part of the Hebrew state and, even more important, whether they were inhabited by Hebrews. There are reasons for doubt in this connection: given that Naphtali, Gilead and Zebulun (and moreover Ephraim) are in origin purely geographical names, the mention of them does not necessarily imply that Hebrews were involved; the Bible itself suggests that they had little (if any) connection with the Hebrew people: the Song of Deborah, which has already been mentioned, is evidence that Dan, Naphtali and Asher were largely extraneous to the history of the Israelites, as were Reuben and Gilead across the Jordan; the first three, and then Zebulun and Issachar, were already almost unknown to the author of Joshua 19, who uses more generic indications for them than those used for the central tribes; the same situation is described in the first chapter of the book of Judges, which does not know of even the existence of Issachar and the tribes across the Jordan. So it is legitimate to suppose that the five northern tribes, if they ever existed, were rapidly assimilated by the Canaanite element. It is certainly no coincidence that the north of Palestine has produced various Phoenician inscriptions but not a single Hebrew one.

The same also goes for the two Transjordanian tribes, Gad-Gilead and Reuben, which always remained outside the history of Israel and of which there are neither archaeological nor epigraphical traces. Rather, we need to add that the geographical position of Reuben, decidedly to the south, rules out the possibility that this tribe had been part of the northern kingdom; if it belonged anywhere, it would have belonged to Judah. The same thing is true of Simeon, and with more reason, settled as it was south of Judah beyond the Dead Sea (cf. Josh.19.1-9).

To sum up, the 'ten tribes' of the kingdom of Israel prove to be an invention of the latest strata of the Old Testament: even for those who do not want to take account of what is said about many tribes, the geographical information provided by the Bible shows beyond any doubt that the south was formed of four tribes (Judah, Benjamin, Simeon and Reuben) and the north, possibly, of the other eight.[6] This reality, which in fact does not know of the existence of the twelve tribes, is moreover expressed in the earlier traditions present in the biblical text itself, which speak of just one tribe, Judah, that remained faithful to the Davidic dynasty, and of an imprecise number of tribes which followed Jeroboam

(I Kings 12.20). When the prophet Ahijah, meeting Jeroboam alone in the country, took off his new mantle and, after tearing it into twelve pieces, said to the future king: 'Take for yourself ten pieces, for thus says the Lord, the God of Israel, Behold I am about to tear the kingdom from the hand of Solomon, and will give you ten tribes; but he shall have one tribe' (I Kings 11.31-32), his addition was not quite right; and the twelfth piece of garment remaining in Ahijah's hand shows that the little story was invented late and not very skilfully.

In short, the tribes of Israel were a somewhat fluid historical entity in continual transformation; apart from historical probability, it is the biblical text itself which confirms this (in addition to what has already been said, one thinks of the Calebite and Kenite groups which were transformed into, or fused with, the latest of the tribes, that of Judah: cf. Judges 1). What we are not in a position to reconstruct is the progressive manifestation of this reality, of which the Hebrew tradition has handed down only a late and distorted recollection and of which the extra-biblical sources say virtually nothing. However, it is interesting to note that an Egyptian text of the thirteenth century BC knows two tribes in northern Palestine, the Tayaru and the Rahamu, unknown as such to the biblical tradition. But it should be noted that the name 'Abraham' could be interpreted as 'father of Raham', i.e. as the eponym of the tribe in question.[7] It is certain that the traditions before the exile knew of various Israelite tribes more or less assimilated to local populations, but were totally ignorant of the number twelve.

Having established the time 'when', i.e. the post-exilic period, it is not too difficult to discover the reason for the ideology of the 'twelve tribes'. In Achaemenidean Jerusalem a small group of those who had returned from the Bablyonian exile considered themselves the only legitimate 'remnant', not only of the kingdom of Judah which had disappeared but of the whole people of Israel. Jerusalem represented all the tribes because it considered itself, in polemic against the Israelites of Shechem, to be the sole people of God: a sacred people who had the mission of serving God in his temple and in his dwelling, Jerusalem. That is why the high priest wore on his breast the twelve precious stones, all different and each bearing the name of a tribe (Ex.28.15-21): a people of men had become a people of priests, and like these was sub-divided into a sacred number.

Chapter 11

Joshua's Exploits

Joshua is the conqueror of Palestine, the one who at the head of the twelve tribes took military occupation of the Promised Land and divided it by lot among the various Israelite tribes; Joshua is also the one who had the people circumcised and who renewed the covenant between Yahweh and the Hebrew people. These facts, related in detail in the biblical book which takes its name from the hero, do not allow any doubt about the basic importance of Joshua in the view of history outlined by the Old Testament. Moreover, the existence of a popular tradition according to which Joshua even stopped the course of the sun in a battle reveals the extraordinary position of his figure in Hebrew historical tradition. The precise age of this tradition is difficult to establish: Joshua was a military leader involved in the battle of Gibeon, and his miraculous exploit was recorded in verse in the mysterious *Sepher ha-Yasar*, a book of which we know nothing: even the form of the title is uncertain. Since the supernatural intervention makes the battle of Gibeon resemble that fought by Barak at Taanach and sung of by the prophetess Deborah (Judg.5), it is not too risky to suppose that the two episodes will have had their roots in the pre-monarchical period. However, one should add the further qualification that this proto-historical period should be extended to the period in which the biblical tradition puts the first kings, i.e. the tenth century BC; nor can we exclude the possibility that Joshua was a ruler who lived at the time of rulers we already know. At all events, the fact remains that Joshua was one of the 'saviours' of Israel (as his own name tells us) whose memory was preserved by a relatively early work of which we have only a few verses (Josh.10.12-14). However, what I want now to stress is neither the historical reality of the Hebrew leader nor the antiquity of the traditions relating to him; I am interested in noting how the figure of Joshua is treated in the present text, especially in the book which takes its name from him.

If we compare the achievements of Joshua with those of other military leaders recorded in the Old Testament we can note some differences. Take David, for example. It should immediately be noted that he always acts on his own initiative when deciding on wars and battles; only exceptionally does he consult the oracle of Yahweh (II Sam.5.19ff.). Joshua, however, moves exclusively on Yahweh's orders, which prescribe every one of his actions: crossing the Jordan (1.2ff.; 3.7ff.; 4.2ff.), the circumcision (5.2ff.), the conquest of Jericho (6.2ff.), the punishment of those who have transgressed the ban (7.10ff.), the conquest of Ai (8.1ff.) and the very beginning of the battle (8.18ff.), the battles of Gibeon (10.8ff.) and of Merom (11.6ff.), the partition of Palestine (13.1ff.), and the designation of the cities of refuge (20.1ff.). On the only occasion on which Joshua takes an initiative of his own, when he sends the spies to Ai (7.2ff.) without an order from Yahweh, the enterprise results in a defeat for the Israelites (7.4-5). This close dependence of Joshua on the word of Yahweh has a parallel in the story of the exploits of Gideon, another 'saviour' of Israel (cf.Judg.6-8), though there the relationship between God and the hero is different: whereas Joshua limits himself to listening to the orders of God and putting them into practice, Gideon replies and engages God in conversation; he is the one who asks Yahweh to provide evidence that will guarantee the validity of the divine promises, putting Yahweh's patience to a hard trial (see in this connection the disconcerting episode of Judg.6.36-40). So Joshua remains unique in his custom and in his inability to act by himself; he always carries out orders and his own military strength is sometimes made superfluous by the direct intervention of God, who performs miracles, like the conquest of Jericho, which is also preceded by a supernatural vision (5.13ff.) with a subsequent collapse of the walls, and like the hail of stones in the battle of Gibeon, during which the sun is also stopped in its course.

That Joshua appears so dependent on the divine directives is certainly a sign of his piety, but it is not that which is of interest to the biblical author, whose real aim is to depict Joshua not as a protagonist but as a subordinate. He is subordinate to Yahweh, of course, but not only to him. Right at the beginning of the book Yahweh speaks to Joshua, stressing the fact that Joshua is merely the successor to Moses and in a sense the executor of his testament: Joshua must follow faithfully and punctiliously the law of Moses (1.7-8). When Joshua speaks to the tribes of Transjordan, in a few phrases he repeats three times that the orders that he is giving are in fact orders which had already been given by Moses (1.13ff.); and twice the name of Moses appears in the response given to him by the tribes. The orders of Moses are recalled in the crossing of the Jordan (4.10,12), in the building of the altar on Mount Ebal (8.31ff.), in the bans on Hazor (11.12,15), the northern region (11.20) and the southern region (11.23), in the designation of the cities of refuge (20.2) and the levitical cities (21.2), and in the speech to the tribes of Transjordan (22.2). This continual reference to the orders of Moses simply represents a concern to stress the subordinate role of Joshua over against Moses, even if this is a subordination which is stressed in the phase of the final redaction of the book of Joshua. (It is obvious that in it there are statements from earlier writers, but it is difficult to deny that the book as it is now is a unitary and late work which, while utilizing earlier writings, takes an autonomous position; if it has any connections elsewhere, they are with Judges.)[1] The clearly subordinate role of Joshua over against Moses in the book of Joshua has already been noted;[2] but this is not so much a matter of giving a position of clear pre-eminence to Moses, the liberator and supreme legislator of the Hebrew people, as of laying the ideological foundations for another pre-eminence, that of those who set themselves up as custodians and champions of the law of Moses: Joshua subject to Moses means political power subject to religious power.

That this assertion is not the illegitimate inference of a hypercritical reader but the simple observation of someone who wants to make the text understandable is demonstrated by the second part of the book of Joshua, which speaks of the division of Palestine among the various tribes. In these chapters we find a kind of hierarchy of Hebrew power mentioned three times: 'the priest Eleazar, Joshua son of Nun and the heads of the tribes of the children of Israel' (14.1; 21.1; in 17.4 the heads of families are replaced by the expression 'the notables', neśi'im). It is worth noting that the premises of this situation are to be found in the book of Numbers: on being designated the successor of Moses, Joshua must present himself before the priest Eleazar, who by consulting the oracle of Yahweh decides the actions that Joshua and the people must perform (27.21). In Numbers the hierarchy is 'Moses, the priest Eleazar' and the people, variously represented (cf. 31.12-13 etc.); when he is nominated, Joshua comes after Eleazar (32.28). There is therefore no doubt of the significance of the way in which the work of Joshua is presented: political authority must be subordinated to the Law of Moses, i.e. to religious authority.

A military conqueror *sui generis*, Joshua is moreover additionally credited by the biblical narrative with exploits as it were of a religious nature, like the circumcision of the people and the celebration of the passover (ch.5), the copying and the reading of the law (ch.8), and the renewal of the covenant (ch.24). These and other points which we need not recall in detail here have suggested to various scholars that Joshua is depicted as a king; according to one scholar who has been occupied with the problem most recently, Joshua will have been depicted as the immediate prototype of Josiah, as he appears in the account of the 'Deuteronomistic history'.³ The general opinion which sees the final redactor of the book at work in this 'history'⁴ would thus find a further confirmation; but things are not quite like that. Certainly in Joshua there are elements which make him resemble Josiah; however, this is not the 'Deuteronomistic' Josiah (of the book of Kings) but the 'Priestly' Josiah (of the Book of Chronicles).

The careful reader will also note the stress which the book of Joshua puts on the presence of priests in the episode of the crossing of the Jordan and the conquest of Jericho; a delight in liturgical description quite alien to the narratives of the Book of Kings but typical of that of Chronicles: think of the descriptions of the transfer of the ark to Jerusalem and of the passover celebrations of Hezekiah and Josiah, of the levitical ordering attributed to David. Here, then, are the 'scribes' who advise the people on the passage of the ark across the Jordan; Joshua appears as a pious rabbi who mediates on the law 'day and night' (1.8). All in all these are features which recall the Judaism of the fourth-third century BC. Here we have by no means neglible (though neglected) ideological differences which oblige us to make a connection between Joshua and the Josiah of Chronicles rather than the Josiah of Kings.

When describing Josiah's religious reform, which is presented as having taken place basically in order to centralize the cult in Jerusalem, the author of Kings spends a remarkably long time on details of the religious practices abolished by the pious king (II Kings 23), details which are totally ignored by Chronicles. Among these, the destruction of the altar at Bethel built by Jeroboam acquires some prominence; this is stressed by the dialogue that the king has with the inhabitants of the place about the tombs of two prophets, which are then left intact (II Kings 23.16-19). The dialogue presupposes the episode narrated in II Kings 13: the prophet of Judah who forecasts the end of the altar of Bethel is the one who, deceived by the prophet of Bethel, is killed on his return journey. In II Chron.34 there is not a word of Bethel, Jeroboam and the two prophets. It is clear that the author of Chronicles had reasons not to share the hostility towards Bethel shown by the author of Kings. The latter seems to justify his aversion to a place of worship, sacred to the Hebrews from the time of Jacob (cf.Gen.28.12-19; 35.1-15), by the fact that the abhorred Jeroboam erected a sanctuary here; however, the question remains, if we enter into the logic of the biblical account, what reason Jeroboam, who was at Shechem, would have had for building sanctuaries at Dan and Bethel, two places quite a long way from Shechem but both close to Jerusalem.[5] The impression which emerges from the story is that at Jerusalem a profound aversion was nurtured towards the sanctuaries of Bethel and Dan (cf.Judg,17-18) but that the real reasons were hidden behind the convenient façade of the 'sin of Jeroboam'.

However, not everyone shared the hostility of the author of Kings against Bethel, the oldest Israelite sanctuary; as I have said, it was not shared by the author of Chronicles, and now we know why. Bethel, which after Gilgal and Shechem had been the seat of the ark,[6] was also bound up with a branch of the Hebrew priesthood which claimed descent from Aaron[7] and which can be seen in Chronicles and in certain passages of the Pentateuch (Num.25.10-13). According to an acute textual conjecture which restores the Hebrew original of the text of the Septuagint of Joshua 24.33a, Joshua, too, found a place among the writings of those who did not have a particular aversion to Bethel;[8] this confirms the affinity of Joshua with Chronicles and not with Kings.

With that we return to putting the book of Joshua in a period near to that in which Chronicles was composed and near also to the development of Pharisaic conceptions: let us say in the third century BC. We are in the period of the hierocracy of post-exilic Jerusalem, when the political power, for what it was worth, was in the hands of the priestly class. Against this background, which lasted until the fifth century BC, some of the writings combined in the final redaction were also composed; and that explains the curious episode of the submission of the inhabitants of Gibeon. Not without problems for those who make it a historical fact, the strange alliance of the inhabitants of Gibeon with the Israelites has rightly suggested to someone that the 'slaves who had to cut wood and carry water to the house of God' (9.23) must have had something to do wih the temple of Jerusalem.[9] The manifest anachronism of the mention of the temple is a late addition of the Massoretic text (it is in fact missing in the Septuagint), but the substance of the discussion remains unchanged even without the mention of the temple. The existence of people who in the neighbourhood of Jerusalem (Gibeon was little more than five miles away) gravitated in a subordinate position towards the temple faithfully reflects the situation of the post-exilic period when those who had returned from Babylon assumed an attitude of superiority towards the 'people of the land',[10] i.e. those who had escaped deportation and did not share all the religious ideas developed during the exile.

In conclusion, we may say that the book of Joshua reflects a historical situation markedly later than the exile and an ideology which it is difficult to date before the third century BC. To rely on it and on the book of Judges as a basis for a unitary framework of Hebrew history prior to the monarchy leads to accepting such a historical absurdity as a fairly large social body completely without a head. The often minuscule dimensions of the cities governed by the 'kings' of ancient Syria and Palestine suggest that either the inhabitants of the place then amalgamated with the newcomers or that the Israelite groups settled in Palestine would all have had their valiant 'kings', albeit with different political and religious connotations. Nor can we think that the power vacuum created by the theory which adopts the biblical data uncritically can be filled by the judges: their appearances as saviours only in exceptional cases does not alter the fact that usually the Israelites had no guide. The lack of a head, of a king, while improbable for social groups in Palestine at the beginning of the Iron Age, is, however, conceivable for a small group with a hierocratic government like that of Jerusalem after the exile – a 'Hebrew people' without a 'king' in Palestine existed only before the Hasmonaeans.

Chapter 12

Between Egypt and Babylon

The Letter of Aristeas, a Jewish apologetic work which can be dated to the first century BC,[1] recounts at length a legend relating to the origin of the Greek translation of the Hebrew law (the *Torah*), a translation which on the basis of this very legend has acquired the name 'Septuagint'. In part the legend, which was then taken up, also at length, by Flavius Josephus, who paraphrases the Letter (*Antiquities* 12.11-118), and by other authors who give more or less divergent versions of it, was already known to Aristobulus, a Jewish philosopher who wrote towards the middle of the second century BC;[2] at least he knew that the translation had been made through the good offices of Demetrius of Phalerum. According to this legend, which appears in the letter, Demetrius of Phalerum, head of the library of Alexandria at the time of Ptolemy Philadelphus (285-247 BC) and more specifically in the years during which Queen Arsinoe, mentioned in the letter, was alive (i.e. between 278 and 270 BC) is said to have suggested to the king that he should also enrich his library with a translation of the sacred books of the Jews. Here is a fragment of the conversation which took place between the two: ' "Information has reached me [Demetrius is speaking] that the lawbooks of the Jews are also worth translation and inclusion in your royal library." "What is there to prevent you from doing this?," the ruler asked. "Everything for your needs has been put at your disposal," Demetrius replied. "Translation is needed. They use letters characteristic of the language of the Jews, just as Egyptians use the formation of their letters in accordance with their own language. The Jews are supposed to use Aramaic, but this is not so, for it is another form of language." The king, in answer to each point, gave orders that a letter be written to the high priest of the Jews that the aforementioned project might be carried out' (Letter of Aristeas 10-11).[3]

It emerges from this statement that the translation of the Law of the Jews, i.e. the Pentateuch, will have been made to meet the wish of Ptolemy, who wanted his library to be as complete as possible. Soon afterwards, however, in the letter which king Ptolemy is said to have written to the high priest Eleazar for the purpose of agreeing that the work should be done, the aim of the translation seems to be different, and takes priority over the enriching of the library: 'It is a fact that a large number of the Jews settled in our country after being uprooted from Jerusalem by the Persians during the time of their ascendancy, and also came with our fathers into Egypt as prisoners... we have freed more than one hundred thousand prisoners, paying to their captors the price in silver proportionate to their rank... It is our wish to grant favours to them and to all the Jews throughout the world, including future generations. We have accordingly decided that your Law should be translated into Greek letters from what you call the Hebrew letters, in order that they too should take their place with us in our library with the other royal books' (Letter of Aristeas 35, 37-38).[4] Over and above the apologetic tone of the letter, this seems to suggest that, since the Septuagint version was produced by people who came from Jerusalem, it met the demands of Alexandrian and Egyptian Judaism generally. The ruler's wish is probably just an invention by the author of the Letter, since for Aristobulus the promoter of the translation seems to have been exclusively Demetrius; but the demand of the Egyptian Jews, who had rapidly become Hellenized, for the law to be written in their language, was real. So there is a good reason why the final part of the letter (310-11) confirms the sacred character of the translation and therefore its immutability.

If we accept the as it were official point of view of the Letter we cannot fail to note some inconsistencies: first of all the basic contradiction which emerges as to the motives which led to the translation; it is not clear if the Pentateuch was more necessary for the royal library or for the Jews who lived in Egypt. As for the latter, a good percentage ('one hundred thousand') had come to Egypt recently enough to be ransomed; it is therefore to be supposed that they would have known their own language better than Greek and that a Greek translation would not have been much use to them. Given that in any case Egyptian Judaism would have needed the law in Greek, the part played by Jerusalem in the production of the translation seems exaggerated and improbable: the giving of priestly permission is understandable (though it was not given for the Aramaic translations), but it is hard to understand why the translators had to be Palestinian and not Egyptian: apart from the absurdity of the twelve tribes (were not only ten of them 'dispersed'?) it is hardly probable that around 275 BC Greek was known better in Jerusalem and its environs than in Alexandria. Nevertheless, a recent study[5] has allowed us to affirm that the nomenclature of the legendary translators as given in the Letter of Aristeas is largely paralleled by that in Palestine during the Hellenistic and Roman periods but cannot be found in Egyptian nomenclature of the same period. These considerations lead us to suppose that the Septuagint version (limited to the earliest part, i.e. the Pentateuch) was presented as the consequence of a demand on the part of Egyptian Judaism but in reality corresponded, rather, to certain demands of Jerusalem Judaism which the author in fact defines by means of the figures of the legendary translators.

We find quite a curious passage in the Letter of Aristeas itself which is worth quoting. The written report which Demetrius presents to King Ptolemy about the situation of the library, with particular reference to the Jewish works, says at one point: 'Scrolls of the Law of the Jews, together with a few others, are missing from the library, for these works are written in Hebrew characters and language. But they have been transcribed somewhat carelessly and not as they should be, according to the report of the experts, because they have not received royal patronage' (Letter of Aristeas 30).[6] This passage is extremely interesting with its contradictions and its indirect admissions; it is therefore worth dwelling on it briefly. In the first place we should note two contradictions in it: it is in fact said that the library does not lack many books, but before that, in the conversation between Demetrius and the king (paragraph 10), the librarian had said that the library contained 200,000 volumes but that in a short time he would have increased the number to 500,000. More significant, however, is the contradiction between the fact that the Jewish books are said to be missing (and therefore Demetrius cannot have known them) and the simultaneous assertion that they are inaccurate: this presupposes that Demetrius had quite a deep knowledge of them. At any rate, if the verb σεσήμανται means 'edit', 'interpret', 'translate', the phrase indicates that the author of the Letter knew of the existence of Jewish writings, in Hebrew or in Greek, which did not match up to a certain model which the new version had to reflect. We are not in a position to know precisely what this refers to, but it was certainly something that had to be 'corrected' by the new version; an investigation of the Jewish literature of this period may perhaps help us to understand the situation better.

I have already mentioned a certain Aristobulus, a fragment of whose work attests the existence of a form of legend which associated the translation of the Septuagint with Demetrius of Phalerum and Ptolemy Philadelphus. In the same fragment we also read that 'before Demetrius and before the rule of Alexander and the Persians the things relating to the exodus of our Jewish fellow-countrymen from Egypt and all the events which happened to them and the conquest of the land and the exposition of all the law had been translated'.[7] As we would put it, according to Aristobulus, as early as the neo-Babylonian period (Aristobulus insisted that the Jewish law was known in Greek before Pythagoras, who had been inspired by it), there will have been a Greek translation of Exodus, Leviticus, Numbers, Deuteronomy and Joshua. Leaving aside the chronology, which is controlled by the need to make the work antedate Pythagoras, who lived in the sixth century BC, we can infer from the evidence of Aristobulus that before the third century BC there were various Greek versions of Jewish writings corresponding approximately to what we call the Hexateuch, but with the exclusion of Genesis. 'It is impossible to say for what reason he [viz. Aristobulus] (apparently) does not mention Genesis,' comments Walter in this connection in his work on Aristobulus.[8] But knowledge of a Jewish history which was unaware of the events narrated in Genesis was not limited to Aristobulus: that makes pointless the caution expressed by Walter ('here','[apparently]'), who thought that he had come upon a unique and unprecedented fact.

One piece of evidence is provided by the Letter of Aristeas itself: in the prologue, the person who calls himself Aristeas writes to his correspondent: 'I had previously sent you the account of what I regarded as the most memorable matters. We received this account of the people of the Jews from the most renowned high priests in renowned Egypt' (paragraph 6).[9] This passage seeks to instil in the reader the idea that the author of the Letter is the historical Aristeas, an author a fragment of whose work has come down to us: it is about the exegesis of the book of Job.[10] Since, however, the true Aristeas uses the Septuagint version (for a text translated later than the Pentateuch), it is obvious that he cannot be regarded as the author of the letter. Unless we want to invent a simple homonym, we must suppose that the author of the Letter had only rather a somewhat approximate idea of the Jewish-Hellenistic writers who had preceded him. The important point about the statement that I have quoted is, however a different one: the author presents himself (we do not know whether this is objectively or as a literary fiction) as an Egyptian Jew who had written a history of the Jews, and this history had begun in Egypt: otherwise, in fact, it would not have made sense to say that the earliest information about the Jews had been provided by Egyptian priests. In the historical perspective of the Old Testament as we now have it the Babylonian priests, not the Egyptian ones, would have to have furnished this kind of information.

The evidence of Aristobulus and of the Letter of Aristeas shows that even in the second and first centuries BC the most educated elements of Alexandrian Judaism were aware that before the translation of the Law their history had profound roots in Egyptian soil. A third piece of evidence in this direction is provided by the Jewish Sibylline oracles, in a sentence which belongs to the earliest phase, around the middle of the second century BC; this, too, is a product of Egyptian Judaism. 3.218-318 depicts in broad outline the history of the Jewish people; in the first verse the origin of the Jews is indicated in a city the name of which, however, is completely lacking in every manuscript tradition: the lacuna was evidently in the archetype and was due to a deletion in the text. Although a late glossator has added the annotation ουρχαλδαιω, 'Ur of the Chaldaeans', in the margin, obviously derived from the account in Genesis, it seems quite probable that the deleted name must have referred to an Egyptian city (and this discrepancy with the biblical account explains why it was deleted in mediaeval times);[11] verses 248-9 in fact say that 'the people of the twelve tribes with their leaders sent by God left Egypt and went their way'; but since there had been no previous mention of an entrance into Egypt, it is natural that this exodus from a foreign land was the first in Jewish history (later there is mention of the Babylonian exile and the return of the exiles). A polemical reference to the astrological science of the Chaldaeans (v.227) also confirms the assumption that the Jews originated in Egypt. Finally, we should recall that even around AD 100 Justus of Tiberias wrote a history of the Jews which had begun with Moses.[12]

The Jews of Egypt thus long cultivated the tradition that they had originated in Egypt, even after the translation of Genesis into Greek with its account of their origin in Babylon. It is difficult not to see in this attitude a polemical position over against Palestinian Judaism, which preferred to give itself a Mesopotamian origin; but this has two further connotations: the barely normative role that the Jews of Egypt gave to the historical traditions collected in the Pentateuch and, as a presupposition of this attitude, the lack of antiquity in these traditions. If the Babylonian origin of the Jews and the essential role of Abraham had been part of the earliest national Jewish tradition, the Egyptian Jews, who were often looked down on and despised by the Egyptians, would certainly not have abandoned them, especially when the political power was in Babylon or Susa. On the other hand, it should be remembered that though the Egyptian Jewish traditions that the Jews originated in Egypt are not attested before the second century BC in the evidence that we have noted so far, that does not mean that this evidence is late. There are other confirmations of their antiquity, which can be inferred from the fact that they were not undermined even by the Greek translation of Genesis.

Hecataeus of Abdera, who wrote around 300 BC, has left a fragment[13] which speaks of the origin of the Jews; it says that this was analogous to that of the Greeks, i.e. that they were driven out of Egypt after a plague and that under the leadership of Moses they reached Jerusalem. Since Hecataeus lived at the Ptolemaic court, it is natural to suppose that the source of his information, whether written or oral, can only have been Egyptian Jewish.[14] Jewish tradition about the Egyptian origin of the Jews therefore existed in Egypt as early as the fourth century BC; it was perpetuated not only in the bosom of Judaism, as we have seen, but also in the Hellenistic sphere: it is present in the Egyptian historian Manetho, from the first half of the third century BC,[15] and later in Lysimachus;[16] in the first century AD it was taken up again by other Egyptian writers, like Apion,[17] against whom Flavius Josephus wrote an apologia which includes various fragments from these authors, and Chaeremon;[18] it also recurs in Tacitus who, after summarily recording various theories about the origin of the Jews, asserts that 'most authors agree that once during a plague in Egypt which caused bodily disfigurement, king Bocchoris approached the oracle of Ammon and asked for a remedy, whereupon he was told to purge his kingdom and to transport this race [the Jews] into other lands since it was hateful to the gods. One only of the exiles, Moses by name, warned them not to hope for help from gods or men. They then marched for six days continually, and on the seventh secured a country, expelling the few inhabitants. There they founded a city and dedicated a temple.'[19] If ancient non-Jewish authors generally agree with the Jewish-Egyptian tradition and are completely unaware of the tradition which became canonical with the formation of the Old Testament, there can be only one explanation; we must begin by assuming that the Jews of Egypt, and especially those of Alexandria, were in a privileged position to make their cultural profile known as well; but to this we must add the fact that little, if any, authority was attached to the historical accounts in Genesis by the Egyptian Jews and that the Greek version of the Pentateuch had a very limited circulation, in fact remaining unknown outside the more orthodox Jewish circles.

The historical traditions of the Egyptian Jews were notably different from those collected in Genesis not only as regards the origins of the Jewish people but also and particularly in connection with the figure of Moses. All the authors I have mentioned obviously thought he was an Egyptian; some even thought that he was an Egyptian priest: Manetho, Chaeremon and Apion say as much.[20] That this tradition ultimately goes back to the Jews, even if we have no explicit evidence about it, can be deduced from the kind of 'Moses Romance' which Artapanus wrote some time before the middle of the first century BC.[21] Artapanus was an Egyptian Jewish writer who, without going back on his origins and his creed, did not hesitate to make substantial doctrinal and theological concessions towards both the Egyptians and the Greeks.[22] In short, everything suggests that Egyptian Judaism was totally ignorant, before the Septuagint translation, of that part of Jewish history narrated in Genesis, and that even after the diffusion of the book in the literary complex of the Pentateuch, not all that much importance was attached to this history. The attitude of Artapanus is typical here: while knowing of Abraham, Jacob and Joseph (he gives signs of knowing the Septuagint), he concentrates his attention on Moses, the Egyptian hero. Nor did the anonymous author of the romance 'Joseph and Asenath' act differently at a later date;[23] he inserted the brothers of Joseph into his story but obviously left this hero of the Egyptian-Jewish novella as protagonist. Even Flavius Josephus, who usually limited himself to paraphrasing the biblical text of the Pentateuch, when speaking of Moses (and indeed of Abraham, on whom we shall spend time in due course) inserts details, like for example his war against the Ethiopians,[24] which are taken from extra-biblical sources, probably peculiar to Artapanus.

If we compare the Egyptian Jewish tradition with that of the Jews in Jerusalem as it has been included in the present books of the Old Testament, we can note some substantial differences: rather than originating in Egypt, and therefore in an obscure way, the Jews are given a specific and substantiated origin in Babylon, which is made to go back to the beginnings of humanity. What is certainly quite an old tradition which saw the Jews as slaves in Egypt, but with a famous fellow-countryman like Joseph, was inserted into a story which explained how they came to be in Egypt; the figure of Moses, 'philosopher', commander, liberator and founder of the Jewish state of Jerusalem,[24a] is given radically new dimensions: every possible drop of Egyptian blood having been eliminated from his veins, Moses becomes just anyone, the mere instrument of God, incapable even of speaking fluently (Ex.4.10-16); the man who had made Israel a people and had given Israel the laws and a land was thought unworthy even to set foot in the Promised Land because he was Egyptian by birth. It is difficult to deny that the 'history' developed on the hills of Judah was a frontal attack on the 'history' narrated on the banks of the Nile. No wonder, then, that the Egyptian Jews were unaware of it. Far from the liturgical complications of the temple of Jerusalem, to which a large part of the law was devoted, they felt themselves to be good Jews who observed the laws of Moses – *their* Moses, undoubtedly more imposing than the figure depicted in Jerusalem.

So we begin to understand the real reasons for the Greek 'translation' of the Septuagint and why this was so close to the hearts of the clergy of Jerusalem. It was not a matter of translating already known texts into Greek, texts which Aristobulus and the Letter of Aristeas show already to have been translated; the texts which were to be put into Greek at Alexandria were new texts which gave a new face to Judaism. These were 'the authentic example', which was to correct the 'neglect' and the 'lack of agreement' in the Jewish books which were circulating in Egypt. The Septuagint version was to introduce into Egypt the 'final edition' of the Jerusalem Law. This had made many innovations, not only over Jewish origins and over Moses, but also over Abraham.

In Genesis Abraham appears as a native of Ur of the Chaldaeans, but this tradition was not the only one in circulation. Apollonius Molo wrote in the first century BC that Abraham had been born in a mountainous and desert region of Syria after his ancestors had been chased out of Armenia.[25] The unknown source of Pompeius Trogus, however, had more precise information; according to Justin the Epitomator 'the origin of the Jews is in Damascus, the most noble city of Syria... the name was given to the city by king Damascus. After Damascus the kings were Azelo, then Adore, Abraham and Israel' (36.2). The connection between Abraham and Damascus is confirmed by Nicolaus of Damascus,[26] Herod's historian, who must have been very familiar with the traditions of his city. Nicolaus writes: 'Abraham reigned at Damascus having arrived a stranger with an army from the so-called land of the Chaldaeans which lies beyond Babylon. Not long afterwards he also abandoned this land and settled himself and his people in the land which was then called Canaan and is now called Judaea... Even now the name of Abraham is famous in the region of Damascus, and people point to a village called "house of Abraham".'[27] Despite the late date of this information, it can hardly have been the product of late traditions, especially with its mention of a toponym 'Bet Abraham', which with its northern location can only suggests the tribe of Raham that I have already had cause to note.[28] The existence of a Jewish colony in Damascus in the Hellenistic period might suggest that this was the origin of the legend that had Abraham ruling in Damascus (as we have already seen, the Jews were quite fond of creating historical links with all those with whom they came in contact: I Maccabees 12.21 shows that they even said that they were related to the Spartans!); but it is quite difficult to suppose that a late tradition, connected with a group which certainly cannot have been the most authoritative in the city, succeeded in finding its way into Hellenistic historiography and creating a toponym.

The antiquity of the traditions which linked Abraham with Damascus finds interesting confirmation in the Old Testament itself. Genesis has a recollection of Abraham's journey to Damascus in the figure of the Eliezer of Damascus who would have become Abraham's heir had Isaac not been born (Gen.15.2). Whatever may have been the exact meaning of the controversial expression *ben mešeq* (for which quite recently a parallel has even been proposed with Eblaite),[29] the fact remains that the biblical text explicitly mentions Damascus, albeit only in a corrupt context;[30] and since the corruption is ancient (it is present even in the Septuagint and in Jubilees 14.2), we cannot exclude the hypothesis that it was meant to make obscure a passage which should have clarified relations between the patriarch and the Syrian city.

Another interesting indication of the relationship between Abraham and the north of Palestine including Damascus is given by Amos. In one passage (7.9) there is a poetic parallelism between 'Isaac' and 'Israel', with a reference to the northern Hebrew kingdom. Given the close connection between Isaac and Abraham, here we have explicit evidence of the presence of this patriarchal cycle in the kingdom of Israel, i.e. outside the typically southern ambience presented by Genesis. An attempt was made to eliminate the contrast between the information in Amos and that in Genesis by the later tradents of the text, who transformed the name Isaac by simply changing a consonant, so that it became a similar sounding word which meant 'laugh' (the same thing has been done in v.16 of the same chapter). The retouching of the text succeeded in deceiving the Greek translator and Jerome (who perhaps wanted to be deceived) but has not deceived modern philologists, helped by the Massoretic text (which in this case is superior to the Greek text) and by the fact that in various semitic languages the consonants of the root of which the name Isaac is composed vary quite freely. The parallelism between Isaac and Israel, which recurs twice in ch.7, is supplemented by another parallelism to be found in Amos 3.12; here there is mention of the 'remnant' of Israel and a parallel is drawn between 'Samaria' and 'Damascus'. By now we shall not be surprised to find that here, too, the text has been corrupt since ancient times,[31] accustomed as we are to seeing the text interfered with whenever we meet Abraham outside Judah. Keeping the concepts expressed in 5.3, 6.9 and the terminology of 6.4 we could reconstruct the text as follows: 'Thus says Yahweh; as the shepherd rescues from the mouth of the lion two legs, or a piece of an ear, so shall the sons of Israel be saved: those who are in Samaria a handful of tribes, and at Damascus ten (men).'

Some connection between Abraham and therefore the Hebrews and the area of Damascus is also presupposed by the geographical boundaries set by Genesis to the descendants of Abraham. Genesis 15.18-21 speaks of a land which goes 'from the river of Egypt to the Great River', i.e. the Euphrates, an area which thus stretches from the frontiers of Egypt to those of Mesopotamia and which therefore includes not only all Palestine but also all Syria. The subsequent details to be found in Genesis are, however, vague: there is no mention of other toponyms, but rather recourse to the usual list of more or less historical populations (Canaanites, Amorites, Hittites, Rephaim and so on) who often appear in the Old Testament and who in any case lived only in Palestine; the description therefore remains incomplete. The situation in Jubilees 14.18, which depends on Genesis, is similar; however, the one that we find in the so-called Genesis Apocryphon (21.11-12) is rather more complete from a geographical point of view: 'from the River of Egypt to Lebanon and Senir, and from the Great Sea to Hauran, and all the land of Gebal as far as Kadesh, and all the Great Desert to the east of Hauran and Senir as far as the Euphrates.'[31a] It is evident that this is a description of the whole region between Egypt and Mesopotamia, with the Lebanon, understood in a generic sense as the mountains of the north;[32] this large area, which according to the Genesis Apocryphon Abraham took in with his gaze from the summit of Mount Hazor, just north of Bethel (a literary procedure which curiously is repeated in Stendhal's *Charterhouse of Parma*, whose hero is said to have managed to see the whole chain of the Alps from a small tower in Parma), has its geographical centre in Damascus.

Before ending this discussion of the relations between Abraham and Damascus we must note another significant coincidence. In its voluntary withdrawal to the shores of the Dead Sea the Essene community of Qumran considered itself to be 'exiled in the land of Damascus' (Damascus Document 6.5).[33] The expression derives from Amos 5.27, an author very close to the Qumranic ideology because of the hostility to Bethel which he shared with Qumran, though obviously for different reasons;[34] but Amos is quoted and interpreted (Damascus Document 7.14-20) in the light of Jer.31.31-34: Damascus is not only the place of exile but also the place where the true interpretation of the Law will shine out (polemic against the Jerusalem clergy) and where God will renew the covenant with his just people (i.e. with the Essenes themselves). The new covenant made at Damascus (Damascus Document 19.33-34; 20.12) will be 'the covenant of Abraham' (ibid., 12.11). This conception, quite original in identifying the place of exile with that of the making of the new covenant, is as it were a synthesis of Genesis, Jeremiah and Amos; however, it would have been very difficult to bring about had there not already been a tradition which linked Abraham with Damascus; and perhaps it is also no coincidence that we find Amos again at Qumran, as the only author who is in any way evidence of such links.

In short, we can suppose that the extra-biblical traditions which saw Abraham as being active in northern Palestine and in Syria were not only earlier than the final redaction of the biblical text (which tried to eliminate them) but, given the testimony of Amos, also earlier than those which saw Abraham linked to southern Palestine. The ideological 'restructuring' of the figure of Abraham brought about in Genesis was not limited to removing his northern setting; to achieve its aim better it had to make other changes in the tradition. The enigmatic Genesis 14 shows an Abraham, strangely surnamed 'the Hebrew', in an unaccustomed guise, that of the warrior.[35] Leaving aside the pointless question of the supposed historicity of the episode, what is important to note is the very existence of this erratic mass, which moreover is put outside the economy of the Genesis narratives relating to the patriarch. There is no doubt that this fragment of tradition is typologically different from the rest; but a warrior Abraham appears as out of place in Genesis as he appears fully part of the extra-biblical traditions.

We have already recalled Nicolaus of Damascus, who speaks of Abraham 'with his army'; then there is Pseudo-Eupolemus who tells how Abraham freed his nephew, who had been captured by enemies who had attacked Palestine (called Phoenicia by the writer); these enemies are not Mesopotamian like those of Genesis 14 but 'Armenian'[36] – the episode is substantially the same as that narrated in Genesis, but there is a significant difference in the origin of the eastern kings: the biblical names, with the explicit mention of Elam, point towards Mesopotamia, according to the typical historical perspective of Genesis. That the account of Abraham's war was circulated independently and before the biblical account is demonstrated by the fact that it is narrated both by Philo of Alexandria and Flavius Josephus in an 'Assyrian' setting and with the addition of some details absent from Genesis which are precisely repeated in the two authors[37] and are therefore necessarily drawn from a common extra-biblical source. That suggest that the episode of Abraham's war must have been well known and also quite widespread in written form, to such a degree that the compiler of Genesis felt obliged to insert it into his account although it barely fits in with the context. He changed its setting in the direction of Mesopotamia, as we have seen, but since he did not carry out the work thoroughly he left evident traces of the original setting in the text: Abraham pursues his conquered enemies to Dan and to Hobah 'north of Damascus'.

Although Genesis deliberately stresses the relationships of Abraham and his family (ancestors and descendants) with Mesopotamia, there is an aspect of the tradition that associated Abraham with Babylon about which the biblical account is completely silent. The view was firmly rooted in the Jewish tradition that Abraham was above all a wise man, even a scientist, and that this wisdom derived from his Mesopotamian origin; it is almost superfluous to add that Abraham's wisdom was particularly connected with astrology. This tradition is especially developed in Jubilees (11.15-35; 12.16-18) and extensively taken up by Philo and Josephus;[38] it is explicitly also affirmed by Pseudo-Eupolemus[39] and by Apollonius Molo;[40] it is probably also echoed by Ben Sira, at least in the Greek version,[41] which in this case is thought to keep to the original Hebrew text, a text that has been retouched in the copies in our possession, which do not date from before the tenth century AD.[42] The most interesting aspect of this tradition is that Abraham was not only a wise man but also transmitted his wisdom to the Egyptians during a journey which he made in Egypt (in Genesis it is reduced to the Sarah episode). The story of Abraham's migration to Egypt as a result of famine and the teaching which the patriarch gave there is also reported by Pseudo-Hecateus II,[43] Artapanus,[44] and Nicolaus of Damascus;[45] it also recurs in the Genesis Apocryphon

(19.24-25).[46] This tradition is too widespread to be a late invention, later than Genesis (if we recall the total ineffectiveness of this book in disseminating the account of the Mesopotamian origin of the Jews); its presence also in Qumran and perhaps in Ben Sirach shows that this was not the fantasy of more or less Hellenized writers. We must therefore conclude that it is Genesis that did not include a widespread tradition, and we can also understand very well why not: first of all to rid Abraham of any suspicion of having practised astrology, firmly repudiated by orthodox Judaism (cf. also the anti-astrological allusion which we have recalled from the Sibylline Oracles, directed against Babylon), but also to avoid a positive relationship between Jews and Egyptians; an Abraham who held discussions with Egyptian priests, albeit in a period of superiority elevated the latter to the status of interlocutors, whereas for Jerusalem, Egypt could only the place of slavery and negative experiences. The sole purpose of the episode of Sarah and the Pharaoh (Gen.12.11-20) which is presented as a doublet of that between Sarah and Abimelek (Gen.20) is to put the Egyptians in a bad light.

In conclusion, if we compare the traditions of Genesis with those which were in circulation, and continued to circulate, in the Jewish circles of the Egyptian diaspora but also in Palestine itself and at Jerusalem,[46a] we can easily see that Genesis is characterized by a markedly anti-Egyptian attitude which is at the same time philo-Babylonian, and also by the repudiation of all the traditions which cast doubt on the ideological purity of Abraham and his exclusive activity in the south of Palestine. In other words, it is the assertion of Jerusalem and its priesthood, having returned from exile after being shaped in a Babylonian cultural environment, over Egyptian Judaism and that of northern Palestine, each with its own historical traditions. If this is the fairly evident substance of the ideological message of Genesis, it remains to be seen at what point we should date the message. It is obvious that its development must have already taken place during the Babylonian exile and have begun to become more specific after the return to Jerusalem; but it is one thing to develop traditions for one's own ideology and another to organize them in a homogeneous complex over against other traditions which are regarded as hostile. In terms of biblical criticism, it is not a matter of seeing when the so-called Yahwist puts the origins of Abraham in Ur (we have seen that this happened about the time of Nabonidus), but of when a certain group of texts which were already in existence were revised more or less thoroughly, combined and coordinated in a uniform frame: that is, when the Priestly writer (P) was at work, i. e. the Torah (the Pentateuch) came into being in its present form. From what I have said so far, two facts seem to emerge. The elimination of Damascus and its importance, which emerges from the references in Amos, must have been quite early, given that virtually nothing has remained of this tradition in the biblical texts as we now have them; the removal of the inconvenient information about Abraham as an astrologer, about Moses and relations with Egypt, must have been later, both because this remained in circulation for a very long time, up to the Roman period, and because the biblical text itself offers evidence of pre-existing traditions relating to it (as in the case of Gen.14). However, there are arguments which allow us to be more precise.

It has recently been argued[47] that the source of Hecataeus of Abdera, who wrote at the end of the fourth century BC, derives directly or indirectly from Jerusalem. If this is correct, it means that at least up to the end of the Achaemenidean period there was a tradition in Jerusalem which saw a direct connection between Moses and Jerusalem and that the tradition which we find in Exodus can hardly be earlier than 300 BC. This leads to a conclusion, namely that the final redaction of the Pentateuch should be dated in the third century BC, which is interesting because it confirms what I said to begin with, namely that the translation of the Septuagint must also have served to put into circulation in the Greek-speaking world the latest 'edition' of the Law; in other words, the final redaction of the Pentateuch and the Septuagint almost coincide on a chronological level. This statement will sound strange to the majority of biblical scholars, but not to G.Larsson, a scholar who has recently studied[48] the dates attributed to the patriarchs, from Adam to Abraham, and has come to the conclusion that the Priestly writer will have been at work in the second half of the third century BC.[49] As for the Greek translation, a major specialist puts it between the end of the third and the beginning of the second century BC.[50]

To the arguments adduced above we can add another which is of some weight in dating the final redaction of the Pentateuch. In the Letter of Aristeas there is often stress on an apparently insignificant fact: the Law of the Jews is written 'in the Hebrew language and in Hebrew letters', quite different from Aramaic (see the quotation at the beginning of this chapter, from para.11, and that from para.30 soon afterwards; and also: 'fine skins on which the Law had been written in letters of gold, in Hebrew characters', 176).[51] The importance of this detail is such that it is mentioned at the very beginning of the letter: 'Our deputation (waited upon him) with a view to the translation of the divine

Law, due to its being written by them on parchments in Hebrew characters' (3).[52] This stress on 'Hebrew' characters, as distinct from the Aramaic characters used for writing Hebrew, would have remained incomprehensible had not fragments of the Pentateuch (and of Job, which was also regarded as being of Mosaic origin) been found at Qumran written in 'palaeo-Hebraic' characters, imitating those used in the pre-exilic period. So it seems clear that the author of the Letter knew of the existence of palaeo-Hebraic texts, obviously used by the official priesthood of Jerusalem until this usage was discouraged by the assertion of Samaritan scripture, which also revived an archaic model.[53] The problem is to know when 'palaeo-Hebraic' writing came into use. On an official level it was used for the first time on coins and amphora seals around 200 BC,[54] and for the last time during the second revolt against the Romans (AD 135); this dating is confirmed by the Qumran manuscripts, which do not go back before the second century BC, and by Samaritan writing (a direct development of Jewish 'palaeo-Hebraic'), which does not make its first appearance before the first century AD and only defines itself in the third.[55] If we allow a reasonable amount of time between the earliest archaeological evidence for 'palaeo-Hebraic' writing and the time of this first use, we come back at most to the beginning of the third century BC. In the course of a few decades, which if Larsson's hypothesis is correct we can put in the second half of the third century BC, we would have the final redaction of the Torah, its drafting in 'palaeo-Hebraic' characters which returned to fashion even in secular use, and finally the Greek translation of the new Law which had been developed in Jerusalem.[56]

If we remember that Chronicles and, in my opinion, the 'Memoirs of Nehemiah', were written in the third century BC along with the texts which were then combined in the first part of Ezra (for these see the next chapter), we cannot but ask what was happening in Jerusalem in this period, when quite a number of traditional historical perspectives were being put in question and radically transformed. The paucity of both archaeological and historiographical documentation leaves considerable scope for the imagination of anyone who seeks to make a historical reconstruction of this period. However, it is not so much a matter of reconstructing precise historical events as rather of trying to define the climate of the milieu which produced the texts, i.e. the hierocratic oligarchy in Jerusalem.

From our investigation there has emerged a decidely anti-Egpytian attitude which manifested itself in the repudiation of the Egyptian origins of the Jewish people and in the new image of Abraham and Moses; this is the same attitude which made the author of Chronicles regard the famous daughter of the Pharaoh whom Solomon married as almost impure and therefore unworthy of living in the 'city of David', where the ark of God was placed (II Chron.8.11). This attitude is quite consistent with Exodus, which sees Egypt as the place of slavery, and with the historical view of the so-called Deuteronomistic redactor of the historical books,[57] and contrasts clearly with the role played by Egypt as a place of refuge which is presupposed by so many biblical episodes: it is Egypt which feeds Abraham (Gen.12.10-20) and then the sons of Jacob (Gen.42ff.); only an explicit divine prohibition prevents Isaac from going down there (Gen.26.2). In order to escape unfavourable political situations, various people take refuge in Egypt: Jeroboam before ascending the throne (I Kings 11.40; 12.2) and the Edomite Hadad with his men (I Kings 11.17-22); the prophet Uriah (Jeremiah 26.20-23), the anti-Babylonian rebels and with them the prophet Jeremiah (Jer.41.16-18; 42ff.), and later Onias IV (*Jewish Antiquities* 12,387-8; 13,62). Refuge in Egypt becomes a literary theme which even the New Testament does not escape.[58] However, there is a way of explaining the information provided by the biblical text, which makes the contrast seem more apparent than real: despite the mythical exodus, Egypt continued to offer itself as a place of refuge, even in Christian times, especially for those who ran into difficulties in Jerusalem; and Jerusalem did not make war against the Egypt of the Egyptians but against the Egypt of the Jews who took refuge there: the Jews of Egypt, not the Egyptians, were the real objects of the attacks on Egypt. While it is quite natural that there are no passages in the Bible about the Jewish colony of Elephantine, which by virtue of its position was remote and hardly important, what is said about the refugees who escaped to Egypt with Jeremiah after the conquest of Jerusalem by Nebuchadnezzar (Jer.42ff.) is important: they are all doomed to death, precisely because they wanted to take refuge in Egypt (Jer.42.17-18; 44.26-29). This is in fact a total repudiation, a *damnatio memoriae*. So it is with some amazement that we read a passage like Isaiah 19.18-25;[59] the explanation of its presence in the Old Testament is perhaps the great authority of the text of Isaiah (at least its earliest part), from which people did not dare to delete an inconvenient passage, even at the time of the major literary revisions in the third century BC.

So Egyptian Judaism was the real rival of the Judaism of Jerusalem. The illuminating pages which A.Momigliano has written on Egyptian

Judaism and its relations with that of Jerusalem from the second century BC on[60] even speak at one point of 'religious separatism'; this situation, however, had very ancient roots, even if it is only in the second century that the sources become quite explicit about it. Against this separatism there was promulgated in Jerusalem the new Law which was meant, though evidently it had no success, to bring an excessively independent Judaism into line. But how was such a situation created?

The crisis which exploded in the third century BC within Judaism did not arise out of nowhere. Alexander's achievements, especially with their after-effects in the last decades of the century, had revolutionized the generally tranquil situation of Western Asia under Persian rule. When Ptolemy I presented himself at Jerusalem, the most authoritative part of the population was very happy to open its gates to him; somewhat later a different version of the facts was put into circulation, according to which the Greek king is said to have found his way into the city by guile, exploiting the sabbath.[61] But Pseudo-Hecataeus I, quoted by Flavius Josephus,[62] shows that there was an agreement between Ptolemy and the inhabitants of Jerusalem when he speaks of a group of Jews which, with the 'high priest Hezekiah' (so they are from Jerusalem), voluntarily went to Egypt with various followers; the fact that this Hezekiah was 'very expert in business matters' says a good deal about the whole affair. Egyptian Judaism, which was probably beginning to take on a certain character with Jeremiah's refugees, and then consolidated itself during the Achaemenidean period (the military colony of Elephantine was only a marginal episode but certainly not an isolated one), must have been quite numerous and qualified even before its dominant presence in Alexandria, even if we know virtually nothing about it before the Ptolemaic period.[63] Once extracted, narrative texts like the episode of Sarah and the Pharaoh (Gen.12.10-20, obviously retouched in its present form), the Joseph story (Gen.37; 39-48; 50) and the infancy of Moses (Ex.1-2), give evidence of its intellectual vitality (at any rate Egyptian culture did not favour the consideration of problems of the kind developed by Babylonian culture in the Judaism of Babylonia); these stories are incorporated in the Pentateuch as we now have it, but a series of features, not least linguistic ones, suggest that they originated in Egypt.

Egyptian Judaism, far from the fetters of liturgical ritual, economically prosperous, intellectually capricious, in accordance with the Egyptian tradition – in short, too free – could not but contrast at one point with the Jerusalem hierocracy, shut up in a city which seemed to have lost all political authority and was even excluded from livelier commercial activity[64] (it is significant that Josephus did not find even one source for the third century BC). The priestly class of Jerusalem, especially preoccupied with the internal quarrels which divided it ('sons of Zadok' against 'sons of Aaron', priests against Levites), turned in on itself and within its own walls (the composition in this period of the 'Memoirs of Nehemiah', written on the model of Hellenistic autobiography, which relate the rebuilding of the walls of Jerusalem, seems to me to be symbolic), thinking back on the tradition from which it was born, in Babylon. This is the withdrawing into their own past typical of cultures in decadence, but there is also something new, interpretation in terms of present interests: from here arises the profound 'Priestly' stamp, in fact indistinguishable from that of the 'Deuteronomist', which characterizes almost all the biblical books. Love of the past is expressed in the exclusive use of the Hebrew language, dead for centuries, for religious texts which previously had also been written in Aramaic, the living language which was now in the process of becoming rapidly Graecized (an Aramaic ostracon of the third century BC found at Jerusalem has five words on it of which two are Greek);[65] it is also expressed in the exhumation of 'palaeo-Hebraic' script. But the third century BC is also stubbornly closed to the new world which was coming into being; some people obstinately left out Hellenism, which opened up new horizons to all the people of the Near East, Jews included, of a traditional world which became increasingly restricted. Pious priests, preoccupied with their modest economic privileges and their liturgical prerogatives, expressed to God, in psalms based on models learned in Babylon, their own laments about improbable enemies (probably priests who were otherwise pious but who belonged to the opposite party) but no longer managed to think about the great problems of evil and human existence in the world, problems which had been raised in Babylon and then developed in works which were rejected (apocalyptic literature). In the new Law the problem of evil is evaded in an ambiguous sexual sphere and the problems of the Book of the Watchmen are condensed into a few incomprehensible lines (Gen.6.1-4).

If we compare Genesis and Exodus with the extra-biblical traditions, we may think in terms of a victory of Babylon over Egypt; but if we take all the Jewish literature of that period together we must admit that the third century BC marks the first great victory of Jerusalem, over both Egypt and Babylon.

Chapter 13

Ezra

'With Ezra, the Judaism which, through Pharisaism, has come down to our own days, takes clearer form';[1] 'From Ezra onwards, the Torah was Judaism and Judaism was the Torah. It is impossible to understand anything that happened within Judaism from this point on without understanding this identification. Without it, little of the New Testament seems comprehensible, especially the thought of the apostle Paul; and without it, it is impossible to understand the Pharisees, the Sadducees, the Zadokites, the Essenes or even the various apocalyptic groups';[2] 'Later Judaism saw Ezra as the true founder of the new order and exalted him even to the stature of a second Moses. The name of Ezra remained indissolubly bound up with the Torah and its interpretation; here special note should be taken of the fact that this is already a specific interpretation of the written Torah and therefore that the later assumption that Ezra was the father of scriptural science is not unjustified.'[3] These verdicts, expressed recently from different positions, shows a significant agreement on the importance still attached today to the figure of Ezra in the history of Judaism, an importance echoed in ancient times even by the Koran, in which we can read (Surah 9, v.30): 'The Jews said: "'Uzayr [Ezra] is the son of God."'[4] So here we find ourselves confronted with a figure of a magnitude which cannot be ignored, especially in a book of this kind.

The biblical book which takes its name from Ezra and puts his activity in Jerusalem in the seventh year of Artaxerxes, i.e. in 458 BC,[5] speaks at length of him, the second Moses and one like God. Ezra was a priest, but also a scribe skilled in the law of Moses;[6] he was a friend of Artaxerxes, who sent him to Jerusalem with full political, administrative and religious powers (Ezra 7.25-26); Ezra made use of these to give a new face to the community of those who had returned from Babylonian exile. One assumes that a figure of such stature would have left deep traces of himself in the biblical books after the fifth century BC, but these seem to be totally ignorant of Ezra.

Ezra is presented in the Old Testament as belonging to the most important priestly family, the one which, claiming to go back to Aaron, had provided the dynasty of the high priests (Ezra 7.1-5). However, when in I Chron. 5.27-41 we find all the genealogy of the high priests, from Levi to the Babylonian exile, we read in the penultimate position the name of Seraiah, Ezra's father, and in last place not the name of Ezra but that of Jozedek, the priest who lived in exile and was the father of the priest Joshua who returned from Babylon along with Zerubbabel. The silence of Chronicles, a work composed around the third century BC, about a priest as important as Ezra, who is sometimes even called 'high priest',[7] seems surprising. Even more surprising is another marked absence of Ezra, his omission from the list of famous men of Israel in the poem written by Ben Sirach[8] about the beginning of the second century BC (Sirach 44-50); from Enoch to Simon the Just, through Abraham, Moses, David, Elijah, Isaiah, Zerubbabel, Joshua the son of Jozedek (Ezra's nephew!) and Nehemiah, to mention only some of them. What strikes one even more is that Ben Sirach not only ignores Ezra but gives Zerubbabel and Joshua the credit for having restored the cult: that means that the author is ignorant of the law promulgated by Ezra. II Maccabees relates, as a kind of liturgical prologue in the form of a letter, the story of the sacred fire miraculously rediscovered in Jerusalem after the exile (1.18-36); this is a way of alluding to the continuity of the cult and the resumption of the sacred functions of the Jerusalem temple which had just been rebuilt. But the hero of the account is not Ezra but Nehemiah, who came to Jerusalem after him, and the protagonists are the priests gathered around him, of whom Ezra is naturally not one. When soon afterwards (II Macc.2.1-8) we are told of the Law entrusted to those who were deported during the exile it is Jeremiah, not Ezra, who is compared to Moses; and I am not taking account of the contradiction between the fact of preserving the Law in Babylon and making it known in Jerusalem only after the return.

In short, no Jewish work, whether in the Bible or not, shows knowledge of the great Ezra before Flavius Josephus: and he speaks of Ezra only as a paraphrase of the biblical text.[9] Towards the beginning of the second century BC the redaction of the Apocalypse of Ezra took place, a reworking of an earlier Apocalypse of Salathiel with the addition of material relating to a Legend of Ezra;[10] the Christian addition which forms the first two chapters of IV Ezra and which speaks of 'Ezra the prophet' belongs to the second half of the century. It is from this work that the fortunes of the figure of Ezra grew in the first centuries of the Christian church. If we consider that more than half a millennium elapses between the moment when Ezra is said to have written his 'Memoirs', which were inserted into the biblical text, and the time when he began to be known in a fairly wide circle, we cannot but admit that we find ourselves faced with a quite remarkable phenomenon: it is as if Pericles were mentioned by name for the first time in Lucian of Samosata.

The biblical book which speaks of Ezra presents itself as a historical book which reports historical facts and adduces original documents; therefore it must be taken seriously because, according to the somewhat irritable words of an American historian, 'any proposal to contradict an apparently historical document must carry the burden of proof'.[11] However, it is worth drawing attention to some aspects of this 'apparently historical document'. The book presents itself as the account of the events which took place on the return from the Babylonian exile: the rebuilding of the temple, the presentation of the Law of Moses by Ezra and the rebuilding of the walls of Jerusalem by Nehemiah.[12] Apart from the fact that this raises the question what religion the Jews had professed from the time of Moses to 458 BC, the year in which the law of Moses seems to have been known for the first time, this is the sequence of Achaemenidean rulers offered by our historical book: Cyrus, Xerxes, Artaxerxes, Darius (the actual sequence was Cyrus, Cambyses, Darius, Xerxes, Artaxerxes, Darius II). As well as this ignorance of the order of succession and the omission of Cambyses (things which suggest that the author was at a considerable remove from the events he narrates), there is a very serious contradiction relating to a fact of primary importance like the rebuilidng of the Jerusalem temple: first it is said that Artaxerxes had the work on the rebuilding of the temple stopped throughout his reign (465-424 BC)(Ezra 4.24) – the temple was completed under his successor Darius (522-486 BC if this was Darius I; 423-404 BC if it was Darius II); then it is said that Ezra came to Jerusalem in the seventh year of Artaxerxes (458 BC)(Ezra 7.7) and found the temple already built (Ezra 8.33). So we can see how many scholars place Ezra's activity in the time of Artaxerxes II (404-359 BC), i.e. after Nehemiah;[13] however, this ingenious expedient to eliminate such a major contradiction goes against both the spirit and the letter of the biblical text. It seeks first of all to assert that Ezra went to Jerusalem before Nehemiah (it is enough to think of the sequence of the two books, which have been unified in the Massoretic text); and secondly that he went there very soon, immediately after the official end of the exile, indeed that Ezra the son of Seraiah, like his 'brother' Jozedek, belonged to the generation which lived in exile and which, as Ezra 3.12 narrates, having seen the temple of Solomon, wept when the foundations of the new temple were laid. It is more than clear that in the historical perspective of the author of the book of Ezra the interval of time occupied by 'Artaxerxes' between Cyrus and Darius must have been rather short – precisely the roughly six years of the reign of Cambyses (529-522 BC), whose name Flavius Josephus (who knew Persian history better than the biblical author) substitutes for that of Artaxerxes (*Antiquities* 11,21).

The inevitable conclusion is that the author of Ezra had remarkably confused ideas about the historical period in which his narrative is set, and therefore falls into innumerable contradictions and errors, an inexhaustible source of hypotheses and inferences (as useless as they are unjustified) by biblical scholars who want at all costs to find a historical foundation in a text which is only 'apparently' historical. However, we must add that the inevitability of this conclusion has been felt, for a century at least, only by the tiniest minority of scholars who have regarded Ezra as a purely literary creation by the Chronicler,[14] who will have taken Nehemiah as his model (Nehemiah is historically much better attested than Ezra, as we shall see). This position, which is called 'radical' in the United States, was manifested for the first time in France by M.Vernes in 1889[15] and was immediately taken up by Ernest Renan;[16] the latter, in a chapter entitled 'Légende d'Esdras', argued on the basis of the passages already noted in Ecclesiasticus and II Maccabees that the religious reform of the fifth century BC was the work of Nehemiah and that later religious circles, who could not bear the fact that this was the work of a 'lay official', wanted 'a scribe, belonging to the priestly family, to have made at least an equal contribution to this great work of restoration'.[17] Renan's position was taken up a few years later by a young American student, C.C.Torrey, who in 1896 published in Germany a short but thorough monograph[18] in which he approached the problem of the composition and historical value of Ezra-Nehemiah on a strictly philological basis, contesting with linguistic arguments the authenticity of the so-called 'official documents' contained in the first chapters of Ezra and denying the biblical book and the figure of Ezra all historical value, arguing that it was a pure invention based on the figure of Zerubbabel. Whereas Renan was brushed aside, since his book made no academic claims, the attacks of the biblical scholars and the traditionalist historians focussed on Torrey, who continued his philological studies (also rebutting the argument in favour of the authenticity of the documents put forward by the historican E.Meyer), which were then collected in an important volume.[19] But developments did not support him: the position of Renan and Torrey was also taken by G.Hölscher in 1922,[20] approved in 1924 by Theodor Nöldeke, who was almost a nonagenarian (he noted how little impact had been made by Torrey's book) and in 1933 by Alfred Loisy, who was almost eighty;[21] and it was partly taken up again by R.H.Pfeiffer in 1941.[22] Renan is completely forgotten, while Torrey is still sometimes remembered for bibliographical completeness, but his views are no longer discussed.[23]

Despite the now general silence on the problem of the historicity of Ezra, I think that an objective evaluation of the evidence cannot lead to any other result than the denial of the historical existence not only of a person by the name of Ezra in the fifth century BC but also – and here I would differ from the views of Renan and Hölscher but agree substantially with that of Torrey – of the religious and social reforms which are attributed to him. The silence of the sources on Ezra up to the first century AD and the late date of the composition of Ezra, which is betrayed by its total historical improbability, agree in indicating that behind the figure of Ezra and the book which bears his name there lies something, evidently a religious reform, which took place not before the second century BC. The comparison by ancient Jewish circles of Ezra with Moses is significant in this connection: in both cases we have figures closely bound up with the Law, founders in the historical and religious sense of the term, and therefore nearer to myth than history. It is certainly no coincidence that both are elusive on a historical level and that both begin to be spoken of only many centuries after their supposed existence: Moses, who in modern terms would be said to have lived in the thirteenth century BC, began to be 'put to use' only in the exilic period,[24] whereas his name appears in probably pre-exilic texts only as an indirect reference (a Kenite 'father-in-law' or 'kinsman' of Moses, Judg.1.16; 4.11; the 'bronze serpent which Moses made', II Kings 18.4). To understand the significance of Ezra we must see how the book and the person are presented in specific terms, in the historical documentation.

The fact that the earliest evidence, that of Flavius Josephus, speaks of Ezra exclusively as the protagonist of the book gives us an important point of reference: the figure of Ezra was created by the book of the same name; he did not have an autonomous existence as a person who, if not historical, was at least legendary, before the writing of the book.

The earliest appearance of the figure of Ezra outside the book of Ezra is in IV Ezra 14, which is an addition to the preceding Apocalypse of Salathiel (chs.3-13), transformed by the redactor into the Apocalypse of Ezra. It is probable that this addition is the work of the redactor himself, who wanted in this way to strengthen his work of transference; whether it is redactional or not, the date to be assigned to ch.14 still remains the beginning of the second century AD or at most the end of the first century AD. What is interesting to note is that in these pages Ezra is presented as a second Moses, in that he receives directly from God the revelation which he is to transmit, in various ways, to the people. The equivalence of Ezra to Moses, implicit at the end of the Apocalypse of Ezra, becomes explicit in the later Christian addition put at the beginning of the book. Here we find 'the prophet Ezra' (1.1) who affirms: 'I, Ezra, received from the Lord on Mount Horeb the command to go to Israel' (2.33). So Ezra is just like Moses, as we find in the Mishnah in connection with the ceremony of the red heifer (Parah 3,5) and in the Babylonian Talmud, which attributes to Ezra ten ordinances (Baba Qamma 82a), in evident parallel to the ten commandments of Moses.

So it seems clear that when around the beginning of the second century BC the figure of Ezra began to be disseminated, it had two aspects: in apocalyptic literature Ezra represents exile (like Ezekiel, Daniel, and Salathiel,[25] who were in Babylon, and like John on Patmos and Hermas in Rome), but here too he did not lose his close link with the Law, stressed by rabbinic literature. The problem whch arises is as follows: given that Ezra is not a substitute for Moses but simply stands beside him, what is his relationship to the Law? Why was Moses not enough to represent the Torah? It could be supposed at first sight that Ezra was to symbolize as it were the oral law of the Pharisees alongside the written law of Moses. However, that is ruled out by the rabbinic tradition itself, as is shown by the Mishnah, which is very clear in this connection: the Law (oral) was given to Moses on Sinai, and Moses transmitted it to Joshua by whom it was transmitted to the Men of Old; from them it passed to the prophets, who handed it down to the 'men of the Great Synagogue' (Aboth 1,1-5), i.e. according to rabbinic tradition, to those who returned from exile with Ezra.[26] The silence about Ezra, at the very moment of alluding to his companions, is very important because it seeks to indicate how Ezra stands outside this transmission of the oral law; this outside position is confirmed by an abbreviated version of the same tradition which is also in the Mishnah, according to which the links of the chain were formed by Moses, the prophets and the *Zugoth*, i.e. the pairs of most authoritative rabbis in every generation from about 160 BC (Peah 2.6): the Great Synagogue was a less essential element than the 'pairs'.[27]

If in the eyes of rabbinic Judaism Ezra represented directly neither the written Law (which was represented by Moses) nor the oral law, then what did he represent? If we think about the historical moment (around the beginning of the second century BC) at which Ezra appears like Moses, we cannot but agree with Wellhausen that Ezra was seen, according to the indication of the rabbinic tradition itself, as the founder not of the Law but of the biblical canon.[28] It is no coincidence that the fourteenth and last chapter of the Apocalypse of Ezra ends with an account of the miraculous composition of ninety-four books of which only the first twenty-four are to be divulged: according to one way of calculating there are in fact twenty-four books in the Hebrew canon.[29] So Ezra emerges as a basic figure of Judaism as a consequence of the definition of the rabbinic canon of the Old Testament – that canon endorsed by the legendary council of Jamnia at the end of the first century AD. It is from this that the fame of Ezra arose within Judaism: quite a different fame, as we shall see, from that attributed to him by Christians, ancient and modern. As a result the historical problem shifts: though we have identified the origin of the success of the figure of Ezra in the Christian era, the fact remains that at a certain moment, when problems of the canon did not exist, a book called Ezra was written whose protagonist was connected with the Law: why?

It is obvious that at this point we must face the problem of the book of Ezra directly. This is a strictly philological problem which it is impossible to treat adequately in a few pages; for that very reason I have devoted a university course to the subject which I hope to illustrate in the not too distant future with a specific monograph at present in preparation. Here I shall limit myself to presenting briefly the results of my investigation.

In the first place we should note the original independence of the book of Ezra from Nehemiah and Chronicles. The unity of Ezra and Nehemiah is affirmed by the rabbinic tradition, but it is denied by a series of internal and external facts: on the internal level the presence of the same list of those returning both in Ezra 2.1-70 and in Neh. 7.6-72 shows that the two works were originally independent, since there would have been no point in presenting the same document twice. On the level of external evidence we should note that while the Greek version presents Ezra and Nehemiah as a single book (II Esdras) it gives a special title to the second part, i.e. to Nehemiah; that Flavius Josephus, in his paraphrase of these books (*Antiquities* 11,1-183), does not follow, as he usually does, the order of the Hebrew text (which in this case puts the end of the narrative of Ezra in the middle of the book of Nehemiah, specifically 7.73b-8.13a) but uses different and distinct sources for Ezra and Nehemiah; that in Jerome's Latin version the two books are distinct (Ezra = I Ezra, Nehemiah = II Ezra); and that Jerome explicitly states: 'among the Jews the stories of Ezra and Nehemiah are combined in a single volume'.[30] Finally, we should note that the insertion of the last part of the story of Ezra into the middle of the book of Nehemiah, which I have already mentioned, makes an unnatural break in the latter account, which proves to be a redactional expedient to bind the two books more closely together. That Ezra and Nehemiah form the last part of Chronicles is only a hypothesis of the German J.D.Michaelis, who put it forward in 1783; it immediately became almost a dogma for biblical scholars. In fact there is no foundation for it (it is obvious that all the historical books of the Old Testament are ideally bound in a kind of unity, from Genesis to Nehemiah or to I Maccabees), and the simple observation that in the Hebrew Bible Ezra and Nehemiah precede Chronicles should be enough to discredit it; moreover, it must be noted that there are ideological differences (so far not noted) between Ezra and Chronicles, over the position and function of the Levites, which show that the two works do not belong to the same period. In recent times, to tell the truth, the old hypothesis of the unity of Chronicles, Ezra and Nehemiah seems to be losing ground.[31]

A second extremely important point is the relationship between the canonical text of Ezra and the redaction of the same text known as I Esdras (in the Greek text) or III Ezra (in the Latin text). There is quite a widespread view, which also goes back to Michaelis, that I Esdras represents a fragment of a Greek redaction of what is supposed to be the one text Chronicles-Ezra-Nehemiah (the first chapter of I Esdras corresponds to II Chronicles 35-36). This view not only has no *raison d'être* from the moment when, as we have seen, Chronicles, Ezra and Nehemiah are distinct works, but has various major arguments against it. The independence and the completeness of the book of I Esdras as a separate work is demonstrated by its presence as such in all the ancient versions of the Old Testament, alongside canonical Ezra; by the use made of it by Flavius Josephus (who in his account follows I Esdras and not Ezra); by the explicit testimony of Jerome ('here there are not the delights of the dreams of the apocryphal III and IV [Ezra]')[32] that he refused to translate it; not to mention the total gratuitousness of the so-called 'fragmentary' hypothesis and the profound ideological coherence of I Esdras, a coherence which, moreover, no one has taken the trouble to study. So not only is I Esdras a complete book in itself, but it also represents the original version of the book of Ezra; the greater antiquity of I Esdras (of which the Hebrew original has not come down to us directly)[33] over against canonical Ezra is demonstrated by a series of facts: by the greater antiquity of the Greek version; by the external quotations (I Esdras is quoted by Flavius Josephus, by the Greek fathers down to the eighth century AD and by the Latin fathers down to the fifth; Ezra begins to be quoted by the Greek fathers only in the fifth century and by the Latin fathers, with the exception of Jerome, only after the sixth);[34] by the fact that a Qumran text of the first century BC which deals with the priestly sphere presents a person called *(š)nybṣr*, a form close to that of I Esdras (*sanabassaros*) and Josephus (*sanabasaros*, etc.), and not to that of Ezra (*ššbṣr*).[35] Finally there are various arguments which I need not note here which show clearly that the canonical Ezra represents a quite radical revision of I Esdras, a revision which is to be connected with the definition of the canon and therefore can be dated towards the end of the first century AD.

As for the composition of I Esdras (which from now on will be our point of reference, given its greater antiquity), it has to be said that this is an extremely composite book which does not have an organic literary form, following sources pedantically with minimal interventions in the text (usually for ideological reasons, but sometimes for literary taste). It is therefore evident that neither the historical narrative in itself nor the literary coherence derive from the origin of the work, conceived as an ideological message, transmitted indirectly through a pseudo-historical narrative which is not concerned to avoid either the repetitions or the contradictions that so disturb biblical scholars, a consequence of the juxtaposition of various sources relating to the same events.[36] It is a meta-historical, mythical narrative which provides the basis for a certain religious reality: the reform attributed to Ezra.

When this took place can be deduced on a philological basis: the sources used by I Esdras do not go back beyond the third century BC, which therefore forms the *terminus post quem*; as the *terminus ante quem* before Flavius Josephus there is an indirect allusion in Philo of Alexandria.[37] On the other hand we should remember that at this point the silence of the authors of the second century (Ben Sirach and II Maccabees) takes on a different significance; this silence could indicate that I Esdras was not yet written, but it could also indicate a refusal to recognize a reform and the person who embodied it. That means, essentially, that we cannot exclude a date for I Esdras in the second century. To discover more, we must finally turn to the book itself, and what it tells us about the reform with which it deals.

I Esdras begins with the account of Josiah's passover (taken from Chronicles) and ends with the promulgation of the Law of Ezra, in connection with the feast of Tabernacles. These points of reference are enough to help us to understand the nature of the work, delimited by the two most important Jewish feasts centred on the temple (and also rules out the bizarre hypothesis of the 'fragmentary redaction'): the book is primarily interested in certain liturgical aspects, and it is important that it refers back to Josiah (and not to Hezekiah, though he celebrated a passover which is described in detail in II Chron.39). It is for this reason that Ezra is always called 'priest' and even, in the last part of the book, where the promulgation of the Law is described, as 'high priest' (I Esdras 9.39-40: the expression is absent from the corresponding part of the canonical text, Neh.8.9, which moreover does not coincide exactly). The importance of the liturgy in I Esdras (the Greek version of it which has come down to us is rather less detailed than that in Ezra, perhaps because it was also intended for circulation in a non-Jewish environment: Flavius Josephus also skips over details of the cult) is revealed in the care taken to describe religious ceremonies: but it is significant that the description is not so much of the ceremonies in themselves as of the functions, the tasks and the areas marked out for each individual priestly class: priests, Levites, cantors, gatekeepers. The aim of the book is to show clearly the role of each priestly category, in particular that of the Levites: it is in this respect that I Esdras puts itself under the shadow of Chronicles. However, certain details, which amount to allusions and textual variants (that is why they have not so far been noted) show that here we have a situation which does not match that in Chronicles.

In I Esdras the Levites are in fact put on the same footing as the priests, as in Chronicles, but in comparison with the latter we can see an accentuation of the function of a link between the priesthood and the people which the Levites perform. I Esdras 1.5 (= II Chron.35.5) is particularly important in this connection: there we have a significant variant from the Hebrew text, which moreover is obscure and perhaps retouched. It reads: 'stand in the temple... before your brothers, the sons of Israel';[38] this is the same 'before the people' as in v.12 (here, too, the

II Chronicles

"Judaean levitical party"

Hebrew has a textual variant[39] which does not make any sense). Another detail worth noting, because it shows the complementary aspect of the assimilation of the Levites-priests to the people, namely the assimilation of the people to the priests, is the statement made in I Esdras 5.61,63; in the account of the laying of the foundations of the new temple and the consequent great joy of the Jews present, it is said -- and this detail is repeated twice because it is evidently important -- that as a sign of rejoicing, the multitude of the people sounded the trumpets: this detail of the trumpets is absent from the canonical text Ezra 3.11-13, which limits itself to saying that the people 'shouted with a loud voice' and therefore without trumpets in their mouths: because the trumpets were sounded by the priest (Ezra 3.10). This is a very important piece of specific information, because it indicates that the function of sounding the trumpets was denied even to the Levites, at least in this context.

These only apparently insignificant details (and there are others in I Esdras which will be illustrated in the work which I am preparing) are indicators of a situation which has changed from that in Chronicles: the Levites are even more important, but the people enters directly into the liturgical celebration and is no longer separate from the priests: these can now stand directly 'in front' of them. We can now see when, where and how the ceremony of the promulgation of the Law by Ezra took part: we are at the beginning of the seventh month (Tishri, according to liturgical computation), i.e. at the beginning of the autumn, in connection with the feast of Tabernacles, the greatest of the Hebrew festivals in the period of the second temple, with the temple as its point of reference. The people gather together 'in the open square before the east gate of the temple' (I Esdras 9.38), i.e. outside the main entrance (the Jerusalem temple was orientated from east to west) which led to the sacred area to which only men and priests were admitted (therefore the text repeats many times that Ezra stood before 'men and women').[40] This reading of the law is therefore different from that of Josiah, which takes place in front of all the people but 'in the temple', near one of the columns of which the king makes a covenant with Yahweh (II Kings 23.2-3; II Chron.34.30-31). The 'high priest' Ezra comes out of the temple, really goes into the midst of the people, which also includes women (something quite revolutionary); and Ezra, as it were *primus inter pares*, in order to make himself seen and heard, 'stood on the wooden platform that had been prepared' (I Esdras 9.42), 'for he had the place of honour in the presence of all' (9.45).[41] This is an artificial dais improvised for the occasion, with a purely practical purpose: the significance of all these details is that although Ezra is high priest, he is not above the others because the others are also worthy of taking part in the liturgy itself. Before beginning to read, Ezra 'blessed the Lord God Most High, the God of hosts, the Almighty; and all the multitude answered, "Amen". And they lifted up their hands, and fell to the ground and worshipped the Lord' (I Esdras 9.46-47). The scene is illuminating, but it is this 'amen' pronounced by the people which makes it exceptional: it is perhaps the only time that we see the people participating directly in a liturgical ceremony.[42] All this indicates that there are no longer substantial barriers between the officiating priest and the people[43] and that we are at exactly the opposite pole from Ezekiel 44.19, where there is a prescription that the priests shall take off their liturgical garments 'lest they communicate holiness to the people'. With Ezra, the 'sons of Aaron' bring to completion their revolution, begun with Chronicles, against the 'sons of Zadok' who recognized themselves in Ezek.40-48.[44] If we find the culmination of the liturgical reform in the choral benediction in front of the temple, its premises are brought out in the account of the first celebration of the passover by those who had returned from Babylon (I Esdras 7.10-11): on this occasion 'the priests and the Levites were purified together, and all of the returned exiles were also purified, because the Levites were all purified together'.[45]

In short, with the subtle interplay of allusions and recurrent references to the festivals and liturgical celebrations, projected on to a passage which we can define as 'mythical' (it is the moment of the foundation, in every sense, of the new temple of Jerusalem) the author of I Esdras makes himself the herald of a liturgical reform implemented among the Jerusalem clergy. It is a reform of enormous ideological significance, because for the first time the people, including women, is called to take an active part in the celebration of the cult, which was hitherto reserved to the priestly class. But we need to stress the profound significance of this reform: it is not a 'laicization' of the cult but a 'sacralization' of the people, all of whom are elevated to priestly rank. It is in this perspective that we need to put the facts prior to the promulgation of the Law of Ezra, namely the repudiation of foreign wives: in our eyes this ideological position (which in fact will have been much less rigid than that which is narrated in I Esdras) can seem racist because we are accustomed to thinking in lay terms, but in a society like that of Palestine (or, better, of Jerusalem), where Hellenization remained superficial, it was possible to talk of 'sacred seed' (I Esdras 8.67) without raising a smile. In certain religious spheres, like the priestly sphere to which expression is given in

I Esdras, a concept like 'people of God' was taken literally - and the people had to behave in such a way as to be worthy of belonging to such an exalted company.

The Law of Ezra, i.e., the new 'popular' liturgy that we think we have been able to identify in I Esdras, must have had a degree of success; otherwise the book of I Esdras would not have been successful. That it was then progressively (but much later) supplanted by a revision, the canonical Ezra, means that at a certain point this reform was no longer as pleasing as it had been: but in the meantime even the temple had ceased to exist, and so the problem relates to a historical period later to that in which we are interested. So if the reform performed under the name of Ezra succeeded in establishing itself, as everything leads us to believe, we must ask whether it may also have left traces in other Jewish texts: it is most improbable that no one would have talked about such an important fact.

I Maccabees 9.54-56 tells how the high priest Alcimus ordered that the wall (τεῖχος) of the courtyard within the temple should be pulled down; from the point of view of the author of the book this must have been virtually a sacrilege: the paralysis which struck Alcimus after the beginning of the work and which brought him to a speedy death is presented almost as a divine punishment, even if that is not explicitly stated; and it is also said that the work was stopped. The ambiguity, or better the reticence, of these words does not escape us; a demolition like that would never have been left half done: the wall would have either had to be completely pulled down or to be rebuilt. We have reason to suppose that the wall was pulled down after the death of Alcimus, but the important thing is to know which wall it was. A number of scholars have argued that this was the wall which separated Jews from Gentiles; but this supposition is quite unfounded, first of all because the text speaks explicitly of the 'court within the sanctuary' and then because it would be absurd to think of the ideological and material elimination of a wall like that which prevented the Gentiles from entering the temple proper:[46] to do that would have been to betray the essence of Judaism and in fact to destroy the temple itself (marked out as such precisely by the wall which isolated it from the area in which even those who were not Jews were allowed to circulate). The wall which Alcimus knocked down, within the temple, was something which divided various categories of Jews; we would never have known which wall it was had not this breaking down of barriers proved successful, so that it was also maintained in the great temple which Herod built at Jerusalem, evidently respecting the ideological structures of the previous temple built by Zerubbabel and Joshua.

The Mishnah, in the tractate Middoth, gives us ample details of Herod's temple. Here we read that within the great court to which Gentiles were also admitted stood the temple proper marked out by a wall with seven gates in it and formed by a series of successive courts. The first, furthest to the east, was that 'of the women'; from this fifteen steps led up to the 'court of the Israelites' which bordered directly, to the east, on that 'of the priests'; after this there was the court with the altar and then the sanctuary. What must be stressed is that the 'court of the Israelites' (about 11 cubits wide and 135 cubits long: the 'court of the priests' had identical dimensions) was divided from that 'of the priests' only by the paving which characterized the latter (the 'court of the Israelites' evidently had none) (Middoth 2.6); at the entrance to the 'court of the priests' there was a low stone dais, which recalls Ezra's wooden platform. So everything suggests that the wall which Alcimus wanted to have pulled down was that which, within the temple, separated the priests from the Israelites (male) and which Herod omitted to rebuild.

If we put the various pieces together, the pattern becomes clear: I Esdras reflects, but we can also say provides propaganda for, a liturgical (and ideological) revolution which assimilated the people to the priesthood; Alcimus had a wall knocked down within the temple; Herod's temple had no division between the court of the people and that of the priests: it is impossible to avoid the conclusion that in all probability the redaction of I Esdras represents the ideological projection of what Alcimus began to do in 159 BC.

We have seen that Alcimus' reform did not please the authors of I Maccabees; and since the reform was successful, we begin to understand why I Maccabees, while narrating the glorious achievements of a great Hebrew family, did not find a place in the rabbinic canon. However, it is clear that others were utterly delighted with the reform: indeed, the date of the knocking down of the wall became a national festival. We read in Megillat Ta'anit: 'on the twenty-third of Marheshwan the dividing wall of the inner court was broken down';[47] so rabbinic Judaism celebrated something similar to the action of Alcimus. And since it is difficult to suppose that the same event took place twice in the history of the second temple at Jerusalem, we can note with reasonable certainty that the rabbis in fact celebrated the breaking down of the wall by Alcimus. This is confirmed by the date: the rabbinic text speaks of the month of Marheshwan, which would have been the eighth (October-

November) according to the liturgical calendar, whereas I Maccabees speaks of the 'second month'; but the apparent contradiction disappears when we remember that I Maccabees uses two reckonings: the traditional Jewish one ('first month' = Nisan = March-April) for liturgical events and the Seleucid one ('first month' = Tishri = September-October) for political events.[48] This usage, endorsed by the Mishnah,[49] confirms the ideological attitude of the author of I Maccabees, who is utterly opposed to Alcimus, regarding him as a foreign king (he is said to have been made high priest by Demetrius, son of Seleucus IV, cf. 7.5-25; this, however, is incorrect, because II Macc. 14.3-4 indicates that Alcimus was already high priest at the moment when he went to ask for Demetrius to intervene). Megillat Ta'anit provides an interesting detail: the word used for 'dividing wall', *swrygh*, in itself denotes a 'trellis': this therefore indicates that the wall must have been very light, even if it was stonework, having the function of providing a theoretical rather than a material division (rather like the iconostasis of Eastern Christian churches).

It now remains to be seen why Alcimus' reform, which in a certain sense continued the tendency reflected by Chronicles with its references to Josiah, should have been associated with a non-existent person like Ezra. Of course we shall never be able to provide an adequate reply to this question; we can, however, follow up some reflections. It is normal for a religious reform to be legitimated with a reference to a tradition which is claimed already to exist and to be associated with an important person. The starting point was provided by the Josiah of Chronicles, explicitly associated with the Josiah of the book of Kings, but in some way a chronological point had to be fixed towards the beginning of the post-exilic period, which was rightly felt to be the beginning of the new way of being Jewish. To find a figure adequate to the task when one was living around the middle of the second century BC was not, however, very simple: the Jewish historical tradition was now fixed firmly from Abraham to the exile; the ancient prophetic texts had now acquired their authority and for the most part also their definitive form; the priestly movement which, victorious, had entrusted its position to Chronicles had largely used the historical texts (Kings) and the later prophetic texts (Haggai and Zechariah in particular), making substantial additions to the latter;[50] the figure of Joshua was now established for the period immediately after the exile, to the detriment of Zerubbabel, and towards the third century BC the figure of Nehemiah had emerged, in whose name 'Memoirs' had been composed in imitation of a Hellenistic literary genre, which celebrated the rebuilding of the walls of Jerusalem (and codified the prebends and and privileges of the priests and Levites). It is no coincidence that these three individuals (Zerubbabel, Joshua and Nehemiah) in that order open the list of those who returned from Babylon which has been preserved in I Esdras 5: it would have been inopportune to draw on the same list for a fourth figure, because that meant producing an obscure personage like Zarhai; so it was necessary to invent a new one.[51] But why was he called Ezra?

The name of Ezra is never attested in Hebrew before the composition of I Esdras (the two 'Ezras' of Nehemiah 12.1 and 12.33 appear in a text which is later than I Esdras, as I have already said); apparently it did not exist even in the nomenclature of neghbouring peoples, since the Moabite seal on which the name Ezra appears, which was published in 1977,[52] is probably a modern forgery, as are so many seals published in recent years containing the names of biblical figures.[53] The name (*'zr*) is a hypocoristicon which means 'He (God) is help', a name which calls to mind the Greek Alcimus (attested as such independently of the second-century Jewish high priest), an adjective formed from ἀλκή, 'force, courage, protection, help', which means 'strong, brave'.[54] But the name Ezra is also virtually identical to the word *'azarah*, which in the later priestly texts (Ezek.40-48 and Chronicles), in Ben Sirach and in rabbinic Judaism means 'inner court of the temple'.[55] Is it only a coincidence that in the name of Ezra we could find allusions to Alcimus and his liturgical revolution?

We turn now to the latter. The demolition of the wall in the inner courtyard of the temple, which delighted the Pharisees as much as it displeased the followers of the Maccabees, also profoundly irritated other people. Those 'sons of Zadok' who recognized themselves in Ezek.40-48[56] and against whom Chronicles set forth the dominant role of the 'sons of Aaron' found themselves at a certain point expelled from power, and began to write against their opponents. These came to be called 'traitors', 'transgressors of the covenant' and 'lustful': somewhat generic accusations which could have been directed against anyone. But there were also more precise accusations: the enemies of the 'sons of Zadok' had 'justified the wicked and condemned the just, and they transgressed the covenant and violated the precept. They banded together against the life of the righteous' (Damascus Document 1.19-20); they made Israel depart from 'the ways of righteousness... removing the boundary with which the forefathers had marked out their inheritance' (1.16; the same expression also occurs in 5.20 and 19.15); they are those who 'profane the temple because they do not observe the distinction in accordance with the Law' (5.6-7); finally, they are those who 'have not kept apart from the people' (8.8; 19.20). In the light of what what I have said above, these references, which hitherto have remained obscure or vague, become quite clear: those who confuse the just and the wicked, i.e. the sacred and the profane, eliminating the distinctions and shifting the boundaries with the aim of not keeping apart from the people, cannot be other than the priests who approved or even suggested Alcimus' reform. In particular it is the excessive proximity to the people, which risks causing confusion, that is rejected; and to seal the attitude of the clergy of Jerusalem, which they regard as demagogic (whereas we have seen that it is concerned with something else), the 'sons of Zadok' borrow from their beloved Ezekiel the expressions which the prophet had invented to denote the false prophets who deluded the people: 'builders of the wall' (4.19; 19.31) and 'builders of the wall and daubers of whitewash' (8.12; 19.24-25), direct quotations of Ezekiel 13.10.

The religious reform carried out by Alcimus thus leads us to the discovery of that part of the priesthood which did not share that tendency the initial moment of which is reflected by Chronicles. The breaking down of the wall within the temple that divided the clergy from the male faithful was regarded as an intolerable act, such as to provoke the priests, 'the sons of Zadok', to abandon the temple, which they now regarded as having been desecrated, and indeed Jerusalem itself; they preferred to go to live in the desert near the Dead Sea, at Qumran. Here they founded the community which was later known as that of the Essenes.

The story of the Essenes is complex and still far from clear; we can even say that it is still shrouded in obscurity because so far it has proved impossible to give names to the various figures like the 'Teacher of Righteousness', the 'Wicked Priest', and so on. The main reason for this is the lack of a historical approach to the problem of the origins of the sect, which therefore seems to have grown out of nothing.[57] Something that needs to be remembered in a general evaluation of the Qumran movement is that it came into being in a priestly environment but was soon to be transformed into something profoundly different since at a time when a Jew could not conceive of a temple other than that in Jerusalem, and that was in hostile hands, a priesthood without a temple could not survive as such. What has emerged from our analysis is that Alcimus' liturgical reform (159 BC) provides a negative but essential point of reference in a text, the Damascus Document, which is one of the most significant Essene writings from Qumran (at least ten copies of it have been found, even if often in fragments). This means that the year 159 BC is a fundamental date in the history of the sect: even if it is not the date of its beginning (the revolt of the 'sons of Zadok' against the 'sons of Aaron' certainly began before that date), it in fact coincides with the beginning of the Qumran community, the earliest archaeological evidence for which can be dated in the middle of the second century BC. Even if it does not seem possible to identify the 'wicked priest' with Alcimus, since the former was 'given into the hands of his enemies to humiliate him' (Habakkuk Commentary 8.8-13; 9.9-12), a reference to the later is to be seen in the passage of the Nahum commentary which recalls that king Demetrius was summoned to Jerusalem by deceitful men (this seems to be a summary of I Macc.7.1-25). So it seems probable that Alcimus is the 'man of lies', the ideological adversary of the 'Teacher of Righteousness'; the fact that the 'man of lies' is often replaced, especially in the Isaiah commentary, with a collective expression, the 'assembly of those who pursue lies, who are at Jerusalem', 'the assembly of the arrogant who stand at Jerusalem', and that this group is said to have transgressed the Law, leads us to suppose that it is in the priestly environment that the enemies of the 'Teacher of Righteousness' are to be found, also independently of the 'wicked priest'. If the emendation of the Isaiah Commentary 4Q163 which reads 'as a band of robbers is the association of priests, they have repudiated the law'[58] is correct, this supposition becomes a certainty.

In this general context, the identification of the 'wicked priest' with Jonathan Maccabaeus, which has found widespread approval,[59] seems fully justified on a chronological and ideological level: the common rejection of Alcimus' reform both by the 'sons of Zadok' (Damascus Document) and the Maccabees (I Maccabbees) did not prevent the two groups from later becoming enemies. This explains how although the library of Qumran is so rich, the Hebrew original of I Maccabees has not been found in it nor have the books of the 'sons of Aaron', Chronicles and I Ezra:[60] the books of hostile parties were not admitted.

But Qumran has also kept another surprise here. The fabulous caves of the Dead Sea have restored to us the 'Law' of the 'sons of Zadok', which we can read and compare with the 'Law' of the 'sons of Aaron', i.e. the 'Law' of Ezra. It is the achievement of C.Houtman and especially of B.Z.Wacholder (in courteous polemic with Y.Yadin) to have recognized in the so-called Temple Scroll the Law of Qumran,[61] which moreover is explicitly defined as such in the text itself.[62] The problem of the law of Ezra has thus been finally resolved, for historians if not for Old Testament scholars:[63] it was none other than a ritual codex proper which also closely involved the people, since it indicated the oblations and the sacrifices which they were to make in the temple of Jerusalem; for this reason it had to be explained by the Levites, point by point (cf.I Esdras 9.48). There was no Pentateuch in the hand of Ezra, then, and no royal Persian law: only a new liturgical manual which will have been substantially identical, apart obviously from some individual details, to the so-called Temple Scroll. This text does not seem to have come down directly, but it was probably the 'scroll of the court' or 'book of Ezra' of which the Mishnah speaks and which had the character of 'not defiling the hands', i.e. of not being included in the canon of sacred books (Kelim 15,6); this character would be really strange had this been, as many would have it, the autograph text of Ezra(!) used for future copies of the Torah.[64]

As a further and final confirmation of my interpretation of Ezra and the events which took place in 159 BC let me quote a passage from the Temple Scroll: 'You shall make a place to the east of the temple... for the *ḥṭ't* and the *'šm* offering, separated one from the other, (one) for the *ḥṭ't* offering of the priests and for the rams, (the other) for the *ḥṭ't* offering of the people and its *'šm*; there shall be no mixing between the one and the other, because their places shall be separated one from the other, so that the priests do not err with any offering of the people' (35.10-14). A last detail: the Temple Scroll never uses the word *'zrh* for 'court', it always uses the more traditional term *ḥṣr*: certain ambiguous terms had carefully to be avoided.

The great liturgical reform which finally endorsed the sacrality and the priestly nature of the Jewish people; the appearance of the first rabbinic *zugah* (then made legendary as the Great Synagogue); the detachment of the Zadokite priesthood from Jerusalem and the foundation of Qumran; the crisis of the Jerusalemite priesthood, which provoked a seven-year vacancy in the post of high priest and therefore the assumption of it by Jonathan Maccabaeus: all this revolves around the year 159 BC and has a name – Ezra. With this name, which no one ever bore, there really came into being that 'Judaism which, through Pharisaism, has come down to our own days', Dead Sea scrolls included.

Chapter 14

Time and History

The title of this final chapter might deceive the reader, led by it to expect difficult speculations on a subject which has been dealt with in a both fascinating and profound way by eminent thinkers and scholars. However, those who have followed me so far will by now have discovered that if they want an abstract discussion of problems they have to look elsewhere, because this book is always limited to pursuing observations, however basic, on particular data; and the same will be true in this case, at the cost of verging on banality.

The idea of 'history' as a succession of events which are in some way interconnected necessarily presupposes a mental scheme in which there is a 'before' and an 'after', in other words, a conception of time of a 'linear' kind. Events are placed one after the other along a line on which it is not possible to travel back, and it does not matter whether the line is straight, curved or even spiral (think of Polybius Book VI or Giambattista Vico): the essential thing is that it avoids being a closed circle. If the circle is closed there is no longer a 'before' and an 'after', because if one goes round in a circle every 'before' inevitably comes to be after an 'after' which thus automatically becomes a 'before'; this is cyclical time, which does not know history and which annuls it. However naive or primitive people may be, no one thinks that an action repeated periodically (getting up every morning, preparing the same Christmas tree each year) is exactly the same, even if one seeks to delude oneself that it is so because one would like it to be, in order to eliminate the agonizing passage of time, Heraclitus's πάντα ῥεί, everything flows. Cyclical time, in which everything is repeated exactly, does not exist in our reality; it exists only in myth: this is the myth of primitive societies[1] or the myth created by philosophers like Chrysippus[2] or Nietzsche.[3] 'Mythical time' is not only ahistorical but a 'revolt against concrete, historical time', a 'will to refuse concrete time... hostility toward every attempt at autonomous "history"'; these words which Mircea Eliade uses in connection with 'traditional societies'[4] are not only valid for these; the same scholar entitles the final chapter of his book, devoted to modern European man, 'The "Terror of History" ', while for Nietzsche the 'eternal return' is not a reality but only a desire that it should be such.[5]

If cyclical time is only a deliberate rejection of historical time which manifests itself on the speculative level (mythopoetic or philosophical), it would seem obvious to infer that its presence in a particular culture necessarily presupposes the existence of linear time; and since no one likes the idea of finitude and death, it will not be difficult to find more or less striking traces of a cyclical conception of time in almost every human society. Every human being and every society participates to varying degrees in both conceptions of time, and the predominance of the one over the other depends on individual states of mind or individual moments; time cannot but be linear, since the past does not return, but that does not prevent one from being able to hope or being able to delude oneself even for a moment that time will go backwards. For the thinking person, one instant follows another and one event comes after another: this continual flux of time can be rejected, by avoiding taking note of or seeking to forget what has been; but it can also be accepted and even endorsed, by fixing in some way the memory of something one does not want to perish, i.e. by writing history. Hence history (historiography) is not only a linear conception of time but also and especially its deliberate acceptance: it is a reflection which forces itself to grasp the meaning of what happens (as one fact is connected with another) and the happening itself: historical causes.

Christianity provided a major force for giving a meaning to history. After rejecting the philosophical theory of cyclical time, St Augustine[6] reduced time to a line the beginning of which he put, with the creation of the world according to Genesis, just under six thousand years previously.[7] However, others before him had also set an end to that line: 'By the same word the heavens and earth that now exist have been stored up for fire, being kept until the day of judgment and destruction of ungodly men... the heavens will pass away with a loud noise, and the elements will be dissolved with fire, and the earth and the works that are upon it will be burned up' (II Peter 3.7,10). But this linear time has a central point, the redemption, which divides time into 'before' and 'after' Christ,[8] according to a providential design which is to save humanity from evil. Around 1912 Benedetto Croce wrote: 'And since with Christianity history becomes the truth of history, escapes both fortune and chance, to which the ancients often abandoned it, and recognizes its own law, which is no longer a natural law... but rationality, intelligence, providence: this concept, too, is not extraneous to ancient philosophy... Providence guides and disposes the course of events, directing it to a goal, allows evils as punishments and means of education, and determines the magnitude and the catastrophes of empires to prepare for the kingdom of God. And this means that for the first time the idea of the circle, of the perpetual return of human affairs to their starting point, is really broken... and that for the first time history is understood as progress: progress which the ancient historians only succeeded in making in rare glimpses.'[9]

To see history as a history of salvation is therefore a demand implicit in Christian thought, which has its foundation in a historical event, the figure of Christ: so it seems obvious that this concept should have been thoroughly studied by biblical theology. However, that theology does not seem to have been satisfied of the newness of Christian thought which was born out of reflection on the death and resurrection of Christ, but began at a certain point to seek extrinsic (and therefore not necessary) causes for this originality, which in fact amounted to diminishing it: there are those who have thought that they could find such causes in the Jewish matrix of Christianity itself. And so there emerged in the period between the two world wars a school of German Protestant theologians which was destined to have considerable influence; it set out to discover in the intrinsic nature of the Hebrew language (which moreover was not spoken by the first Christians) the immediate premises of Christian theological development. Such research obviously relied on investigations of a linguistic kind, but then it went even further, to the point of hypothesizing, on the basis of this, complex forms of typically Hebrew 'thought' which as such was opposed to Greek thought. This was a type of research which found its justification in the particular cultural climate of those years: German biblical theology wanted to react, in perhaps not too intelligent a way, to the dominant antisemitism, and that was one of its merits, probably the only one. Among all the strange ideas which were put in circulation in this period, one is related to my argument: in contrast to the Greeks, who were characterized by 'static' thought which was therefore opposed to history, the Hebrews were said to have had a 'dynamic' view of the world which led them automatically to think in a historical way and therefore to create a historiography as early as the

tenth century with the 'Succession history'. 'The dynamic approach of
the Hebrews to reality is expressed in their interest in history. Their
God is characteristically one who acts in history, and these actions in
history are the core of the religious tradition of Israel. The interest in
history corresponds to and presupposes a realistic view of time. Time is
not an empty vanity but a scene of meaningful action. There is no
distinction between time and eternity, not at any rate in any sense in
which eternity would mean timelessness and be considered a higher
reality than time... For ultimate reality the Greeks turned away from
history into the unchanging. Typically, therefore, it is held, their view of
time became cyclic in the philosophical refinements of thought': this is
how James Barr[10] effectively synthesizes the positions of that biblical
theology. There were even those who, caught up in the gears of *bon mots*
devised to express the presumed merits of the Hebrew language, could
be found to state that 'there is certainly a precise chronological succession
in the Bible[11] from the creation of the world, but without chronology',
thanks to 'this specific Hebrew possibility of feeling past and future as
present'.[12]

These ideas, developed and taken over by scholars of the stature of
O.Cullmann,[13] K.Löwith,[14] and R.Bultmann,[15] could not fail also to
make an impact outside Germany and the environment in which they
came into being. A section of the book by M.Eliade, already mentioned,
devoted to the Hebrews, is entitled 'History considered as Theophany'
and shows a complete acceptance of them. The reaction of Santo
Mazzarino to them is very different: noting the fact that 'the very people
to whom we owe the greatest historical works in the world are considered
to be basically ahistorical',[16] he then goes on to contest, point by point,
with his enormous learning, the affirmations made so lightly by those
who were certainly more at home in Jerusalem than in Athens.[17] Perhaps
the Greeks lacked a 'sense of development', as Croce[18] wrote too
severely, thinking of his 'new historiography', but they certainly did not
lack a sense of historical time. The inconsistency of the linguistic basis
on which the castle of 'Hebrew thought' was built has been demonstrated
now for some time,[19] but there are still those who display a belief in
linear time, if not among the Hebrews at least among the Semites,
finding it precisely where it should not have been, namely in the cultural
environment of Iran, the first to theorize on the linearity of time.[20] As
for the second aspect of the hypothesis of biblical theology, namely the
conception of history as a manifestation of the work of God which would
have allowed the Hebrews to 'invent' history, it had its greatest and last

theorizer in G.von Rad;[21] but here too it has not been difficult to demonstrate its fragility. The fundamental study in this respect has been a book by B.Albrektson,[22] which showed on the basis of texts that the conception which was claimed to be exclusive to the Hebrews was in fact shared by practically all the peoples of Western Asia. The foreseeable criticisms which Albrektson's study encountered, especially from non-theologians,[23] have revealed once again the state of psychological subjection among various orientalists to the positions defended by the most conservative biblical scholars. As Gian Luigi Prato wrote in connection with such criticisms: 'All in all the orientalists seem to be guided by a somewhat summary and common vision of the content of the Old Testament, putting forward again precisely those conceptions which the biblical scholars themselves have cast doubts on or which have been the object of a radical revision. One would almost prefer to think that the orientalists are ignorant of the state of biblical studies, or that the latter are guided by a frantic concern to run in parallel.'[24] However, this theology, too, the presuppositions of which have had a negative effect on works like those of R.de Vaux,[25] is fortunately being surpassed.[26]

At this point we might feel in a position, having cleared the ground of the false problems created by theology, to tackle the problem of Hebrew historiography directly. The Old Testament certainly tells a long and fascinating story, from the creation of the world to the Hellenistic age; but how much of this story can be considered historiography? There are real myths in it (creation, the earthly paradise, the flood), miraculous events (the exodus from Egypt, Jericho), legends developed in various ways (patriarchs, Moses, Balaam), romances (Joseph, Samson, Gideon, Abimelek, Saul, David, Solomon), late fictions (Ezra). Some echoes of ancient traditions can still be found in some parts of Exodus, Numbers, Judges, but they are only echoes, in complex narratives where the enjoyment of the narrator (literature) is never dissociated from the concern to put forward a thesis (ideology), as appears quite evident in the books of Samuel and Kings. Only in these last is it possible to discover the presence, though only between the lines, of a real historical work of an annalistic kind,[27] substantially no different from what must have been produced in Phoenicia[28] and Babylon.[29] The fact that the only biblical data which can be compared with external sources are those relating to the Hebrew monarchies in the period between the tenth and the sixth centuries BC makes it easy to see that Hebrew historiography was closely bound up with the sphere of the court, as it was throughout the ancient Near East.[30] That is so true that after Zedekiah there are no longer Hebrew historical memoirs until another monarchy takes shape, that of the Maccabees and Hasmonaeans, the end of which again put an end to Jewish historiography (Flavius Josephus died soon after Agrippa II, the last Jewish ruler to have official recognition). Without kings, for five hundred years the Jews wrote nothing about their contemporary history (the memory of Zerubbabel is preserved only because he was celebrated by two prophets, who were then used as sources by late compilers), devoting all its energies to a continual revision of the little historical material that had been handed down to them by the hated monarchy. This, if one is prepared to admit it, is a strange fact and one worth investigating; it is as if only one moment had existed, that of the kings, and only that was worthy of revision, each time in a different way and almost always presented as something to be condemned – a love-hate relationship with a moment of their past which was certainly fertile on the religious level but which is difficult to reconcile with a 'historical' view of the world or simply of the Jews themselves.

I have thus drawn attention (and it was not my intention to do more than this) to two problems which seem essential here, that of the actual quantitative consistency of Hebrew 'historiography' (which Hecataeus of Miletus would not have judged by the same standard as all the many Greek narratives which were in circulation before him) and that of the nature of the continual revisions (biblical scholars call them 'redactions') to which the earliest historiographical texts were subjected – to which we would not be inclined to give the name history. However, there remains another great problem, implicit in the assertions of those who argue for 'Hebrew thought' and made explicit in the title of an article by E.A.Speiser:[31] that of the 'biblical' idea of history. To consider (as does Speiser, and so many with him) the whole of the Old Testament as a unitary block to be studied synchronously in the light of a central idea is justified, but only from the point of view of those who created this unity which is called the 'Old Testament'. That is, from the point of view of those rabbis who at the end of the first century AD chose, and when necessary corrected, some works of Jewish religious literature with the criterion and the aim of collecting together writings which were ideologically quite homogeneous and suitable, with appropriate interpretations, for 'forming an opinion'. If we remember the chronological moment (before the Jewish dispersion which resulted in the redaction of the Mishnah), we shall not go too far from the truth in supposing that the demand for the biblical canon of the Old Testament arose out of the need for a distinction, which was to be as clear as possible, between a Judaism which wanted to remain attached to its traditions and a markedly innovative Judaism which was in the process of creating a literature of its own, centred on the message of Jesus of Nazareth. The 'Bible' as a whole has a significance only for theologians, for whom there is an 'Old' Testament which is 'old' only in relation to the New, and for those who, though not theologians, take over the point of view of those theologians who shaped the Tanak.

So from the historical point of view it is not possible to speak of one biblical conception of history (Old Testament) or of one central idea of Hebrew historical thought; rather, we must speak of the historical view of an individual book or group of books which, in their present form, have been clearly conceived as a unitary complex. Since the loss of the majority of ancient Jewish literature (in various languages) forces us to work predominantly with the biblical material, as this is all that has come down to us, we may say that this presents two very different blocks of historical narrative: one is formed by the narratives of Hebrew origins, variously distributed over the so-called Hexateuch;[32] the other brings together narratives relating to the monarchy, starting from the situation which preceded it. These are two narrative complexes which we could call chiastic: the end of the first and the beginning of the second show the Hebrew people settled in Palestine, while the beginning of the first and the end of the second present the Hebrews without a country. The fact that only the second complex preserves traces of historical events which really happened, whereas the first is mythical and legendary, makes it easy to see that the narratives about origins have been organized in their present form only in relation to the second complex and as their specific prelude. This ideal juxtaposition, materially reflected in the arrangement of the various books within the canon, is the manifestation of a late historical view (which can be dated to the third century BC: see what was said in ch.12) and in any case remains limited to the general design produced by the last 'redactor'; within the various narrative units the leading ideas remain quite autonomous.

To identify a uniform, or at least a coherent, historical design within the narrative cycles which extend from Abraham to Joshua is an enterprise in which only theologians succeed – probably because the account is theological and not historical. However, it is worth noting that what is often regarded as the central idea, i.e. the 'promise', is not truly realized in the work, even if it is considered a unity. What God promises solemnly to Abraham (Gen.17.1-14) is not so much the land, which is mentioned only at the end, as rather numerous descendants who will become a great people (cf. also, in an even more incisive way, Gen.12.2-3) and that he will reign over a great land (Gen.15.18-21). However, this promise was not kept because Israel never became 'great' not only in our historical perspective (the greatness of Israel is not political) but even in that of the Jews themselves. At first sight one might suppose that the realization of the promise made to Abraham came about in the time of Solomon: I Kings 5.1-15 (English versions 4.21-5.1) seems evidence to this effect, but apart fom the fact that this historical datum is to be found in a different historical work from that which contains the promise, it should be noted that the passage is the work of a very late redactor and that it serves to stress the greatness not of Israel but only of Solomon. We could therefore say that the promise of God to Abraham is a messianic promise projected into a metahistorical future. The story of Hebrew origins is thus finalized on a particular theological view and can also be dated with reasonable approximation to a period which saw the greatest frustration in a part of Judaism.

The second Hebrew historiographical complex, which is usually designated the 'Deuteronomistic history', develops fully the theme of the historical events associated with the monarchy and therefore its argument has a substantial unity. However, more than one central idea is expressed here: apart from the basic theme of the greater part of the work (or rather the complex, which was put together only at a very late date), the centralization of the cult in Jerusalem (an eloquent indication of the environment and the moment at which the central nucleus was edited – Jerusalem between the fourth and the third centuries BC), it is impossible to reduce to a unity the stress on the concept of the liberation from Egypt and the promise of an eternal monarchy made to David (II Sam.7.1-17). It is easy to see in this last another messianic promise analogous to that of the great people promised to Abraham; because in this case the lack of a historical realization is manifest in an even more evident way than in the previous case (and the chronological element is even more evident: the messianic projection of the Davidic dynasty was certainly not developed immediately after Zerubbabel had been discarded). As for the liberation from Egypt, this too is a theological vision, given that there never was an exodus like that narrated by the book of the same name, while we have seen in ch.12 how a certain view of Egypt came into being. In its present form the Deuteronomistic work shows more theological than historical reflection; however, it is important to stress that there are residues of historiographical material in it, because this demonstrates the existence, at a period and in a form which is still impossible to specify, of a historiographical work relating to the Hebrew monarchy which could have been something more than a mere annalistic repertoire. Its utilization by authors who now no longer had any real interest in history is a significant indication of the presence, in this first history work,[33] of a kind of historical thought which was perhaps asking itself about the end of the Hebrew state. Here one might like to think that the close relationship which can still be seen in the books of Kings between the faults of the monarchy and the end of the kingdoms of Judah and Israel could already be found in the original work; in that case it is in the prophetic sphere (of Babylon or Egypt?), still tenaciously anti-monarchical, that we should seek its origins. This would provide further confirmation of what we noted at the end of ch.6 on the partially common origin of Greek and Hebrew historiography, arising out of the sphere of ideological and religious reaction to the respective traditional societies of the seventh century BC.

Thus we have arrived at a perhaps unexpected conclusion: the narratives which are to be found in the Hebrew Bible are all less than historical, and therefore it is useless to look for an 'idea of history' in them;[34] but regardless of the Bible, the Hebrews probably had a historiography, even if it was not a rich one, comparable to and roughly contemporaneous with that of Herodotus. And even if the verbal system of their language (with its two aspects of 'fulfilment' and 'incompleteness') was not in a position to distinguish the past from the future, they were perfectly well aware that 'before' the exile was much better than 'after'. It was only to console themseves for this 'after' that they wanted to forget the present and began to look for the return of the 'before'.[35]

NOTES

Chapter 1 The History of Israel

1. A profile from the prehistory to 586 BC was outlined by S.Moscati, 'Siria antica', in G.Tucci (ed.), *Le civiltà dell'Oriente* 1, Rome 1956, 59-91 (the work had already appeared, as an anticipatory extract, in 1954).

2. For this great scholar see the American journal *Semeia* 25, 1983, which contains various studies inspired by the centenary of the *Prolegomena* in 1978.

3. Words written by Stade in 1887 are still fully valid today: 'The nature of our task [viz. to write a history of Israel] means that it has mainly been the occupation of theologians, whereas to pursue it properly, profound philological and historical training is needed. But theologians in these disciplines have tended, rather, to go backwards at the very time when philological and critical methods are reaching the apogee of their development' (Vol.I, 51). Stade's comments are, of course, addressed to Protestant theologians, but he goes on to make equally relevant criticisms of both Catholic and Jewish theologians.

4. J.A.Soggin, 'The History of Ancient Israel. A Study in Some Questions of Method', *Eretz-Israel* 14, 1978, 44*-51*, has made a critical survey of histories which appeared betwen 1940 and 1970.

5. M.Noth, *The History of Israel*, London and Philadelphia 1958, second edition in a revised and corrected translation 1960, 2f.

6. J. Barr, *The Semantics of Biblical Language*, Oxford 1961 reissued London 1983.

7. Noth also stresses the historicity of the exodus on p.119.

8. S.Herrmann, *A History of Israel in Old Testament Times*, London and Philadelphia 1975, revised and enlarged edition 1981.

9. Herrmann's book is not without its inaccuracies. Today it is not easy to claim the existence of fortified cities isolated in a territory, i.e. a countryside, which is in hostile hands (118); the ongoing provision of food supplies for the city also presupposes military control of the countryside. And in connection with the countryside, Herrmann says of Solomon's great enterprises that 'the king probably made use during the summer of people who were free while there was no work in the fields' (177); evidently the author does not know that the most important agricultural work is in fact done during the summer – as is also evident from the famous Gezer 'calendar'.

10. The popular nature of the book and perhaps over-hasty editing probably underlie

a series of errors and approximations which somewhat detract from the work of one who for many years has been the leading German Old Testament scholar. Thus on p.8 we find attributed to the Sumerian *lugal* the functions of the *en* (he was the priest-king, not the other) and on pp.19f. a reconstruction of Semitic history in which it is hard to find a correct statement: 'Among the most important waves of migration mention should be made of the Akkadian-Egyptian (after 3000), though it is not clear whether this reached Syria; the "ancient Amorite" (around 2500-2300), not accepted by all historians, though we do not know at what point this was a concern in Syria; the Canaanite (around 2100-1700) which had a beneficial influence on the west with the foundation of states (Alalakh, Carchemish, Aleppo, Qatna, Ugarit and so on) and the development of an autonomous culture (with the discovery of alphabetic writing) and a religion of its own.' The total omission of Ebla, with all that the discovery of this city has contributed to the history of Syria, certainly does not increase the reader's confidence. Soon afterwards (25), Fohrer recalls the 'many myths and legends' in Genesis of Mesopotamian inspiration, to conjecture a 'period of direct cohabitation [of the proto-Israelites] with the Sumerians'; there are certainly less costly hypotheses to explain the affinities between Genesis and Mesopotamian literature. It is easy to challenge the statement that Josiah's reform transformed the monarchy 'from an absolute to a constitutional one' (175).

11. W.F.Albright, *From the Stone Age to Christianity*, Baltimore 1940, ²1957; *The Biblical Period from Abraham to Ezra* (1949), New York 1963; *Archaeology, Historical Analogy, and Early Biblical Tradition*, Baton Rouge 1966.

12. M.Liverani, *Oriens Antiquus* 15, 1976, 145-59.

13. P.Sacchi, 'Israele e le culture circonvicine', *Rivista di Storia e Letteratura Religiosa* 19, 1983, 216-28.

14. Quoted from the tenth edition, Turin 1884, 237.

15. Quoted from the Naples edition of 1843, 95.

16. Ibid., 290.

17. First edition, Turin 1932, English translation Milwaukee, 1955.

18. Ricciotti, op.cit., 111f.

19. *La Sacra Bibbia* II, Florence 1957, 9f.

20. J.A.Soggin, *A History of Israel. From the Beginnings to the Bar Kochba Revolt*, London and Philadelphia 1984.

20b. The positions which Soggin has adopted more recently are more acceptable in terms of methodology; cf. 'La storiografia israelitica più antica', in *La storiografia nella Bibbia. Atti della XXVIII Settimana Biblica*, Bologna 1986, 21-7.

21. The essentials of the inaugural lecture appeared in the volume *Storia e religione nell'Oriente semitico*, Rome 1924, 43-55. It was reprinted, with other historical works by Levi Della Vida, edited by F.Gabrieli and F.Tessitore, in G.Levi Della Vida, *Arabi ed ebrei nella storia*, Naples 1984; here the lecture is on pp.78-85; the quotations will follow the page numbering of this volume.

22. 'Biblical science, which with more than a century of intense work has achieved its autonomy, setting itself free from the fetters of these formulae [the dogmatic ones], approaches the sacred texts with full independence, not that it does not understand and does not appreciate the practical value of the individual religions in a positive way or opposes them deliberately in order to be a substitute for them, but because by a necessary prejudicial methodology it cannot consider documents

of a historical character with a criterion which is not that of historical method' (78).

23. Reprinted in *Arabi ed ebrei nella storia*, 213–62; the quotations are on 216.

24. S.Moscati, in the *Storia universale* edited by E.Pontieri and published by Editore Francesco Vallardi; the first volume, with the ancient Near East, appeared in 1959, but Moscati's contribution was also published independently under the title *L'Oriente antico*, Milan 1952.

25. M.Liverani, *Introduzione alla storia dell'Asia Anteriore antica*, Rome 1963.

26. G.Buccellati, *Cities and Nations of Ancient Syria*, Rome 1967.

27. A. Momigliano, 'Fattori orientali della storiografia ebraica post-exilica e della storiografia greca', in *La Persia e il mondo greco-romano*, Accademia Nazionale dei Lincei – Quaderno 76, Rome 1966, 137–46. Cf. also *The Development of Greek Biography*, Cambridge, Mass. 1972, 36.

28. Momigliano shows the same attitude of complete trust in the reliability of the data provided by the Old Testament in the chapters devoted to Judges in his book *Alien Wisdom: Limits of Hellenization*, Cambridge 1975.

29. 'I dodici intendenti di Salomone', *Rivista degli Studi Orientali* 45, 1970, 177–207; 'Osservazione sulle vie e l'orientamento dei commerci nella Siria-Palestina meridionale dall'inizio del I millennio all'anno 841 a.C', in *Studi orientalistici in ricordo di F.Pintore*, Pavia 1983, 257–93 (the article was written in 1968).

30. I have to confess that to the list of scholars mentioned here I must add myself, as author of a juvenile review article on 'Israele e gli Aramei di Damasco' (in connection with a book by M.F.Unger), which appeared in *Rivista Biblica* 6, 1958, 199–209. – There is no substantial difference between the position of the Catholics and that of the 'laity' on the way in which a history of Israel should be planned and written. However, an important exception should be recorded, even if this is an attitude which is not expressly declared. In 1906 Ignazio Guidi published an article on the historiography of the Semites, 'L'historiographie chez les Sémites', *Revue Biblique* 1906, 509–19; in it the author illustrated some methods of historiography with examples drawn from Arabic and Ethiopic writings and concluded by stating that the same methods had been applied by the Syriac writers: there was no reference to Hebrew historiography. For the Catholic Guidi this omission must have had a significance: probably that Hebrew history was too sacred to be considered just history.

31. M.Liverani, 'L'histoire de Joas', *Vetus Testamentum* 24, 1974, 438–53; C.Grottanelli, 'Horatius, i Curiatii e II Sam.2.12–18', *Annali dell'Istituto Orientale di Napoli* 35, 1975, 547–54; id., 'Spunti comparativi per la storia biblica di Giuseppe', *Oriens Antiquus* 15, 1976, 115–40 (the opening pages are important in terms of method); id., 'Possessione carismatica e razionalizzazione statale nella Bibbia ebraica', *Studi Storico Religiosi* 1, 1977, 263–88; M.Liverani,' Le "origini" d'Israele progetto irrealizzabile di ricerca etnogenetica', *Rivista Biblica* 28, 1980, 9–31; A.Catastini, 'Il quattordicesimo anno del regno di Ezechia (II Re 18.13)', *Henoch* 4, 1982, 257–63. After the articles cited here the sketch of Jewish history outlined by M.Liverani (in A.Giardina, M.Liverani, B.Scarcia, *La Palestina*, Rome 1987, 38–70) causes some surprise. Again projected on a wider background, in this history we again find the twelve tribes united in a confederation (at the time of David), a Davidic empire which includes Damascus, Solomon's twelve districts, the 'imposing buildings' in the capital of Jerusalem, Tarshish equated with Tartessus, and the

edict of Artaxerxes regarded as authentic. The historical course suggested by the Bible is faithfully followed by Liverani, who in fact does not seem ever to have moved from the conservative positions that he adopted in 1963.

32. In the course of a somewhat severe review of Fohrer's *Geschichte Israels* (which I discussed above), G.L.Prato has written, among other things: 'The basic question is not in fact that of the most up-to-date results but of the general approach of a history of Israel for which, at least in the pre-Davidic period, the biblical material itself must not be the starting point for a reconstruction which at many points does not fit in with the data of Near Eastern history', and again: 'It is more than ever essential to define clearly the nature of the sources that can be used, and the specific historical perspective from which the material is discussed. Otherwise one is forced to follow the biblical canvas, filling it with more or less solid information depending on the period and above all basically on a criterion of verisimilitude applied to individual blocks of biblical material' (*Civiltà Cattolica* 1981, III, 610).

33. A.Momigliano, 'Biblical Studies and Classical Studies. Simple Reflections upon Historical Method', *Annali della Scuola Normale Superiore di Pisa* III.11, 1981, 25.

34. C.Grottanelli, 'Un passo del libro dei Giudici alla luce della comparazione storico-religiosa: il giudice Ehud e il valore della mano sinistra', in *Atti del 1° Convegno italiano sul Vicino Oriente antico, Roma 1976*, Rome 1978, 35-45.

35. Cf. M.Liverani, in *Rivista Biblica* 28, 1980.

36. M.Guidi, *Storia e cultura degli Arabi fino alla morte di Maometto*, Florence 1951, 114.

37. This conviction underlies the two meetings of Old Testament scholars organized by the Italian Biblical Association at Bocca di Magra in 1983 and in 1985, which were entitled 'The Hebrew World in the Light of Extra-Biblical Sources'. The proceedings of the first of these, which covered the period from the beginnings to the fall of Jerusalem, have been published in *Rivista Biblica* 32, 1984, 3-151; those of the second, relating to the post-exilic period, have been published in *Rivista Biblica* 34, 1986, 1-238.

38. Only sparse fragments of Phoenician historical writings from the Hellenistic period, written in Greek, give us any idea of what Phoenician historical literature must have been like. In the 'Annals of Tyre' and the work of Philo of Byblos and Mochus it is not difficult to detect the traces of a literature which served as a model for Hebrew literature.

39. Cf. J.A.Fitzmyer and D.J.Harrington, *A Manual of Palestinian Aramaic Texts*, Rome 1978, 184-7, for the text of the Megillah.

40. As I said earlier, the Hebrews left virtually no strictly historical documents. The 'virtually' consists for the most part of seals bearing the names of various senior officials or ministers which have sometimes told us the name of their ruler. Thus some names which have vanished from the face of the earth can be discovered underground – given that the seals have always been found in tombs. The best known is a fine seal from Megiddo depicting a lion with the name of Shema, minister of Jeroboam, inscribed on it; this is the second ruler of this name, who reigned for much of the first half of the eighth century BC. Much less well known is the seal with Egyptian religious symbols of an official of Ahaz (second half of the eighth century BC). Various imprints of another seal, found on vases in various parts of Judaea, do however record the name of an official of Jehoiachin, a king who will concern us in due course; the stamp of a seal bears the name of an official

of Hezekiah, while two seals to which we shall be returning belong to two ministers of an Uzziah king of Israel.

41. It is worth recalling that the Samaria ostraca are also written in Phoenician, not in Hebrew; the same goes for the seals of the northern kingdom. As for all the inscriptions of Tell Qasileh, the one with the mention of Ophir is Philistine (as is all the rest of the culture on the site), while the seal and the ostracon which are said to have been found on the surface before the digging began are respectively a forgery and an object of unknown provenance; cf. A.Catastini, 'Hebraica dubiosa I-III', *Egitto e Vicino Oriente* 7, 1984, 121f.; id., 'Note di epigrafia ebraica I-II', *Henoch* 6, 1984, 135-7. Only the ostracon of Yabneh Yam bears witness to the presence of Hebrew epigraphy near the coast (seventh century BC).

Chapter 2 David's Empire

1. In fact the histories of Phoenicia written by Philo of Byblos and Mochus also begin with a cosmogony.
2. It is understandable that Jerusalem should produce apologetic works with historical arguments for the less curious and that fundamentalist attitudes should predominate in the bibliography; but even where it is not possible to write histories of Israel, the attitude is no different: the re-evocation of the Davidic empire is replaced, as a homage to material culture, by a more modest but specific analysis of its politics. Cf. A.Malamat, 'Aspects of the Foreign Policies of David and Solomon', *Journal of Near Eastern Studies* 22, 1963, 1-17; id., 'A Political Look at the Kingdom of David and Solomon', in T.Ishida (ed.), *The Period of David and Solomon*, Tokyo 1982, 183-204. At the beginning of the first article it is said in connection with the extent of the Solomon's dominion from the Euphrates to the Egyptian frontier (according to I Kings 5.1,4) that those who have not believed in such an empire 'have not, however, offered any convincing explanation of how the so-called "legend" of the far-flung empire of David and Solomon came into being.' On the other side cf. A.M.Gazov-Ginzberg, 'Sekret prashchi Davida' [The secret of David's sling], *Palestinskij Sbornik* XV, 78, 1966, 54-9.
3. Cf. e.g. J.A.Montgomery and H.S.Gehman, *The Books of Kings*, The International Critical Commentary, Edinburgh 1951, 126-9.
4. For the real nature of the sources quoted by Flavius Josephus as 'Annals of Tyre' see my *I Fenici. Storia e religione*, Naples 1980, 71-86. The passages quoted are *Contra Apionem* I, 117 and *Jewish Antiquities* 7,144.
5. The contradiction in which Josephus is entangled has often been noted, and hypotheses about it have been produced, some more improbable than others, to excuse as a mistake in the sources or calculations what was just a simple oversight by a rather muddle-headed historian. Among all the justifications offered for Josephus see H.J.Katzenstein, 'Is There Any Synchronism between the Reigns of Hiram and Solomon?', *Journal of Near Eastern Studies* 13, 1965, 116f. This same scholar has written a *History of Tyre*, Jerusalem 1973, a typical example of extra-biblical historiography carried out on biblical guidelines.
6. Cf. F.Safar, 'A Further Text of Shalmaneser III from Assur', *Sumer* 7, 1951, 3-21.
7. It is almost superfluous to recall that the publication of the Assyrian text with the mention of Ba'li-manzer immediately sparked off a host of studies in defence of

Flavius Josephus and his good faith. The results of the various harangues, each conflicting with the other and all verging on the absurd, can be seen in E.Lipiński, 'Ba'li-ma'zer II and the Chronology of Tyre', *Rivista degli Studi Orientali* 46, 1971, 59-65.

8. In addition to the work cited in n.4 see my review of L.Troiani, 'Commento storico al "Contro Apione" di Giuseppe, Pisa 1977', in *Henoch* 2, 1980, 231-4.

9. Cf. my 'Note linguistico-filologiche', *Henoch* 4, 1982, 166-70.

10. The two sources are Dio and Menander, both quotations at second hand (cf. my *I Fenici*, 73-7).

11. The similarity between the way in which David attains the throne with the history of Idrimi king of Alalakh (fifteenth century BC) narrated by the king himself in an inscription put on his statue has been noted by G.Buccellati, 'La "carriera" di David e quella di Idrimi re di Alalac', *Bibbia e Oriente* 4, 1962, 95-9; the 'fabulous' character of these two and other similar stories of usurpers in the ancient Near East has been stressed by M.Liverani, 'Partire sul carro, per il deserto', *Annali dell'Istituto Orientale di Napoli* 32, 1972, 403-15.

12. F.Pintore, *Il matrimonio interdinastico nel Vicino Oriente durante i secoli XV-XIII*, Rome 1978, with the important review by C.Zaccagnini in *Bullettino dell'Istituto di Diritto Romano 'Vittoria Scialoja'* 82, 1979, 203-21.

13. Pintore himself also asserts, with excessive confidence, that '...the famous marriage of Solomon with a daughter of the Pharaoh Pseusennis II... incontrovertibly also puts the house of Egypt among those who provided foreign royal wives in the first millennium' (78 n.20). This attitude of total subjection to the biblical text is a characteristic of the studies of Pintore, for the most part depriving them of any validity.

14. J.H.Breasted, *Ancient Records of Egypt*, New York 1906, IV, 344-58. I am grateful to my friend Professor Sergio Donadoni for his valuable comments.

15. This applies in particular to the recent monograph by K.A.Kitchen, *The Third Intermediate Period in Egypt (1100-650 BC)*, Oxford 1973, but in general to all works on the history of Egypt, including the various editions of the classical manual by E.Drioton and J.Vandier, *L'Égypte*.

16. W.F.Albright, 'News from Egypt on the Chronology and History of Israel and Judah', *Bulletin of the American Schools of Oriental Research* 130, 1953, 4-8.

17. Cf.B.Z.Wacholder, *Eupolemus. A Study of Judaeo-Greek Literature*, Cincinnati 1974, 155-70.

18. Apart from the Gezer 'calendar' there is just one inscription (a vase with a name on) which like it could be dated to the tenth century BC. However, we cannot exclude the possibility that the current datings, all subjective and uncertain, must be substantially revised, indeed that what is assigned to the eleventh and the twelfth centuries should be brought down to the tenth and that therefore the Gezer 'calendar' shuld be brought down by a century (from the beginning of the tenth to the beginning of the ninth).

19. K.M.Kenyon, *Archaeology in the Holy Land*, London and New York 1960, 256: 'Almost no recognizable imported objects have been found in levels of this period in Palestine proper.'

20. Cf. S.Mazzoni, 'Gli stati siro-ittiti e l'"età oscura": fattori geo-economici di uno sviluppo culturale', *Egitto e Vicino Oriente* 4, 1981, 322-3.

21. Ibid., 324.

22. Cf. G.Garbini, '*Parzon* "Iron" in the Song of Deborah?', *Journal of Semitic Studies* 23, 1978, 23-24. My dating of the Song of Deborah to the tenth-ninth century BC (cf. 'Il Cantico di Debora', *La Parola del Passato* 33, 1978, 5-31), a dating which has found acceptance, perfectly fits the context described here.

23. This situation is generally accepted, but has not met with the approval of P.R.Ackroyd, who has suggested that the Philistines had removed the Israelite artisans (cf. 'Note to **parzon* "Iron" in the Song of Deborah', *Journal of Semitic Studies* 14, 1979, 19-20). Nor am I forgetting the attempt to present the Hebrews as being superior to the Philistines in iron technology, on the basis of archaeology. The rediscovery at Taanach (not far from Megiddo, and therefore in the area in which the battle sung of by Deborah took place) of carbonized iron, i.e. steel, in a stratum dated before 925 BC has been connected with the supposed conquest by David; the presence, simply noted, of a steel sword in the Philistine locality of Farah has not been sufficient to leave the Philistines that primacy which the Bible itself assigns them; for these scholars 'there is no convincing evidence of iron production from Philistine sites'; cf. T.Stech-Wheeler, J.D.Muhly, K.R.Maxwell-Hyslop, R.Maddin, 'Iron at Taanach and Early Iron Metallurgy in the Eastern Mediterranean', *American Journal of Archaeology* 85, 1981, 245-68 (the quotation comes from 260).

24. In the light of these conclusions it is obvious what verdict is to be passed on the validity of the numerous studies which 'Old Testament' specialists continue to publish on the various aspects of the events and politics of David and Solomon; some of these studies are quite acute, as for example that of H.Donner, 'Israel und Tyrus im Zeitalter Davids und Salomos', *Journal of Northwest Semitic Languages* 10, 1982, 43-52, but based exclusively on what the Bible says.

Chapter 3   Stories of the Kings

1. E.Renan, *Histoire du peuple d'Israël* II, Paris 253-6.
2. G.Ricciotti, *History of Israel*, 402ff.
3. M.Noth, *The History of Israel*, 245.
4. A.H.van Zyl, *The Moabites*, Leiden 1960, 138-40.
5. One of the most recent studies, G.Rendsburg, 'A Reconstruction of Moabite-Israelite History', *Journal of the Ancient Near Eastern Society of Columbia University* 13, 1981, 67-73, has a harmonizing tendency, but attaches most importance to the Bible.
6. M.Liverani, 'L'histoire de Joas', *Vetus Testamentum* 24, 1974, 438-53.
7. G.Garbini, 'I sigilli del regno d'Israele', *Oriens Antiquus* 21, 1982, 163-76.
8. G.Rinaldi, 'Quelques remarques sur la politique d'Azarias (Ozias) de Juda en Philistie (2 Chron.26,6ss.)', in *Congress Volume Bonn 1962*, Leiden 1963, 225-35.
9. The basic study on Azariah is H.Tadmor, 'Azriyau of Yaudi', *Scripta Hierosolymitana* 8, 1961, 232-71. The fact that one of the cuneiform fragments in which the name 'Judah' can be read has been seen to belong to a text different from the one which contains it (cf. N.Na'aman, 'Sennacherib's "Letter to God" on his Campaign to Judah', *Bulletin of the American Schools of Oriental Research* 214, 1974, 25-39) does not in any way prejudice the identification of the Assyrian Azriyau with Azariah; apart from the fact that the attribution of the fragmentary text to Hezekiah remains purely hypothetical (only the final part, -*yau*, of the name of the king of Judah

remains, which could be expanded in many ways, including into Azriyau), we are still left with an Azariah who headed the anti-Assyrian league.

That he is not specifically said to be a king of Judah is, if anything, an argument in favour of the identification, given that Na'aman has observed that Tiglath-pileser III did not know of Judah. Na'aman, who had the evident aim of eliminating too inconvenient an Azariah of Judah, has at any rate obviously found supporters: J.A.Soggin, *History of Israel*, 218; R.Gelio, 'Fonti mesopotamiche relative al territorio palestinese (100-500 BC)', *Rivista Biblica* 32, 1984, 135-7 (the conclusion is, however, quite balanced).

10. The Hebrew word translated 'separate' is in fact incomprehensible: *ḥopšit* denotes freedom (and therefore 'free house') but we cannot exclude the possibilty that the reading of the Massoretic text is misleading: the Septuagint, which was unable to translate the Hebrew term, transcribed it in Greek as αφφουσωθ, a form which presupposes a bi-consonantal root *ps* or *pš* or *ps*, not a root *ḥpš*, like that of the Massoretic text.

11. Cf. G.Garbini, *I Fenici. Storia e religione*, Naples 1980, 65-90. I have to correct what I said on 68 n.8: study of the Hebrew text has shown me that the hypothesis of E.Lipiński in connection with Isaiah 23, which then seemed to me valid, is completely unfounded.

12. Cf. H.Donner and W.Röllig, *Kanaanäische und aramäische Inschriften*, Wiesbaden ²1966-9, II, 49f. no.31 (KAI 31). Röllig's dating of this inscription (720-725 BC) is evidently based only on the synchronism of Hiram with Tiglath-pileser III, without taking account of the fact that around 740 BC Mitinna had already succeeded Hiram.

13. E.L.Sukenik, 'An Epitaph of Uzziah King of Judah', *Tarbiz* 2, 1931, 288-92 (in Hebrew); W.F.Albright, 'The Discovery of an Aramaic Inscription relating to King Uzziah', *Bulletin of the American Schools of Oriental Research* 44, 1931, 8-10; E.L.Sukenik, 'Funerary Tablet of Uzziah King of Israel', *Palestine Exploration Fund Quarterly Statement* 63, 1931, 217-21; 64, 1932, 106-7.

14. J.Simons, *Jerusalem in the Old Testament*, Leiden 1952, 194-225.

15. E.L.Sukenik, in *Palestine...*, 221. On the first page of the article Sukenik states (in a passage lacking in the English version) that Archimandrite Antony did not know Hebrew and that he sent notes of Hebrew inscriptions to D.Chwolson: how did this latter not have any note of the Uzziah inscription?

16. W.F.Albright, art.cit.,8.

17. G.Garbini, 'L'iscrizione del re Uzziah', *Oriens Antiquus* 24, 1985, 67-75.

18. It is not without significance that the Uzziah inscription is not in the classic collection by J.-B.Frey, *Corpus Inscriptionum Iudaicarum* II, Vatican City 1952. The authenticity of this inscription was already put in doubt by A.Vincent, *Revue Biblique* 41, 1932, 480, and p.IX of the inscription ('inscription douteuse').

19. J. Barr, 'Which Language did Jesus Speak? Some Remarks of a Semitist', *Bulletin of the John Rylands Library* 53, 1970, 11,27.

20. C.Rabin, 'Hebrew and Aramaic in the First Century', in *Compendia Rerum Iudaicarum in Novum Testamentum* II, Assen 1976, 1013.

21. E.Ullendorff, 'The Knowledge of Languages in the Old Testament', *Bulletin of the John Rylands Library* 44, 1962, 455-65.

22. P.Xella, ' "Mangiare feci e bere urina": a proposito di 2 Re 18:27/Isaia 36:12', *Studi Storico Religiosi 3*, 1979, 37-51.

23. The text of I Esdras has not come down to us in the original Hebrew redaction but in a series of translations of which the earliest is the Greek Septuagint. In this translation the name Jehoiachin is systematically rendered Ιεχονιας.

24. A.K.Grayson, *Assyrian and Babylonian Chronicles*, Locust Valley, NY 1975, 20, 102 (Chronicle 5).

25. E.F.Weidner, 'Jojachin, König von Juda, in babylonischen Keilschrifttexten', in *Mélanges syriens offerts à M.R.Dussaud*, Paris 1939, II, 923-35; W.F.Albright, 'King Ioachin in Exile', *Biblical Archaeologist* 5, 1942, 59-55.

26. Cf. J.B.Pritchard (ed.), *Ancient Near Eastern Texts Relating to the Old Testament*, Princeton ³1969, 308.

27. This is seal no. 108 according to the catalogue by F.Vattioni, 'I sigilli ebraici', *Biblica* 50, 1969, 357-88; the seal is on 371 (correct *ywkyn* to *ywkn*); W.F.Albright, 'The Seal of Eliakim and the Latest History of Judah with Some Observations on Ezekiel', *Journal of Biblical Literature* 51, 1932, 77-106.

28. This is seal Vattioni 149; H.G.May, 'Three Hebrew Seals and the Status of Exiled Yehoiakin', *American Journal of Semitic Languages and Literatures* 56, 1939, 146-8.

Chapter 4   The Origin and Development of Yahwism

1. It is impossible to make even the scantiest bibliographical references to the Decalogue, given the increase in the bibliography which takes place almost daily. But see B.Lang, 'Neues über den Dekalog', *Theologische Quartalschrift* 164, 1983, 58-65. It is not without interest for a reader who is curious to know how 'biblical scholars' work to cast an eye on quite a recent article in which the 'real history' of this tormented text is given, with remarkable confidence: A.Lemaire, 'Le Décalogue: essai d'histoire de la rédaction', in *Mélanges bibliques et orientaux en honneur de M.H.Cazelles*, Neukirchen-Vluyn 1981, 259-95.

2. M.Noth, *Die israelitischen Personennamen im Rahmen der gemeinsemitischen Namengebung*, Stuttgart 1928, 101-14.

3. W.F.Albright, *From the Stone Age to Christianity*, Garden City, New York ²1957, 15f.; H.B.Huffmon, *Amorite Personal Names in the Mari Texts*, Baltimore 1965, 71-3; id., 'Yahweh and Mari', in *Near Eastern Studies in Honor of W.F.Albright*, Baltimore and London 1971, 283-9.

4. A.Finet, 'Iawi-Ilâ, roi de Talhayum', *Syria* 41, 1964, 118-22; 'Réflexions sur l'onomastique de Mari et le dieu des Hébreux', in *Mélanges A.Abel*, Leiden 1978, III, 64-78. Cf. also A.Murtonen, 'The Appearance of the Name YHWH outside Israel', *Studia Orientalia* 16, 1951, fasc.3, 4-6.

5. H.Cazelles, 'Mari et l'Ancien Testament', in *XVᵉ Rencontre Assyriologique International, Liège 1966 (La civilisation de Mari)*, Paris 1967, (82-86) 84: at Ugarit Yaw has been 'challenged without reason'.

6. The hypothesis of Giovanni Pettinato according to which the very numerous Eblaite proper names ending in -*ia* (a sign that can also be read *i*, *li* and *ni*) will have been a composite with the divine name Yah or Yaw has rightly met with universal rejection (cf. A.Archi, 'The Epigraphic Evidence from Ebla and the Old Testament', *Biblica* 60, 1979, 556-60; R.Biggs, 'The Ebla Tablets', *Biblical Archaeologist*, Spring 1980, 82-3; H.-P.Müller, 'Gab es in Ebla einen Gottesnamen Ja?', *Zeitschrift für Assyriologie* 70, 1980, 70-92; the possibility of the presence of

Yah-Yaw at Ebla, as at Fara in the third millennium BC, is based on a sole attestation of the name read *ᵈià-ra-mu* (at Fara *ᵈià*); see for this G.Pettinato, *Testi amministrativi della biblioteca L. 2769*, Naples 1980, 187f.; P.Mander, 'Brevi considerazioni sul testo lessicale SF 23 = SF 234 e paralleli da Abu Salabikh', *Oriens Antiquus* 19, 1980, 190-1. However, these readings have been challenged: A.Archi, '*ᵈà-ra-mu* at Ebla', *Studi Eblaiti* 1, 1979, 45-8; H.-P.Müller, art.cit., 88; id., 'Der Jahwename und seine Deutung Ex.3,14 im Licht der Textpublikationen aus Ebla', *Biblica* 62, 1981, 305-427 (but in this second article the author, who is a theologian, proves to be more possibilist and ends by allying himself with the usual confessional thesis that *yhwh* outside Israel is only a form of the verb 'to be').

7. For these inscriptions, which can be safely dated around the seventh century BC, cf. J.C.L.Gibson, *Textbook of Syrian Semitic Inscriptions* I, Oxford 1971, 57f.; E.Lipiński, 'North-West Semitic Inscriptions', *Orientalia Lovaniensia Periodica* 8, 1977, 93f. That *yah* etymologically, or rather in common linguistic awareness, had the value of 'force, power' could be inferred from the context of Isa. 12.1; 26.4, where God is invoked as 'power' and 'strength'.

8. Cf. G.Garbini, 'La cosmogonia fenicia e il primo capitolo della Genesi', in G.de Gennaro (ed.), *Il cosmo nella Bibbia*, Naples 1972, 14-40.

9. Cf.G.Grottanelli, 'Il mito delle origini di Tiro: due "versioni" duali', *Oriens Antiquus* 11, 1972, 49-51.

10. W.Herrmann, 'Die Göttersohne', *Zeitschrift für Religions- und Geistesgeschichte* 12, 1960, 242-51; J.L.Cunchillos, *Cuando los ángeles eran dioses*, Salamanca 1976.

11. The fullest publication so far available on the discoveries at Kuntillet 'Ajrud is the catalogue of an exhibition held in 1978: Z.Meshel, *Kuntillet 'Ajrud. A Religious Centre from the time of the Judaean Monarchy on the Border of Sinai*, Jerusalem 1978: this is a bilingual booklet (English and Hebrew) with various photographs and a short text; the pages are unnumbered. From the sparse bibliography which has appeared so far on the basic discoveries mention should be made of A.Catastini, 'Le iscrizioni di Kuntillet 'Ajrud e il profetismo', *Annali dell'Istituto Orientali di Napoli* 42, 1982, 127-34.

12. I have not taken into consideration the supposed presence of Ashera in a Hebrew inscription from Khirbet el-Qom suggested by A.Lemaire, 'Les inscriptions de Khirbet el-Qôm et l'Asherah de YHWH', *Revue Biblique* 84, 1977, 595-608, because it is based on a reading of the text which I regard as erroneous.

12a. The article by W.G.Dever, 'Material Remains and the Cult in Ancient Israel: An Essay in Archaeological Systematics', in *The Word of the Lord Shall Go Forth. Essays in Honor of D.N.Freedman*, Winona Lake 1983, 571-87, is important from a methodological point of view. It is also worth noting the study by G.W.Ahlström, 'An Archaeological Picture of Iron Age Religions in Ancient Palestine', *Studia Orientalia* 55, 1984, 115-45.

13. We cannot rule out the existence of a god *ywh*, whatever his nature, among the Arab Nabataean population who left numerous inscriptions in Sinai around the second to third century AD; the theophoric proper name '*bd 'hyw* attested by various inscriptions can be understood in this sense; cf. E.A.Knauf, 'Eine nabatäische Parallele zum hebräischen Gottesnamen', *Biblische Notizen* 23, 1984, 21-8.

14. It is well known that Yahwistic nomenclature is quite widespread in Hebrew epigraphic documentation and it is also known that this nomenclature displays significant differences in the way in which the divine name is written. With some

rare exceptions, it can be said that usually the ending -*yhw* is typical of the south, while the ending -*yw* occurs in the north (the latter als~~o~~ reappears at Kuntillet 'Ajrud, from which, however, unpublished Phoenician inscriptions also come). Since the Hebrew inscriptions of the south are almost all dated to the seventh and the beginning of the sixth century BC it is difficult to avoid the impression that the form -*yhw* represents a late innovation (it is still absent from Kuntillet 'Ajrud) in the south, connected in some way with the explanation of the divine name that is given in Ex.3.13,14. Moreover the epigraphic evidence finds important confirmation in the study that has been made of the names in Y*ᵉho*- and Yo- attested in the Old Testament: the result of a detailed analysis is that the names in Y*ᵉho*- are markedly later than those in Yo- (S.Norin, 'Jô-Namen und Jᵉho-Namen', *Vetus Testamentum* 29, 1979, 87-97; the results of this study have been criticized by A.R.Millard, 'YW and YHW names', ibid. 30, 1980, 208-12, with questionable arguments, as is also evident from Norin's reply, 'Yw- Names and Yhw- Names, A Reply to A.R.Millard', ibid., 239-40; he stresses how the examples adduced by Millard in fact confirm the thesis that he set out to challenge. So it does not seem out of place to connect the introduction and the rapid diffusion of the nomenclature of the *yhw*- type with the religious reform attributed to Josiah, even if the form of the divine name with *h* already existed earlier, as is shown by the attestations at Kuntillet 'Ajrud and the Amorite onomastica.

15. Cf. M.Liverani, 'Il fuoruscitismo in Siria nella tarda Età del Bronzo', *Rivista Storica Italiana* 77, 1965, 315-36.

16. The Old Testament presents a strictly Hebrew view of a fact which the scholar observes as a historical process but which the Christian believer sees as the development of a providential design. From this last point of view it is difficult to understand why the Christian who puts the focal point of history in Jesus Christ should be held to accepting to the letter the late version, with a markedly ideological character, of so universal a fact as the revelation of monotheism on the part of God himself. Now that for some time we have abandoned the 'letter' of the biblical text as far as the world of nature is concerned (the creation of the world in six days, the creation of man from the dust, the sun moving round the earth), the time has come also to abandon the letter as far as the world of human history is concerned, which is too bound up with contingencies to be able to represent the 'truth'.

Chapter 5   From the Anointer to the Anointed: the 'Messiah'

1. A.Cowley, *Aramaic Papyri of the Fifth Century BC*, Oxford 1923, no.30.
2. The basic study on anointing in the ancient Near East is still that by E.Kutsch, *Salbung als Rechtsakt im Alten Testament und im alten Orient*, Berlin 1963.
3. The traditional position which accepts the biblical data to the letter and which was stated at the very moment at which it was being contested by E.Kutsch, by R.de Vaux, 'Le roi d'Israël, vassal de Yahvé', *Bible et Orient*, Paris 1967, 287-310 (it had already appeared in 1964; in an added note de Vaux mentions Kutsch's book, in obviously critical terms) has of course found new defenders in conservative circles: Z.Weisman, 'Anointing as a Motif in the Making of the Charismatic King', *Biblica* 57, 1976, 378-98 (based especially on the Hittite text: however, it recognizes the importance of the 'Spirit of Yahweh', which is superior to that of anointing, for the Israelite king); A.Schoors, 'Isaiah, the Minister of a Royal Anointment?',

Oudtestamentische Studiën 29, 1977, 85-107 (very critical of Kutsch but somewhat inconclusive). The position of P.Xella, 'L'unzione del re a Ebla e nel Vicino Oriente antico', *Studi Storico Religiosi* 4, 1980, 329-35, is more articulate; he denies the existence of royal anointing at Ebla only to allow it in Mesopotamia, on the basis of just one fragmentary Assyrian text used by some Assyriologists as evidence of royal anointing in Mesopotamia along with the somewhat fantastic interpretation of another Sumerian text (334); at any rate P.Xella moves in a traditional direction, led on by the article by Z.Weisman.

4. Moreover there is a fragmentary Hittite text which speaks of the anointing of a ruler, cf. O.R.Gurney, 'The Anointing of Tudhaliya', in *Studia Mediterranea P.Meriggi dicata*, Pavia 1979, I, 213-23. This text, which is not usually noted by biblical scholars, seems to indicate that among the Hittites, too, anointing had a function analogous to that among the Egyptians, i.e. it 'designated'; the text in fact speaks of the anointing of a co-regent who is becoming allied to the reigning sovereign in the expectation of succeeding him on the throne.

5. Cf.C.Grottanelli, 'Healers and Saviours of the Eastern Mediterranean in Pre-classical Times', in U.Bianchi and M.J.Vermaseren (eds.), *La soteriologia dei culti orientali nell'impero romano*, Leiden 1982, 649-70.

6. This is the text KTU 1,119; for a discussion of its interpretation see G.Garbini, 'Note sui testi rituali ugaritici', *Oriens Antiquus* 22, 1983, 53-60, in particular 58.

7. See Haggai; Zechariah 1-8; Sirach 49.11-12; I Esdras 5-7 (= Ezra 2-6).

8. P.Sacchi, *Storia del mondo giudaico*, Turin 1976, 63f.

9. J.H.Charlesworth (ed.), *The Old Testament Pseudepigrapha* 2, London and New York 1985, 666-7.

10. Ibid., 1, 1982, 775-828.

11. C.Grottanelli, 'Da Myrrha alla mirra: Adonis e il profumo dei re siriani', in *Adonis, Collezione di Studi Fenici* 18, Rome 1984, 35-60 and especially 52f.

Chapter 6   Abraham among the Chaldaeans

1. R.de Vaux, *The Early History of Israel*, London and New York 1978, 161-85.

2. T.L.Thompson, *The Historicity of the Patriarchal Narratives*, Berlin and New York 1974.

3. A.Bonora, 'Recenti studi storiografici sui racconti patriarcali', *Teologia* 1983, 83-108. The position of J.J.Scullion, 'Some Reflections on the Present State of Patriarchal Studies', *Abr-Nahrain* 21, 1982-1983, 50-65, is very conservative.

4. J. Van Seters, *Abraham in History and Tradition*, New Haven 1975.

5. T.L.Thompson, 'A New Attempt to Date the Patriarchal Narratives', *Journal of the American Oriental Society* 98, 1978, 76-84.

6. The same thing can in fact also be said of his most recent volume *In Search of History*, New Haven 1983. I have written on this in *Rivista degli Studi Orientali* 56, 1982 [1985], 193f.

7. What always tends to be underestimated is that it is very difficult for an author to use an earlier text without making more or less substantial retouchings.

8. Thompson, *Historicity*, 298-314; Van Seters, *Abraham*, 24-6.

9. R.H.Sack, 'Nebuchadnezzar and Nabonidus in Folklore and History', *Mesopotamia* 17, 1982, 67-131; id., 'The Nabonidus Legend', *Revue d'assyriologie* 77, 1983, 59-67.

10. A.Jeremias, *Das Alte Testmaent im Lichte des alten Orients*, Leipzig ³1916, 276-9.
11. G.Garbini, 'Deux notes sudarabiques, 1. *hnr btrḥ* = "offrir en holocauste un bouquetin")', *Semitica* 28, 1978, 97-100.
12. G.Garbini, 'Paisà', *La Parola del Passato* 39, 1984, 39-41.
13. From this perspective we must ask whether the difficult passage Gen.15.13-16 was not originally an allusion to the Babylonian exile (rather than to that in Egypt) made in such a way as to give a long duration to the Chaldaean dynasty.
14. For the problem of this Jewish bank see n.5 of the next chapter.
15. J.Hoftijzer, *Die Verheissungen an die drei Erzväter*, Leiden 1956, 5-30.
16. J. Van Seters, *Abraham*, 263-78.
17. Cf. the following chapter.
18. This fact should also make us prudent in assuming 'northern' elements as an explanation of divergent points of view within the biblical texts.
19. De Vaux, *Early History*, 169-72.
20. Ibid., 174-5.
21. *In Search of History*, 161-4.
22. M.Liverani, 'Un'ipotesi sul nome di Abramo', *Henoch* 1, 1979, 9-18.
23. S.Mazzarino, *Il pensiero storico classico* I, Bari 1966, 58-70, 75-9.
24. Ibid., 166-72.
25. Ibid., 23-9.
26. C.H.Gordon, *The Common Background of Greek and Hebrew Civilization*, New York 1965.
27. The by no means insignificant role played by the Philistines in the sphere of commercial activity and of Phoenician culture itself has yet to be brought out. The fact that from the beginning of the first millennium BC the Philistines were using Phoenician as a written (and perhaps also as a spoken) language finally led to their being confused with the Phoenicians. For the commercial importance of the Philistines see my lecture ' "Popoli del mare", Tarsis e Filistei', given in 1985 to a conference in Rome on Greek and Phoenician colonization; for the cultural influence exercised by the Philistines on the Hebrews of the kingdom of Judah see my study 'Philistine Seals'; both of these are due to be published.
28. Cf. 'Dati epigrafici e linguistici sul territorio palestinese fino al VI sec.a.C.', *Rivista Biblica* 32, 1984, 78-80, and the previous note.
29. Cf. 'Il Cantico di Debora', *La Parola del Passato* 33, 1978, 5-31.

Chapter 7 A Prophet and the King of Kings

1. Cf. Chapter 4, n.11.
2. It is significant that the name by which the prophets preferred to call their god was 'Yahweh Sabaoth', the god 'of the fighting troops'. It is a name which directly recalls the armed bands of the nomads (cf. M.Liverani, 'La preistoria dell'epiteto "Yahweh ṣbā'ōt"', *Annali dell'Istituto Orientale di Napoli*, NS 17, 1967, 331-4, evidently in contrast to the dynastic god of the ruler (even if this was the same Yahweh) and therefore to the god of the sedentary population.
3. G.Grottanelli, 'Healers and Saviours of the Eastern Mediterranean in Pre-Classical Times', in U.Bianchi and M.J.Vermaseren (eds.), *La soteriologia dei culti orientali nell'impero romano*, Leiden 1982, 649-70.
4. The emergent role of the Phoenician mercantile class has been brought out well

by S.F.Bondì, 'Note sull'economia fenicia. I. Impresa privata e ruolo dello stato', *Egitto e Vicino Oriente* 1, 1978, 141-6. Cf. J.de Geus, 'Die Gesellschaftskritik der Propheten und die Archäologie', *Zeitschrift des Deutschen Palästina-Vereins*, 1982, 50-7.

5. There is as it were an 'underground' debate as to whether or not the Egibi family belonged to the Jewish nation. Since I have not had access to the work by S.Weingort, *Das Haus Egibi in neubabylonischen Rechtsurkunden*, Berlin 1939, I do not know its position on this problem; in the article by A.Ungnad, 'Das Haus Egibi', *Archiv für Orientforschung* 14, 1941-44, 57-64, which appeared in 1941, to take issue with what it claims to be erroneous statements by Weingort, the composition of the family of the Egibi with the relevant nomenclature is treated with extreme competence: the names are almost exclusively Babylonian. However, the problem is that the name Egibi itself is not Babylonian; K.L.Tallqvist, *Neubabylonisches Namenbuch*, Leipzig 1905, 57, cannot explain it, and it is not included in the contents of J.J.Stamm, *Die akkadische Namengebung*, Leipzig 1939. These reticent silences have finally been broken by the clear statement made by S.W.Baron. In his work *A Social and Religious History of the Jews* 1.1, New York ²1952, 109, he writes: 'The fact that the founder of the house Egibi, the greatest of these private firms, bore the unmistakably Hebrew name, Jacob, and that most of the early loans are recorded to have been granted without interest may, indeed, reflect one of the earliest Jewish contributions to mankind's material civilization.' Something worth noting is that whereas the various Jewish encyclopaedias ignore the existence of Egibi and his successors, in the recent *Encyclopaedia Judaica*, Vol.16, Jerusalem 1971, we read these words, evidently taken from Baron's work: 'Whether or not Jacob, the founder of the leading banking house of Egibi, was Jewish – there is some support for this hypothesis in the fact that loans were formerly extended without interest, though the banker collected the revenues from the mortgaged properties including slaves and cattle...'; but we read it not under an entry 'Egibi' but in an entry on 'Economic history' (col.1271) added, with other passages, at the end of the last volume of the encyclopaedia: this is at least a very strange way of giving information about a figure who is certainly not irrelevant to Jewish history. No less significant than the ambiguity of the *Encyclopaedia Judaica* is the total silence on Egibi on the part of Israeli scholars like R.Zadok, a young man who has written some books on Jewish onomastica attested in Babylon in the period in question (works which, it should be said in passing, contain quantitatively and qualitatively much less than their ambitious titles promise): *The Jews in Babylonia during the Chaldean and Achaemenian Periods according to the Babylonian Sources*, Haifa 1979; *Sources for the History of the Jews in Babylonia during the Chaldean and Achaemenian Periods*, Jerusalem 1980), or like I. Eph'al, who has written a work 'On the Political and Social Organization of the Jews in Babylonian Exile', in *XXI.Deutscher Orientalistentag 1980*, Wiesbaden 1983, 106-12. What makes the Jewish origin of the house of Egibi certain is the fact that not only is the name Egibi Jewish (it presupposes a root *'qb*; cf. not so much *Ya'aqob*, 'Jacob', as rather *'Aqqub* and *'Aqiba'*), but so is the surname Purshu (cf. *par'oš*, 'flea') – of course not listed in the book by J.J.Stamm – borne by an Egibi whose proper name is the purest Babylonian; another surname also points to a Jewish environment: Sherku, the Babylonian form of which ('dedicated to the temple') barely hides the late Hebrew term *netinim*. Then mention could be made of other names like

Shula'a and the feminine Nupta and Suqa'itum, which are very difficult to fit in
with Babylonian nomenclature. When we already find among those who 'returned'
from Babylon some names and surnames which we have already found in the Egibi
documents, no further doubt is possible: *Par'oš* (Ezra 2.3 etc.), *Bene 'Aqqub* (Ezra
2.42), a second group of *Bene 'Aqqub* described as being part of the *netinim* (Ezra
2.45). L.Cagni, 'Le fonti mesopotamiche dei periodi neo-babilonese achemenide
e seleucide (VI-III sec.a.c.)', *Rivista Biblica* 34, 1986, 18-20, has spent some time
on the Jewish Egibi; he has also noted a thesis of J.Krecher, discussed in 1970 but
not published. G. van Driel, 'De opkomst van een nieuwbabylonische Familie: de
Egibi's', *Phoenix* 31, 2, 1985, 33-47, adopts the traditional position which
systematically ignores the information and the bibliography about the Jewish origin
of the Egibi.

6. Cf.G.R.Castellino, *Sapienza babilonese*, Turin 1962, 48f.
7. R.Kittel, 'Cyrus und Deuterojesaja', *Zeitschrift für die alttestamentliche Wissenschaft*
18, 1899, 149-62; M.Smith, 'II Isaiah and the Persians', *Journal of the American
Oriental Society* 83, 1963, 415-21. Of these two articles the earlier is undoubtedly
to be preferred; it presents a historical approach which that of the American scholar
lacks completely. S.M.Paul, 'Deutero-Isaiah and Cuneiform Royal Inscriptions',
Journal of the American Oriental Society 88, 1968, 180-6, has brought out affinities,
albeit generic ones, between Deutero-Isaiah and some Mesopotamian royal
inscriptions.
8. P.R.Berger, 'Der Kyros-Zylinder mit dem Zusatzfragment BIN II Nr 32 und die
akkadischen Personennamen im Danielbuch', *Zeitschrift für Assyriologie* 64, 1975,
192-234 (a thorough philological examination of the Cyrus text).
9. A.Kuhrt, 'The Cyrus Cylinder and Achaemenid Imperial Policy', *Journal for the
Study of the Old Testament* 23, 1983, 38-97; the observations of this scholar are
very good indeed.
10. The *Ludlul bel nemeqi* is attested from the seventh century BC on: in the
Assurbanipal library there were new copies of it, along with a commentary. It is
possible to date the poem to the Cassite era (cf.W.G.Lambert, *Babylonian Wisdom
Literature*, Oxford 1960, 21-62) but it more probably belongs to the beginning of
the first millennium BC.
11. The position of R.Kittel (cf. n.7) is substantially confirmed; he saw a common
Babylonian source ('Babylonian court style') for Deutero-Isaiah and the Cyrus
text. Beyond the terminology of the royal inscriptions the Achaemenidean
chancellery in which Babylonian elements were present thus also drew on a literary
text which lent itself well to a certain kind of propaganda. It is obvious that the
basic approach of a wisdom text must have been totally different from that of an
Achaemenidean or even philo-Babylonian political manifesto.
12. But I would like to differ from the view of Morton Smith (art.cit) according to
which Deutero-Isaiah is said to have written his work before that date, having
learned what Cyrus would have written later in his proclamation not through
prophetic qualities but from information provided by Persian agents sent by Cyrus
to prepare for his arrival – agents well enough instructed already to know the
language and the style of the Babylonian chancellery.
13. It should be noted that from the point of view of its constitutive motives the
creation of the world as presented in Deutero-Isaiah appears completely different
not only from that of the Priestly writer (first chapter of Genesis) written at a

period much later than Deutero-Isaiah and drawing especially on Phoenician tradition (cf. G.Garbini, 'La cosmogonia fenicia e il primo capitolo della Genesi', in G.De Gennaro [ed.], *Il cosmo nella Bibbia*, Naples 1982, 127-48), but also from that of the so-called Yahwist, with direct Babylonian inspiration, which moreover presupposes knowledge of the *Enuma eliš*, a work which is not earlier than the eleventh century BC (see in this connection the important article by L.Cagni, 'La destinazione dell'uomo al lavoro secondo Genesi 2 e secondo le fonti sumero-accadiche', *Annali dell'Istituto Orientale di Napoli* 34, 1974, 31-44). The liturgical explanation by T.M.Ludwig, 'The Traditions of the Establishing of the Earth in Deutero-Isaiah', *Journal of Biblical Literature* 92, 1973, 345-57, seems to me to be completely out of court.

14. C.Herrenschmidt, 'Les créations d'Ahuramazda', *Studia Iranica* 6, 1977, 17-58.
15. Cf. G.Gnoli, 'Politica religiosa e concezione della regalità sotto gli Achaemenidi', in *Gururajamañjarika. Studi in onore di G.Tucci*, 1, Naples 1974, 31-43, 85; id., *De Zoroastre à Mani*, Paris 1985, 53-72.
16. C.Herrenschmidt, 'Désignation de l'empire et conceptions politiques de Darius Iᵉʳ d'après ses inscriptions en vieux-perse', *Studia Iranica* 5, 1976, 33-65; cf. also E.Herzfeld, *The Persian Empire*, Wiesbaden 1968, 304-8.
17. For this see now R.P.Merendino, *Der Erste und der Letzte. Eine Untersuchung von Jes 40-48*, Leiden 1981. The two opening verses of Isa.48 are probably not part of the original text.
18. Cf.G.Gnoli, *Zoroaster's Time and Homeland*, Naples 1980, 202.
19. Here we find one of the most characteristic examples of the still persistent tendency to read the Old Testament, even the later parts of it, in the light of Ugaritic literature; without any reference to possible historical relationships, certain scholars compare simple linguistic expressions: P.C.Craigie, 'Helel, Athtar and Phaeton (Jes.14,12-15)', *Zeitschrift für die alttestamentliche Wissenschaft* 85, 1973, 223-25; O.Loretz, 'Der kanaanäisch-biblische Mythos vom Sturz des Šaḥar-Sohnes Hêlêl', *Ugarit-Forschungen* 8, 1976, 133-6.
20. G.Gnoli, 'Ašavan. Contributo allo studio del libro di Ardā Wirāz', in G.Gnoli and A.V.Rossi (eds.), *Iranica*, Naples 1979, 412.
21. In addition to the observation made in n.13 and many others that could be made, I would comment here only that the very summary story in Gen.6.1-4 would remain almost incomprehensible without the text of Enoch (see below) which tells the story of the Watchmen; it is therefore obvious (if not to all) that the Genesis pasage presupposes the Book of the Watchhmen. Cf.also J.T.Milik, *The Books of Enoch. Aramaic Fragments of Qumran Cave 4*, Oxford 1976, 30-2.
22. G.Gnoli, 'Un particolare aspetto del simbolismo della luce nel mazdeismo e nel manicheismo', *Annali dell'Istituto Universitario Orientale di Napoli*, NS 12, 1962, 95-128.
23. Cf. Pss.4.7; 29.2; 44.4; 89.16; 104.1-2.
24. G.Garbini, 'La creazione della luce (Gen.1,3-5)', *Bibbia e Oriente* 11, 1969, 267-71.
25. G.Gnoli, in *Studi...G.Tucci*, 76.
26. The psalm literally says 'today I have begotten you', as in Ps.110.
27. The reading of the psalm is, according to the Hebrew text: 'I have begotten you in the holy splendour of the womb of the morning', without taking account of some Massoretic retouching; the Greek differs notably.

28. S.Spiegel, 'Noah, Danel, and Job Touching on Canaanite Relics in the Legends of the Jews', in *Louis Ginzberg Jubilee Volume* I, New York 1945, 305-55.
29. P.Sacchi, *Apocrifi dell'Antico Testamento*, Turin 1981, 451.
30. Cf. G.Gnoli, in *Annali dell'Istituto Universitario Orientali di Napoli*, 116.
31. Rev. 19.11-12; cf. E.Corsini, *Apocalisse prima e dopo*, Turin 1980, 471-5.
32. Cf. G.Gnoli, in *Annali dell'Istituto Universitario Orientali di Napoli*, 118.

Chapter 8 Moses' Anger

1. See for example M.Noth, *Exodus*, Old Testament Library, London and Philadelphia 1962, 243-52. For some aspects of the destruction of the golden calf cf. O.Hvidberg-Hansen, 'Die Vernichtung des goldenen Kalbes und der ugaritische Ernteritus', *Acta Orientalia* 23, 1971, 5-46.
2. Cf. J.A.Soggin, *Introduction to the Old Testament*, London and Philadelphia ²1980, 105-9.
3. H.H.Schmidt, *Der sogenannte Jahwist*, Zurich 1976; R.Rendtorff, *Das überlieferungsgeschichtliche Problem des Pentateuch*, Berlin and New York 1977; J.van Seters, *In Search of History*, New Haven and London 1983. My own personal belief is that there never was a 'Yahwist' as a document or a writer (nor an 'Elohist' for that matter) and that a number of the passages attributed to them were written in Babylon during or after the exile.
4. Cf. e.g. Judg.5.4f.; II Sam.22.8-11.
5. A.H.Gunneweg, 'Bildlosigkeit Gottes im alten Israel', *Henoch* 6, 1984, 257-70.
6. I Kings 22.19.
7. H. Danthine, 'L'imagerie des trônes vides et des trônes porteurs de symboles dans le Proche-Orient ancien', in *Mélanges syriens offerts à M.R.Dussaud*, Paris 1939, II, 858-66; R.de Vaux, 'Les chérubins et l'arche d'alliance, les sphinx gardiens et les trônes divins dans L'ancien Orient', *Bible et Orient*, Paris 1967, 251-9 (an article already published in 1961); G.Garbini, 'Troni, sfingi e sirene', *Annali dell'Istituto Orientale di Napoli* 41, 1981, 301-7.
8. Hostility towards the Samaritans is a relatively late datum of Jewish history; it began with the return from the exile, probably became specific when Alexander the Great agreed to the rebuilding of the temple on Gerizim, and exploded virulently with John Hyrcanus. Cf. J.D.Purvis, *The Samaritan Pentateuch and the Origins of the Samaritan Sect*, Cambridge, Mass. 1968. Most recently cf. F.Dexinger, 'Der "Prophet wie Mose" in Qumran und bei den Samaritanern', in *Mélanges bibliques et orientaux en l'honneur de M.Delcor*, Neukirchen-Vluyn 1985, 97-111.
9. G.Castellino, *Libro dei Salmi*, Turin 1955, 185-6.
10. I do not agree with the statements on Exodus 32 and on the relationship between Levites and Aaronic priests made by A.Cody, *A History of the Old Testament Priesthood*, Rome 1969, 146-74.
11. J.Meier, 'Die alttestamentlich-jüdischen Voraussetzungen der Zelotenbewegungen', *Bibel und Kirche* 37, 1982, 82-9.
12. It is significant that in none of the oriental codices, from the Sumerian to that of Hammurabi, from the Assyrian to the Hitite, are cases contemplated which in one way or another can be connected with the religious behaviour of the individual. This total absence of references to specifically religious situations can only be interpreted in one way: in the exercise of his religious practices the subject, whether

free or slave, was in no way bound by the state. To profess one's own religion was a basic right of the individual, like eating and sleeping, to the degree that the civil authority did not feel any need to intervene in it. This religious freedom, the existence of which seems to me difficult to doubt, appears all the more remarkable in that the degree to which the sphere of religion came to be identified in ancient Near Eastern society with that of politics and society generally is well known.

13. This is the opinion expressed, for example, by E.Renan: 'l'intolérance des peuples sémitiques est la conséquence nécessaire de leur monothéisme', 'L'histoire d'Israël', in *Études d'histoire religieuse*, Paris 1857 (the article had originally appeared in 1855). The quotation is taken from p.78 of the reprint edited by J.Gaulmier (E.Renan, *Judaïsme et christianisme*, Paris 1977).

14. See Chapter 4 above, 'The Origin and Development of Yahwism'.

Chapter 9   The Blood of the Innocent

1. The expression 'innocent blood' tends to take the place of 'blood of the innocent', which is probably earlier. The latter is attested only in Deut.19.13, in some manuscripts of Deut.19.10, in Jer.22.17 and in II Kings 14.4; Jer.19.4 has 'blood of the innocents'. In the Greek version 'blood of the innocent' appears only in Prov.6.17, and there only in some manuscripts.

2. Cf. R.Gelio, 'Sangue e vendetta', in *Atti della Settimana Sangue e antropologia biblica*, 1980, Rome 1981, 515-28, with a discussion of earlier works on the subject.

3. Note the use of the root *b'r*, 'burn, consume'.

4. One feature of the ceremony envisaged causes some surprise, namely that the heifer must be killed near running water in an uncultivated area. The scarcity of streams in Palestine must have made this sacrifice of lustration virtually impracticable over large areas of the territory. The suspicion arises that the regulation was made in a different geographical area, i.e. in Babylon.

5. From the bibliography on this type of sacrifice I limit myself to selecting for reference an article of my own in which I explain my way of understanding this religious phenomenon ('Il sacrificio dei bambini nel mondo punico', in *Atti della Settimana*, 127-34) and the extensive study by F.Martelli, 'Il sacrificio dei fanciulli nella letteratura greca e latina', ibid., 247-323. Recently articles have begun to appear which seek to substantiate with more or less specious arguments the view that perhaps the Phoenicians, and certainly the Hebrews, did not practise child sacrifice: the matrix of such an idea is not difficult to identify.

6. It is probably on the basis of this new conception of 'innocent blood' that we are to explain the Massoretic addition of the adjective 'innocent' to the noun 'blood' which occurs in Isa.59.7 (the adjective is absent from the Septuagint). The tampering with the text of vv.19 and 20 in the same chapter is to be seen in the same perspective: where the original text (Septuagint), after a long invective against the faithless people who with their sins have banished justice, announces the arrival of the divine punishment ('from the west they will fear the name of the Lord and from the east his glorious name; the anger of the Lord will come like a rushing river, it will come with wrath; and it will vindicate the cause of Zion and punish the impiety of Jacob') the Hebrew text (not only the Massoretic text but also that attested at Qumran) changes the sense and reads: 'So that men should fear the name of Yahweh from the west, and his majesty from the rising of the sun.

For he comes like the rushing stream when the wind of Yahweh drives it; yet he comes for Zion as Redeemer and for those in Jacob who have turned from apostasy.'

7. The 'servant of Yahweh' ideology was developed in Babylon in the course of the fifth century BC. The expression was first referred to Cyrus, who was also called 'messiah' (Isa.42.1-9), and was then transferred to the people of Israel, or better to the élite group which was preparing in Babylon for the return from exile (Isa.49.5f.). The awareness of its own privileges, despite its misadventures (Isa.50.4-9), was then transformed into an attitude in which the aspect of the victim now prevailed, in spite of what was now a decidedly messianic vision (Isa.52.13-53.12). The Song of Moses in its original form fitted perfectly into Deuteronomistic thought, but at a certain moment, probably quite late, the tone of reproof for the people was lessened by the insertion of two verses which in their present context contradict all the rest. Verse 36 speaks unexpectedly of the mercy that God will have on his servants, right in the middle of the final indictment on Israel which has been abandoned by Yahweh (v.30); to repair the contradiction the whole sentence is understood, wrongly, as threats against foreign peoples rather than against the Hebrew people. The final verse, which speaks of the 'blood of his servants', is even more out of place: that it is a later addition is, moreover, shown clearly both by the bad textual tradition of the Hebrew text and the divergence of the Greek version.

8. See the documentation in M.Ellenbogen, *Foreign Words in the Old Testament*, London 1962.

9. The strong words of this verse have created difficulties for orthodox Judaism which has reacted, as usual, by interfering with the text. Instead of 'they legislated' (*hwrw*) the present Massoretic text reads an improbable 'they dominated' (*yrdw*); the Septuagint reads 'they applauded' (ἐπεκρότησαν) for 'they dominated' (ἐπεκράτησαν), a form indicated by one manuscript. Here we can see a preoccupation with avoiding the use of the verbal root *yrh*, from which the word *torah*, 'Law', is formed.

10. Note that in this passage the Septuagint uses the word 'false prophet'; this expression is unknown in Hebrew but is based on the episode of Jer. 28. It is superfluous to dwell here on the questions raised by the existence of true prophets and false prophets.

11. It is obligatory in this connection to cite Morton Smith, *Palestinian Parties and Politics that Shaped the Old Testament*, New York 1971, reissued London 1987; if it is difficult to agree with the American scholar in his identification of the 'parties', one must recognize the substantial validity of his basic thesis, which is that 'the Hebrew Bible is the product... of a long series of partisan collections and revisions' (11/8).

12. Despite the promise of its title, the real problem in the argument is not dealt with in the article by F.O'Fearghail, 'Il rendiconto per il sangue dei profeti (Lc 11,50s)', in *Atti della Settimana*, 675-88.

13. The reference to the sacrifice of children by sacred trees does not seem relevant; from what we know of *molok*, whether from written sources or from archaeological discoveries, there is no connection between him and trees. This is probably an error in the prophetic text from a late date, prompted by the loss of any recollection

of the real course of this type of sacrifice, to which there are simple allusions in the earlier texts; it had not been practised for a long time.

14. For another example of textual manipulation with the aim of weakening the anti-prophetic position cf. P.G.Borbone, 'L'uccisione dei Profeti (Osea 6,5)', *Henoch* 6, 1984, 271-92.

15. In all probability this is the climate in which in some Jewish quarter the legend arose of the martyrdom of the prophet Isaiah, attested by the apocryphal Martyrdom of Isaiah, which was later partially included in the composite Christian writing known as the Ascension of Isaiah (cf. E.Tisserant, *Ascension d'Isaie*, Paris 1909; R.H.Charles, *The Apocrypha and Pseudepigrapha of the Old Testament in English*, Oxford 1913, II, 155-62). It is worth noting that according to this text Isaiah was killed in the presence of false prophets, who mocked him. Another legend created by Christians on the model of that of the martyrdom of Isaiah but clearly with a polemical function, and relating to the death of Jeremiah, had less good fortune: the writing prophet, who in importance came directly after Isaiah, is said to have been killed in Egypt by his fellow-believers from Judah. Cf. also B.H.Amaru, 'The Killing of the Prophets. Unravelling a Midrash', *Hebrew Union College Annual* 54, 1983, 153-80.

16. Cf. J.Jeremias, *Heiligengräber in Jesu Umwelt*, Göttingen 1958.

17. The juxtaposition of Abel and Zechariah is usually justified as a kind of ideal synthesis of all the innocent victims mentioned in the Old Testament: Abel is the first victim of the first book of the Bible, Genesis, Zechariah is one of the victims (but not the last; here the anonymous son of King Ahaz, killed in *molok* – II Chron.28.3 – and the sons of Manasseh – 33.6) mentioned in the last, Chronicles. However, this explanation does not seem very convincing when one considers that at the time of Jesus, when there is mention only of the Law and the Prophets (i.e. only of the first two parts of the Old Testament), the canon had not yet been fixed, far less the sequence of the books, especially that of the third group, the Kethubim. The Alexandrian canon has a sequence notably different from that of the Massoretic Bible and there are no arguments for claiming that right from the beginning Palestine had known only the sequence adopted by the school of Tiberias.

18. Cf.E.Corsini, *Apocalisse prima e dopo*, Turin 1980, 224-8 (interpretation of 6.9-11; the fifth seal), 437-40.

Chapter 10　The Twelve Tribes

1. An account of the problem of the tribes can be read in P.Capelli, 'Note sul sistema delle dodici tribù di Israele nel libro dei Numeri', *Egitto e vicino Oriente* 7, 1984, 125-35.

2. A sub-division of the united Hebrew state into districts is more conceivable in the eighth century BC, when there was a period of union between the two kingdoms, than at the time of David and Solomon.

3. G.Pettinato, *Ebla, un impero inciso nell'argilla*, Milan 1979, 132: the state was divided into twelve districts, each administered by a 'king' (*lugal*), plus the capital city, which formed two districts by itself; cf. also A.Archi, 'La civiltà di Ebla alla luce degli archivi reali del III millennio a.C', *Il Veltro* 28, 1984, 290.

4. M.Noth, *Das System der zwölf Stämme Israels*, Stuttgart 1930.

5. G.H.J.de Geus, *The Tribes of Israel*, Assen 1976.
6. In the light of this information the words written in all seriousness by someone who is generally considered a great historian cause some surprise: 'What happened to the ten tribes in Assyria and Media? Did they build temples and high places to the Lord on foreign soil?... We do not know' (E.J.Bickermann, *The Cambridge History of Judaism* I, Cambridge 1984, 343).
7. Cf. M.Liverani, 'Un'ipotesi sul nome di Abramo', *Henoch* 1, 1979, 9-18.

Chapter 11 Joshua's Exploits

1. These statements indicate that I do not accept Noth's theory about the Deuteronomistic history work: I regard as absurd the idea of the literary work conjectured by the German scholar which, leaving aside some additions, runs from Deuteronomy to Kings, if only because of its dimensions. A Deuteronomistic history work can be conjectured for the book of Kings, but at a time rather later than the exilic date supposed by Noth. As for Joshua and Judges, they seem to me to be works conceived in the spirit of the Chronicler, and therefore to be dated to the third century BC. See also the conclusions reached in this chapter.
2. A.G. Auld, *Joshua, Moses and the Land*, Edinburgh 1980, 83-5.
3. R.D.Nelson, 'Josiah in the Book of Joshua', *Journal of Biblical Literature* 100, 1981, 531-40.
4. Cf.J.A.Soggin, *The Book of Joshua*, Old Testament Library, London and Philadelphia 1972.
5. If the mention of a sanctuary at Dan (I Kings 12.29f.) is not a late textual insertion, as some scholars believe, we are faced with a sanctuary in the old southern Dan. Dan in the far north would have been of little interest to the priests in Jerusalem.
6. We are not in a position to say what may have been the real historical substance of the ark (or arks). What is certain is that in late historiography the peregrinations of the ark served to give historical justification, i.e. a certain retroactive legitimacy, to sanctuaries frequented by the Israelites. When the centralization of the cult at Jerusalem was achieved in the fifth century BC (recall the coolness of the Jerusalem clergy towards the requests of the Jews of Elephantine for their temple) the situation of these sanctuaries changed: in the historical perspective of the author of Kings they were violently destroyed by Joshua; in that of the author of Chronicles the end of their legitimacy was sanctioned by Josiah's invitation to the Levites to deposit the ark in the temple.
7. L.Yarden, 'Aaron, Bethel, and the Priestly Menorah', *Journal of Jewish Studies* 26, 1975. Cf. also, on various positions, A.Cody, *A History of Old Testament Priesthood*, Rome 1969.
8. A.Rofé, 'The End of the Book of Joshua according to the Septuagint', *Henoch* 4, 1982, 17-36, esp. 27. It is interesting to note how the attitude favourable to Bethel in some quarters has been successively eliminated from the biblical texts by means of textual emendations (like those which removed the mention of Bethel both from the Massoretic text and from the present text of the Septuagint; other examples have been adopted by Rofé, who indicates the starting point of this tendency in the Mishnaic passage Zebahim 14,5-8, which speaks of various seats of the ark but entirely omits any mention of Bethel). In this connection there is another significant fact; when the original list of the thirty cities conquered by Joshua

(12.9-24) was retouched so that the number thirty disappeared (it recalled the number of days in the solar month and gave offence in Pharisaic and then rabbinic circles, which favoured the lunar month, cf. G.Garbini, 'Proverbi per un anno. Il libro dei Proverbi e il calendario', *Henoch* 6, 1984, 139-46), whereas the Massoretic text duplicated the expression 'Aphek of Sharon', making this name of a region into the name of a city (the cities thus become 31), the Septuagint suppressed the mention of Bethel, reducing the number of cities to 29.

9. Cf. J.Liver, 'The Literary History of Joshua IX', *Journal of Semitic Studies* 8, 1963, 227-43.

10. The most reasonable comments on the significance of this expression, which is generic and has particular meanings in individual contexts, have been written by E.W.Nicholson, 'The Meaning of the Expression *'m h'rs* in the Old Testament', *Journal of Semitic Studies* 10, 1965, 59-66. It is interesting to note that whereas in Hag.2.4 the 'people of the land' denotes the population of Judah who had escaped deportation (cf. v.2 of the same chapter), in the books of Ezra and Nehemiah the expression takes on a deprecatory value by identifying the Jews who remained behind as foreigners presumed to have been deported into Judah by an Assyrian king(!) (Ezra 4.2). Late Judaism considered anyone who had not returned from Babylon a 'foreigner' and unworthy of being united in marriage with a good Jew. For the significance of the expression in the rabbinic period cf. A.Oppenheimer, *The* 'Am ha-aretz, Leiden 1977.

Chapter 12 Between Egypt and Babylon

1. F.Parente, 'La Lettera di Aristea come fonte per la storia del giudaismo alessandrino durante la prima meta del I secolo a.C', *Annali della Scuola Normale Superiore di Pisa*, ser.III,2, 1972, 177-237, 517-67. Cf. also F.Vattioni, 'Storia del testo biblico: l'origine dei LXX', *Annali dell'Istituto Orientale di Napoli* 40, 1980, 115-30.

2. N.Walter, *Der Thoraausleger Aristobulos*, Berlin 1964; for his relationship to the Letter see 88-103; id., in Jüdische Schriften aus hellenistisch-römischer Zeit, III,2, Gütersloh 1975, 261-79.

3. The English translation is taken from J.H.Charlesworth (ed.), *The Old Testament Apocrypha* 2, New York and London 1985, 12.

4. Ibid., 15.

5. B.S.J.Isserlin, 'The Names of the 72 Translators of the Septuagint (Aristeas 47-50)', *Journal of the Ancient Near Eastern Society of Columbia University* 5, 1973, 191-7.

6. Charlesworth, op.cit., 14f.

7. In Eusebius, *Praeparatio evangelica* 13,12,1-2.

8. N.Walter, op.cit., 89.n.1: the wording of his comment on the translation of the fragments in Jüdische Schriften is almost identical.

9. Charlesworth, op.cit., 12.

10. F.Jacoby, *Die Fragmente der griechischen Historiker*, no. 725.

11. The earliest manuscripts do not go back beyond the fifteenth century. The emendation often adopted, 'Camarina', on the basis of a statement by Pseudo-Eupolemus (Jacoby, 724), according to whom Camarina was another name for Ur of the Chaldaeans, could be correct, not because it is equivalent to Ur (it seems probable that the identification was made by Pseudo-Eupolemus to harmonize an

extraneous piece of information with Genesis) but because the Jewish writer may have handed down the correct reading. Given the absence of a Camarina in Egpyt it can be presumed that the city mentioned was that in Sicily; in that case the author of the Oracles would have wanted to connect the Jews with the Pythagoreans, as Aristobulus already had.

12. Jacoby, 734, 2.

13. Jacoby, 264, 6.

14. D.Mendels, 'Hecataeus of Abdera and a Jewish "patrios politeia" of the Persian Period (Diodorus Siculus XL,3)', *Zeitschrift für die alttestamentliche Wissenschaft* 98, 1983, 96-110, argues that Hecataeus' source is oral and that it reflects the ideas of Jerusalem at the end of the fourth century BC. It is possible that that is true in the last analysis, but it is difficult to doubt that the direct source of Hecataeus is to be found in Alexandria.

15. Cf. Flavius Josephus, *Contra Apionem* 1, 89-90; 2, 228, 232-250.

16. Cf. ibid., 1, 304-11.

17. R.B.Motzo, *Ricerche sulla letteratura e la storia giudaico-ellenistica*, Rome 1977, 737-58 (a study which originally appeared in 1913).

18. Cf. *Contra Apionem* 1, 288-91. Also P.W.van der Horst, *Chaeremon, Egyptian Priest and Stoic Philosopher*, Leiden 1984.

19. Tacitus, *Histories* 5.3, Loeb Classical Library, London and New York 1931.

20. Cf. *Contra Apionem* 1,238; 1,290; 2,10 respectively.

21. Jacoby, 726.

22. N.Walter, in Jüdische Schriften, 121-36.

23. C.Burchard, *Joseph und Aseneth*, Jüdische Schriften, II, 4, Gütersloh 1983.

24. Josephus, *Jewish Antiquities* 2,238-53. Also J.G.Gager, *Moses in Greco-Roman Paganism*, Nashville 1972.

24a. The Old Testament itself has kept some traces of the traditions which had Moses entering the Promised Land, cf. G.W.Ahlström, 'Another Moses Tradition', *Journal of Near Eastern Studies* 39, 1980, 65-9.

25. Jacoby, 728, 1.

26. B.Z.Wacholder, *Nicolaus of Damascus*, Berkeley and Los Angeles 1962.

27. Cf. Josephus, *Antiquities* 1, 159-60.

28. See p.84.

29. F.Pomponio, '*Mešeq* di Gen.15,2 e un termine amministrativo di Ebla', *Bibbia e Oriente* 25, 1983, 107-9.

30. The expression 'Abraham said' is also repeated, after the opening of v.2, at the beginning of v.3. The incomprehensibility of the second part of v.2 is reflected both in the Septuagint and in Jubilees 14.2.

31. Modern translations presuppose a preposition before the word '*rs* which is not in the text.

31a. Geza Vermes, *The Dead Sea Scrolls in English*, Harmondsworth ²1975, 221.

32. Various scholars see Gebal and Kadesh not as Byblos and Kadesh on the Orontes, as I personally believe, but as southern Kadesh (Barnea); they further stress the southern perspective, of biblical inspiration, by arbitrarily identifying Gebal with Seir, i.e. the desert of the Negeb.

33. Cf.Vermes, *Dead Sea Scrolls*, 102.

34. Amos was in direct confrontation with the priesthood of Bethel (cf. Amos 7); for the Essene community see chapter 13 below.

35. Y.Muffs, 'Abraham the Noble Warrior: Patriarchal Politics and Laws of War in Ancient Israel', *Journal of Jewish Studies* 33, 1982, 81-107, approaches the argument from a fundamentalist point of view.
36. Jacoby, 724,1. Cf.B.Z.Wacholder, 'Pseudo-Eupolemus' two Greek Fragments and the Life of Abraham', *Hebrew Union College Annual* 34, 1963, 83-113; G.L.Prato, 'Babilonia fondata dai giganti: il significato cosmico di Gen.11.1-9 nella storiografia dello Pseudo-Eupolemo', in *El misterio de la palabra. Homenaje al profesor L.Alonso Schökel*, Valencia and Madrid 1983, 121-46.
37. Philo, *De Abrahamo* 233; Josephus, *Antiquities*, 177. The detail relates to the killing of enemies found asleep.
38. Philo, *De Abrahamo* 68-71; Josephus, *Antiquities*, 1,149-53.
39. Jacoby, 724, 1.
40. Jacoby, 728, 1.
41. G.L.Prato, art.cit, 145f.
42. The secondary character of the present Hebrew text is demonstrated by the existence of two different readings corresponding to the Greek ὅμοιος, 'similar': alongside *mwm* one manuscript has *dwpy* in the margin (both Hebrew words mean 'scrub'); it is difficult to doubt that the earlier form is *dwpy* (in this manuscript the marginal glosses are often superior to the text; cf. F.Vattioni, *Ecclesiastico*, Naples 1968, XXII), a deliberate distortion of the original *dwmh*, 'like' (Sirach 44.19).
43. Cf. Josephus, *Antiquities* 1, 165b-168 = Jacoby, 264, 24.
44. Jacoby, 726,1.
45. Cf. Josephus, *Antiquities* 1,161.
46. B.Z.Wacholder, 'How Long did Abraham stay in Egypt?', *Hebrew Union College Annual* 35, 1964, 43-56.
46a. For a correct evaluation of these traditions cf. G.L.Prato, 'Cosmopolitismo culturale e autoidentificazione etnica nella prima storiografia giudaica', *Rivista Biblica* 34, 1986, 143-82.
47. D.Mendels, 'Hecataeus of Abdera' (see n.14).
48. G.Larsson, 'The Chronology of the Pentateuch: A Comparison of the MT and LXX', *Journal of Biblical Literature* 102, 1983, 401-9.
49. Larsson comments on the Priestly writing – as I think, correctly – like this: 'P never existed as an independent unity but rather is the final collection of older and newer source material of the Pentateuch, supplemented with new-written texts and formed into a work of unique consistency and importance' (408).
50. J.W.Wevers, *The History of the Greek Genesis*, Göttingen 1974; for dating cf. 186.
51. Charlesworth, op.cit., 24.
52. Ibid., 12.
53. K.A.Mathews, 'The Background of the Paleo-Hebrew Texts at Qumran', in *The Word of the Lord Shall Go Forth. Essays in Honor of D.N.Freedman*, Winona Lake 1983, 549-68.
54. Cf.G.Garbini, *Storia e problemi dell'epigrafia semitica*, Naples 1979, 63, with a discussion of the problems. Palaeographical analysis of this script as it appears in the Qumran manuscripts demonstrates its artificial and late origin: it is in fact a mere cursivization of the signs on monuments of the seventh to sixth century BC without any internal evolution comparable to that attested for Phoenician and Aramaic. Palaeo-Hebraic script on coins with the names *Yhd* and *Yhzqyw* needs further investigation and is not taken into consideration here.

55. J.Naveh, *Early History of the Alphabet*, Jerusalem-Leiden 1982, 123f. For the schism and the Samaritan Pentateuch, the redaction of which is put in the Hasmonaean period, see J.D.Purvis, *The Samaritan Pentateuch and the Origin of the Samaritan Sect*, Cambridge, Mass. 1968.

56. At this point it is worth drawing attention to a major problem which might find a solution in what I have just written above. For a long time biblical scholars have noted the contradiction between the existence of the Mosaic Pentateuch as we have it now (the 'five books' were a characteristic of Jewish literature of a certain period: one might think of the 'Enochic Pentateuch', the five *megilloth*, the five books of Psalms, and so on) and the fact that the Pentateuch is inconceivable as it is without Joshua, that is, the account of the conquest, which is the logical, historical and theological culmination of all the promises contained in the five books; hence the use of the concept of the Hexateuch, especially towards the end of the last century, when biblical scholars were more sensitive to philological demands. In the perspective of our investigation, which sees Genesis attached to the complex of normative books at the last moment, it is possible to give a historical explanation of the fact that has been noted: to begin with there were five books (certainly very different from those we have now) roughly corresponding to the sequence Exodus-Joshua, with the promise (made to whom?) put at the beginning (all this in a purely conjectural way). The addition of Genesis, which probably formed only an abnormal amplification of what was contained at the beginning of the original book, forced a different distribution of the material, which was justified on the literary level with the figure of Moses the lawgiver. The weight of literary tradition, which did not want a collection of more than five books, left Joshua in an intermediary position (even in the Samaritan tradition).

57. It has now become a commonplace to associate the thought of the 'Deutero-nomistic historian' (with his exclusively theological judgment based on the centrality of the cult at Jerusalem) with Josiah's reform (621 BC). That is quite wrong, because Josiah's reform, as I noted when discussing it, was not concerned with the centralization of the cult. If we were to abandon the procedure of assigning impossibly early dates to the text, we could see that there is an interesting ideological parallel with the 'Deuteronomistic historical conception': the so-called 'Demotic Chronicle' from Egypt, compiled in the third century BC, but referred to the fifth and sixth centuries, has rightly been defined as a 'continual judgment of God on the rulers of Egypt: but between the lines one can clearly read a judgment on the temple' (S.Donadoni, 'L'Egitto achemenide', in *Forme di contatto e processi di trasformazione nelle società antiche. Atti del convegno di Cortona (24-30 maggio 1981)*, Pisa-Rome 1983, 37. I do not want to insist that the 'Demotic Chronicle' is the direct model of the 'Deuteronomistic history', both because of its late date and because of the difference in literary genre. But given that this Egyptian text will not have been either the only one or the earliest one of its kind, it is not out of place to suppose that a certain Egyptian way of seeing history (from the priestly perspective) was echoed in Jerusalem at a time earlier than that which experienced the crisis described in these pages. The centrality of the cult in Jerusalem was in fact achieved only in the post-exilic period and became a theme of polemic only after the reconstruction of the sanctuary on Gerizim, towards the end of the fourth century BC.

58. In this discussion I shall not go into the political attitude held by the Israelite

kings towards Egypt, which was certainly inspired by contingent rather than ideological motives; nor should excessive importance be attached to the invectives against Egypt launched by various prophets like Isaiah (chs.19-20), Jeremiah (ch.44) and Ezekiel (chs.29-32;46); it was a custom of prophetic literature to hurl curses against all foreign peoples (and also against one's own people).

59. According to Josephus, *Antiquities* 13.64,68, it was on the basis of this very passage in Isaiah that Onias wanted to build the temple at Leontopolis, in the name of Heliopolis, where there were many Jews (cf. paragraph 65).

60. A.Momigiliano, *Saggezza straniera*, Turin 1980, 120-4.

61. Josephus, *Antiquities* 12, 3-6.

62. *Contra Apionem* 1, 186-89.

63. L.Fuchs, *Die Juden Aegyptens in ptolemäischer und römischer Zeit*, Vienna 1924, speaks of 'prehistory' for the pre-Ptolemaic period (3-4).

64. P.Sacchi, *Storia del mondo giudaico*, Turin 1976, 63.

65. Cf.F.M.Cross, 'An Aramaic Ostracon of the Third Century B.C.E. from Excavations in Jerusalem', *Eretz-Israel* 15, 1981, 67*-9*.

Chapter 13   Ezra

1. P.Sacchi, *Storia del mondo giudaico*, Turin 1976, 51.

2. J.S.Sanders, *Torah and Canon*, Philadelphia 1972, 51.

3. J.Maier, *Das Judentum*, Munich ²1973, 129.

4. Cf. *The Koran*, translated by N.J.Dawood, Harmondsworth 1959, 313.

5. For the philological problems connected with this book see below. For the moment the quotations follow the Massoretic text.

6. Cf.G.Garbini, 'Aramaico *gᵉmîr* (Esdra 7,12)', in *Studi in onore di E.Bresciani*, Pisa 1985, 227-9.

7. I regard as fundamental to the dating of this book the concordant evidence of the Greek, Latin and Syriac versions, against the Massoretic text, in I Chron.3.19ff.: the eleven generations after Zerubbabel of the original text, kept by the versions, are reduced to six in the Massoretic text by means of textual retouching whch has corrupted the text, as seems evident from the Leningrad manuscript reproduced in the various Hebrew Bibles.

8. The title appears in the text of I Esdras, see below.

9. In reality Josephus paraphases not Ezra but I Esdras, see below.

10. R.Kabisch, *Das vierte Buch Esra*, Göttingen 1889; G.H.Box, in R.H.Charles, *The Apocrypha and Pseudepigrapha of the Old Testament* II, Oxford 1913, 542-624; W.O.E.Oesterley, *II Esdra (The Ezra Apocalypse)*, London 1933; E.Brandenburger, *Die Verborgenheit Gottes im Weltgeschehen. Das literarische und theologische Problem des 4.Esrabuches*, Zurich 1981. The theological and therefore not philological approach to this work which claims that it is a unity (its composite character, at least at the level of its sources, is evident) has influenced the judgment of J.Schreiner, *Das 4.Buch Esra*, Jüdische Schriften aus hellenistisch-römischer Zeit V,4, Gütersloh 1981.

11. Morton Smith, *Palestinian Parties and Politics that Shaped the Old Testament*, New York 1971, 121, reissued London 1987, 91. Smith's judgment relates expressly to Ezra.

12. The Jewish tradition expressed in the present Massoretic text regards Ezra and Nehemiah as a single work.

13. The discussion of the chronology and sequence of Ezra and Nehemiah is defined precisely by H.H.Rowley, 'The Chronological Order of Ezra and Nehemiah', a study which originally appeared in 1948 and was republished, in an updated form, in *The Servant of the Lord and Other Essays on the Old Testament*, Oxford ²1965, 137-68; the discussion is further updated in J.A.Soggin, *Introduction to the Old Testament*, London and Philadelphia ³1979, 420-5 (with relevant bibliography).

14. The prevalent opinion from the end of the eighteenth century to the present day is that Ezra and Nehemiah are an integral part of Chronicles; the whole is said to be the work of just one author, who is referred to as the Chronicler. Of course there have been those who have seen Ezra himself as the Chronicler.

15. However, I have not been able to gain access to this scholar's *Précis d'histoire juive*, 1889, which mentions Ezra on p.582; nor have I been able to see the work by C.Ballangé, which appeared in the same year, where a similar judgment is expressed.

16. E.Renan, *Histoire du peuple d'Israël* IV, Paris 1893, 96-106.

17. Ibid., 97.

18. C.C.Torrey, *The Composition and Historical Value of Ezra-Nehemiah*, Beihefte zur Zeitschrift für die alttestamentliche Wissenschaft 2, Giessen 1896.

19. C.C.Torrey, *Ezra Studies*, Chicago 1910. L.W.Batten, *The Books of Ezra and Nehemiah*, Edinburgh 1913, was very critical of Torrey: this is probably the worst volume of the prestigious Anglo-American series, the International Critical Commentary.

20. G.Hölscher, *Geschichte der israelitischen und jüdischen Religion*, Giessen 1922, 140-1. H.P.Smith, *Old Testament History*, 1903 (which I have not been able to see), seems to have adopted the same position; cf. N.H.Snaith, in H.H.Rowley (ed.), *The Old Testament and Modern Study*, Oxford 1951, 113 n.3.

21. T.Nöldeke, 'Zur Frage der Geschichtlichkeit der Urkunden im Esra-Buche', *Deutsche Literaturzeitung* 45, 1924, 1849-56; A.Loisy, *La religion d'Israël*, Paris ³1933, 27-28, 288.

22. R.H.Pfeiffer, *Introduction to the Old Testament*, New York 1941 (the subsequent editions, the second American edition of 1948 and the English edition of 1952, do not make any changes of interest here). The American scholar does not deny the historicity of Ezra but stresses the improbabilities of the account which narrates his achievements; the Chronicler (Pfeiffer, too, presumes him to be Ezra) 'exaggerated the role of Ezra in such a fantastic way that it is difficult to recover the real historical framework of his contribution through the dense mist of imagination' (256). This moderately critical position (cf. also 828) has not saved Pfeiffer from the violent conservative criticism of R.K.Harrison, *Introduction to the Old Testament*, Grand Rapids, Michigan 1969, 1139-40.

23. As is the case in H.H.Rowley (cf.n.13), 145, or R.K.Harrison (see the preceding note). J.A.Soggin, *History of Israel*, London and Philadephia 1984, 276, devotes a paragraph to the problem of the existence of Ezra, recalling Torrey's position (he mentions only the 1910 volume) and anticipating my own view, communicated in the course of a friendly conversation; his verdict is that 'such a radical theory also presupposes the rejection of much of the tradition that we possess as being an artificial construction; moreover, the arguments used are anything but conclusive

(e.g. the lack of any mention of Ezra in Sir.49.13, where Nehemiah appears alone)'. In this situation it is good that in 1970 there was a reprint in New York of *Ezra Studies*, with a long introduction by W.F.Stinespring in which there is a recollection of, among others, Torrey's predecessors (the 'French radicals') and the few followers of his ideas on Ezra.

24. J.A.Soggin, *History*, 133-7.

25. The choice of Salathiel as a recipient of apocalyptic visions can be explained by the historical and social importance of his figure; in fact, according to the tradition in I Chron.3.17, he was the firstborn of Jehoiachin, the king of Jerusalem in exile, and in turn father of Zerubbabel (Hag. 1.1; Ezra 3.2; against, I Chron.3.19).

26. Cf.I.Loeb, 'La chaîne de la tradition dans le premier chapitre du Pirké Abot', in *Bibliothèque de l'École des Hautes Études. Sciences religieuses* 1, Paris 1889, 307-22.

27. This can be fully justified because, as will emerge, chronology shows that the beginning of the Great Synagogue corresponds exactly to the beginning of the 'pairs'.

28. J.Wellhausen, *Prolegomena to the History of Israel*, 1883; the reference is to the edition by Meridian Books, Cleveland and New York 1957, 409-10.

29. According to another the books themselves amount to twenty-two.

30. Jerome, *Praefatio in Ezram*, in *Patrologia Latina*, ed.J.P.Migne, Vol.28, Paris 1889, 1471-4.

31. S.Japhet, 'The Supposed Common Authorship of Chronicles and Ezra-Nehemia Investigated Anew', *Vetus Testamentum* 18, 1968, 330-71; H.G.M.Williamson, *Israel in the Book of Chronicles*, Cambridge 1977; P.Sacchi, *Apocrifi dell'Antico Testamento* I, Torino 1981, 102-10.

32. Jerome, *Praefatio in Ezram*, 1472. The autonomy of I Esdras has found various supporters, usually in the Catholic sphere; cf.E.Beyer, *Das dritte Buch Esdras und sein Verhältnis zu den Büchern Ezra-Nehemia*, Freiburg im Breisgau 1911; B.Walde, *Die Esdrabücher der Septuaginta*, Freiburg im Breisgau 1913; P.Sacchi, op.cit.

33. On the basis of my studies I can affirm that initially the parts of the text which are now written in very bad imperial Aramaic (also considered as such by T.Nöldeke, 'Semitic Languages', in *Encyclopaedia Britannica*[11] 24, 624) were once written in Hebrew. The existence of the Hebrew original is confirmed by Yadaim 4.5.

34. T.Denter, *Die Stellung der Bücher Esdras im Kanon des Alten Testamentes*, Freiburg CH 1962.

35. Cf.M.Baillet, in *Les 'Petites Grottes' de Qumran*, Oxford 1962, 126-7.

36. I Esdras used (i.e. substantially reproduced) the following sources: 1. II Chronicles 35-36 (= ch.1); 2. the 'Letters of kings about votive offerings' (a work cited by II Macc.2.13, with an epistolary structure) composed at the end of the fourth century BC after Alexander had had the Samaritan temple built; this work is centred on the temple, has Zerubbabel as its protagonist and recalls the prophets, especially Haggai and Zechariah, on whose information ('in the second year of Darius') the narrative is constructed (= chs.2; 6-7.5); 3. a second narrative of the return constructed by using an Aramaic wisdom text of about 300 BC (Darius' three pages); it is interested in the rebuilding of Jerusalem, has Joshua as its protagonist (Zerubbabel is replaced by his son Jehoiachim), puts the return exclusively in the time of Darius, can be dated towards the middle of the third century BC and can be found inserted in the letters when they begin to talk of Darius, according to a

scheme of composition which is also followed by Josephus. The literary unity of this source is also demonstrated by its complete absence from the canonical Ezra (= 3-5.6); 4. a list of those returning, of Levitical inspiration, centred on the return in the time of Cyrus, with Zerubbabel and Joshua as protagonists; it can be dated towards the beginning of the third century BC (= 5.7-71). The original narrative by the author of I Esdras begins in 7.6 and is constructed in imitation of the 'Memoirs of Nehemiah', the original draft of which corresponds to that paraphrased by Josephus (*Antiquities* 11,159-183), i.e. in chs.1-7.73a; the last part of this work has been confused by the considerable revision of the canonical Nehemiah (chs.9-13) at a time which is at present uncertain but is in any case late (cf. C.C.Torrey, *Ezra Studies*, 248-50).

37. Philo, *De confusione linguarum*, 149; the reference is to I Esdras 8.29. The possible use of I Esdras by the writer Eupolemus (middle of the second century BC in connection with the description of the temple of Jerusalem has often been noted (C.C.Torrey, *Ezra Studies*, 82-3; S.S.Tedesche, *A Critical Edition of I Esdras*, Leipzig 1928, 14f.; B.Z.Wacholder, *Eupolemus. A Study of Judaeo-Greek Literature*, Cincinnati 1974, 154, 160-1). The derivation is very probable, but it must be remembered that Eupolemus did not draw on I Esdras but on its earlier source, namely the 'Letters of kings on the votive offerings'.

38. The exact reading of the Greek is not that to be found in the critical editions of A.Rahlfs and R.Hanhart, but that given in the manuscripts of the R recension (cf. P.Vannutelli, *Libri synoptici Veteris Testamenti*, Rome 1931, 643) and by the Ethiopic and Armenian versions. The reading involves the deletion of τῶν after the word 'Levites'. The Vulgate omits and changes various words.

39. 'The sons of the people' instead of 'before the people'; a *p* has been replaced by a *b*.

40. In this connection the canonical text of Ezra-Nehemiah has a very interesting textual variant: instead of 'east gate' it speaks of the 'water gate' (Neh.8.1). This 'water gate' does not correspond to the 'east gate' because it was on the south side of the temple, and immediately in front of it was the largest space within the area delimited by the outer wall. For this reason it was the favoured place for meetings (Middoth 1.4; 21.1; 2.6). This is the information provided by the Mishnah, which, however, refers to the temple built by Herod; that means that the text of canonical Ezra-Nehemiah does not antedate the first century AD.

41. The translations quoted basically follow the Revised Standard Version.

42. Some repetition of the ceremony is described in Neh.9.2-5, but there the scene is not a choral one and there is no explicit mention of the contribution of the people; there is only a long prayer of Levites which is not followed by the people's 'Amen'.

43. Something similar was done about twenty years ago in the Catholic rite when the old altar which forced the officiating priest to turn his back on the faithful was abandoned or even eliminated in all churches; with the new altar, much simpler than its predecessor, the celebrant stands facing the faithful. The people also has a more active role in the rite of the new Catholic liturgy.

44. Ezekiel 40-48 correspond too well to the reality to which the Levites are opposed, first with Chronicles and then with I Esdras, to be far from the Jerusalem of the third century BC. Historically, it seems very probable that they were composed in Jerusalem in the fifth century BC.

45. This is the exact reading of the text in accordance with its internal logic and the textual variants. The reading usually adopted ('not all the sons of the exile purified themselves', with οὐχ instead of ὅτι; the latter is to be found in the Vatican and the Alexandrine texts) is justified by A.Rahlfs with a reference to II Chron.30.17-18: but here the mention is of Hezekiah's passover, the very one challenged by I Esdras, which counters it with Josiah's passover.

46. A copy of the Greek inscription, from the Herodian temple, has been rediscovered, with the text of the warning to Gentiles not to cross the enclosure within the temple, cf. *Inscriptions Reveal*, Jerusalem 1972, 76, no.169.

47. Cf.J.A.Fitzmyer and D.J.Harrington, *A Manual of Palestinian Aramaic Texts*, Rome 1978, 184-7, 248-50.

48. Cf. R.de Vaux, *Ancient Israel*, London and New York 1961, 185f. It is worth noting that the text of I Maccabees, which at present has a not very coherent system in its mention of months (sometimes only the name, sometimes only the number, and sometimes both: 4.52; 16.14) has interventions in precisely this area, perhaps to conceal what was said in the original text; at any rate it is a fact that Sinaiticus omits the number in 4.52 and the name in 14.27.

49. Rosh ha-Shanah 1.1: 'There are four "New Year" days: on the 1st of Nisan is the New Year for kings and feasts; on the 1st of Elul is the New Year for the Tithe of Cattle...; on the 1st of Tishri is the New Year for the [reckoning of the] years [of foreign kings]; and the 1st of Shebat is the New Year for [fruit] trees', H.Danby, *The Mishnah*, Oxford 1933, 188.

50. Cf.W.A.M.Beuken, *Haggai-Sacharja* 1-8, Assen 1967.

51. In all probability the invention of the figure of Ezra was accompanied by the redaction of a new prophetic text, that of Malachi, which seems to provide a counterpoint to Ezra's reform: polemic against a certain priestly class (evidently the 'sons of Zadok' are the ones who perform the sacrifices, not the priests), a polemic against mixed marriages, an exhortation to pay the tithe and to respect the Law. We can see clearly why according to a rabbinic tradition 'Malachi' was simply a pseudonym for Ezra (Babylonian Talmud, *Megillah* 15a).

52. N.Avigad, 'New Moabite and Ammonite Seals at the Israel Museum', *Eretz Israel* 13, 1977, 108-10 (in Hebrew).

53. For the reservations over much material published after 1976 I would refer to the report 'Nuovi documenti epigrafici dalla Palestina' which I have published periodically in *Henoch* from the first year. Doubts about the authenticity of the Moabite seal (which is moreover considered Ammonite by R.Hestrin and M.Dayagi Mendeles, *Ḥotamot miymey Beyt Ri'son*, Jerusalem 1978, 122 no.97) are raised by a series of features: the writing is too archaic for a date like that suggested, around the year 700 BC, on the basis of the iconography of a Mesopotamian kind; the position of the star put above the lunar crescent is unusual; the execution of the figure is too rough compared with the accuracy of the script. I have to admit that I did not raise these doubts when I presented the seal in *Henoch* 1980, 351.

54. According to Josephus, *Antiquities* 12,385, the original name of Alcimus will have been Joachim or Jachim (with different variants in the Greek manuscript tradition).

55. The close link between the two names, on the formal linguistic level and on that of religious content, is confirmed by the textual variant 'book of Ezra' which appears alongside the 'scroll of the inner court of the temple' in Moed Qatan 3,4 and in the Tosephta of Kelim 15,6.

56. Cf. Damascus Document 3.21-4.4.

57. From the boundless bibliography on Qumran I shall limit myself to mentioning J.A.Soggin, *I manoscritti del Mar Morto*, Rome 1978, as a general introduction; L.Moraldi, *Il Maestro di giustizia*, Fossano 1971, for a detailed examination of the problems; G.Vermes, *The Dead Sea Scrolls in English*, Harmondsworth ²1975, for a translation of the texts; B.Z.Wacholder, *The Dawn of Qumran. The Sectarian Torah and the Teacher of Righteousness*, Cincinnati 1983, one of the most acute analyses of the Qumran movement. On the basis of Qirqisani (cf. B.Chiesa and W.Lockwood, *Ya'qūb al-Qirqisānī on Jewish Sects and Christianity*, Frankfurt am Main 1984), Wacholder sees Zadok, the disciple of Antigonus of Socoh, as founder of the Qumran sect, even if Qirqisani in fact asserts that Zadok, with Boethus, was the leader of the Sadducees; Zadok, who died around 170 BC, was probably the initiator of that Zadokite opposition to the priesthood of the 'sons of Aaron' which flared up into an open schism only in the time of Alcimus.

58. L.Moraldi, *I manoscritti di Qumran*, Turin 1971, 535; the uncertainty of the reading relates to the words 'the association of priests'.

59. Cf. most recently F.García Martínez, '¿Judas Macabeo Sacerdote Impío? Notas al margen de 1 QpHab VIII,8-13', in *Mélanges bibliques et orientaux en l'honneur de M.M.Delcor*, Neukirchen-Vluyn 1985, 169-81.

60. It is usually said that all the books of the Bible with the exception of Esther are attested at Qumran, but that is not true. F.M.Cross said in 1953 that a small fragment of Chronicles had been found in Cave 4 (cf. 'Le travail d'édition des fragments manuscrits de Qumrân', *Revue Biblique* 63, 1956, 58), but we have heard no more about it. If it did really exist, it was probably a sentence from Samuel or Kings: similarly, J.A.Fitzmyer, *The Dead Sea Scrolls*, Missoula 1975, 159, says that I Chron.17.9-13 is attested, whereas in reality this is part of Nathan's prophecy taken from II Sam.7 and inserted into one of the so-called Florilegia (4Q174). Since all this was clear to Fitzmeyer (cf.p.33), we must ask whether the citation of Chronicles was not made with the aim of indicating that something was at Qumran which was not in fact there (nor, given the fact that the Florilegium comes from Cave 4, can we rule out the possibility that this is the very fragment noted by Cross). As for I Ezra (which for the biblical scholars does not exist – they talk only of Ezra-Nehemiah), Cross himself affirms in the passage that I have quoted the existence of a fragment, in Cave 4, of Ezra 4 and 5; these too, if they ever existed, have remained unpublished for more than thirty years after their discovery and identification: but this is not yet Ezra but his principal source, the 'Letters of the kings' (see n.36), which was also known to Eupolemus.

61. C.Houtman, 'Ezra and the Law', *Oudtestamentische Studiën* 21, 1981, 91-115; B.Z.Wacholder, *The Dawn of Qumran*, 1-32.

62. Temple Scroll 56, 20-21 ('this law'); 57,1 ('this is the law'). Note that Deut.17.17 and Josh.8.32 speak of 'a copy of the Law' in the hand of the rulers.

63. For the position of theologians see recently A.H.J.Gunneweg, 'Zur Interpretation der Bücher Esra-Nehemia', in *Congress Volume Vienna 1980*, Leiden 1981, 146-61; R.Rendtorff, 'Esra und das "Gesetz"', *Zeitschrift für die alttestamentliche Wissenschaft* 96, 1984, 165-84.

64. Cf. to this effect H.Danby, *The Mishnah*, Oxford 1933, 210 n.15.

Chapter 14   Time and History

1. M.Eliade, *The Myth of the Eternal Return*, London 1956.

2. Belief in the exact repetition, with the same persons and the same events, of the course of history after the 'conflagration' (ἐκπύρωσις), is generally attributed to all the Stoic school. That seems to me to be incorrect because, unlike the 'conflagration', which moreover had already been a hypothesis among the Pythagoreans, the affirmation of the 'return of the same' is exclusive to Chrysippus. It is in fact in fragments of his works that such a theory is mentioned (J.von Arnim, *Stoicorum veterum fragmenta* I-IV, Leipzig 1921-24, nos.623-31, in particular 625 and 626), despite the attribution to Zeno of a similar fragment (op.cit., 109); this attribution is due to Tatian (*Contra Graecos* 3) but in all probability is wrong (the fathers of the church often confused their sources: one can recall in the Jewish sector the two Pseudo-Hecataei and Pseudo-Eupolemus). In favour of the attribution to Chrysippus of the phrase which Tatian refers to Zeno it can be noted that in practice it amounts to a paraphrase of the fragments of Chrysippus, with the addition of burlesque figures like Anitus, Meletus and Busiris who, while they do not go with the serious figure of Zeno (as he is presented by Diogenes Laertius, *Lives of the Philosophers*, 7.1), do fit Chrysippus, who was criticized 'because in his writings he deals with many arguments in a scandalous and brazen tone', as Laertius states (op.cit., 7.7). The playful tone of Chrysippus and the omission of the theory of the conflagration and the return by Laertius, though he devoted a great many pages to the presentation of Stoic doctrine (op.cit., 7.1), make one suspect that Stoic ἐκπύρωσις and 'return' are overvalued, for polemical reasons, by the Christian apologists and therefore by modern scholars who use their testimony as a basis.

3. K.Löwith, *Nietzsches Philosophie der ewigen Wiederkehr des Gleichen*, Stuttgart ²1956 (Italian translation *Nietzsche e l'eterno ritorno*, Bari 1982).

4. Eliade, op.cit., ix.

5. Löwith, op.cit., 'Nietzsche wanted to believe in the eternal return of the identical', Italian ed., 161.

6. *City of God*, 12.11 and 13.

7. *City of God*, 12.10-13; St Augustine follows the chronology of the Septuagint, which is notably longer than that of the Massoretic text. Cf. also the article cited in Chapter 12, n.48.

8. O.Cullmann, *Christ and Time*, London and Philadelphia ³1962.

9. B.Croce, *Teoria e storia della storiografia*, Bari ⁴1941, 196.

10. J.Barr, *The Semantics of Biblical Language*, Oxford 1961, reissued London 1983, 11.

11. The German text, which uses words of Germanic and Latin origin, says 'eine bestimmte zeitliche (= sukzessive) Reihenfolge'.

12. T. Boman, *Das hebräische Denken im Vergleich mit dem griechischen*, Göttingen ⁴1965, 123 (this passage does not appear in the English translation, *Hebrew Thought Compared with Greek*, London and Philadelphia 1960, which was made from the 1954 edition).

13. The original German edition of *Christ and Time* appeared in 1946: pp.51-60 of the English translation are devoted to the conceptions of time.

14. K.Löwith, *Meaning in History*, Chicago 1949; ch.XI is devoted to 'The Biblical View of History'.
15. R.Bultmann, *History and Eschatology*, Edinburgh 1956.
16. S.Mazzarino, *Il pensiero storico classico* I, Bari 1966, 3.
17. Ibid., II, 2, 412-61. To quote the final words of this long study: 'However, if in Livy's narrative the battle of Sentino is also characterized by a motive that could be said to be totemic, that means that the totemic mentality survived, in an almost subconscious way, the disappearance of totemism as such, and could still produce forms of thought in which "sacred time" and "historical time" continued to be fused in an obvious way' (461).
18. B.Croce, op.cit., 182.
19. J.Barr, *The Semantics of Biblical Language*: id., *Biblical Words for Time*, London 1962 (a chapter is devoted to criticism of Cullmann). Still attached to traditional theological positions (the expression 'the insatiably iconoclastic spirit of Barr' on p.197 of the second article cited here is significant), M.Perani no longer speaks of linear and cyclical time in two works which appeared a few years ago: 'La concezione ebraica del tempo: appunti per una storia del problema', *Rivista Biblica* 27, 1978, 401-21; and 'La concezione del tempo nell'Antico Testamento', *Sacra Doctrina* 87, 1978, 193-242.
20. Cf. R.N.Frye, 'Islamic Sources for the Pre-Islamic History of Central Asia', in J.Harmatta (ed.), *Prolegomena to the Sources on the History of Pre-Islamic Central Asia*, Budapest 1979, 221-9, who at the beginning of his study resorts to the linear conception of time, which in his view is peculiar to the Semites, to justify the development of Islamic historiography in Iran and Central Asia. This position has rightly been criticized by Gherardo Gnoli in a review (*Orientalistische Literaturzeitung* 78, 1983, 536). Gnoli recalls how the first linear conception of time was in fact developed in Iran by Zoroastrian thought. The analogy which Gnoli himself sees, in *Zoroaster's Time and Homeland*, Naples 1980, 197, between this aspect of Zoroastrianism and the equivalent aspect of Hebrew prophecy and Jewish messianism can be explained historically as a direct influence of the former on the latter (cf. also D.Winston, 'The Iranian Component in the Bible, Apocrypha, and Qumran: A Review of the Evidence', *History of Religions* 5, 1965-1966, 183-215). The idea of God as 'first and last', typical of Deutero-Isaiah (Isaiah 41.4; 44.6; 48.12), and taken up as such in Rev.1.17, though the book also replaces it with 'alpha and omega' (A.Skrinjar, '—*Ego sum* α *et* ω', *Verbum Domini* 17, 1937, 10-20)(Rev.1.8; 21.6; 22.13), literally adopts a Zoroastrian conception (G.Gnoli, *Zoroaster*, 202); cf. also G.Garbini, 'Le serie alfabetische semitiche e il loro significato', *Annali dell'Istituto Orientale di Napoli* 42, 1982, 403-11.
21. G.von Rad, *Old Testament Theology I. The Theology of the Historical Traditions of Israel*, Edinburgh 1966, reissued London 1975.
22. B.Albrektson, *History and the Gods*, Lund 1967.
23. In particular mention should be made of two articles by the Assyriologist W.G.Lambert: 'History and the Gods: A Review Article', *Orientalia* 39, 1970, 170-7, and 'Destiny and Divine Intervention in Babylon and Israel', *Oudtestamentische Studiën* 17, 1972, 45-72.
24. G.L.Prato, 'Dalla "rivelazione come storia" alla "storia teofanica"', in *Parola e Spirito. Studi in onore di S.Cipriani*, Brescia 1982, 549-73: the quotation comes from pp.566f.

25. I would like to recall the words which Fr de Vaux wrote in his article on von Rad; 'If this resumé of "sacred history" is contradicted by "history", if this confession of faith does not correspond to the facts, the faith of Israel is vain, and so is ours', *Bible et Orient*, Paris 1967, 185. Even if the position of the French scholar seems all in all somewhat critical of that of von Rad on the theological level, it cannot be denied that his attitude as a historian begins from presuppositions analogous to those of the German scholar, namely substantial trust in the historical credibility of the Old Testament.

26. For the position of modern scholars I would refer to the article by G.L.Prato cited in n.24; however, I would recall that here too there was an assessment by J.Barr, 'Revelation through History in the Old Testament and in Modern Theology', *Interpretation* 17, 1963, 193-205. J.A.Soggin, 'La storiografia israelitica più antica', in *La storiografia nella Bibbia. Atti della XXVIII Settimana Biblica*, Bologna 1986, 21-7, has now argued for a substantial reassessment of the antiquity and the value of Jewish historiography.

27. This was not the 'Annals of Judah' cited by the compiler of Kings but an annalistic work relating to Jerusalem, probably beginning with David: cf. G.Garbini, 'Le fonte citate nel "Libro dei Re"', *Henoch* 3, 1981, 26-46.

28. For the so-called 'Annals of Tyre' see the chapter 'Gli "Annali di Tiro" e la storiografica fenicia' in my volume *I Fenici. Storia e religione*, Naples 1980, 26-46.

29. Cf. A.K.Grayson, *Assyrian and Babylonian Chronicles*, Locust Valley, New York 1975.

30. My position is precisely the opposite to that put foward by J.van Seters, *In Search of History*, New Haven 1983, who says (p.355): 'Only when the nation itself took precedence over the king, as happened in Israel, could history writing be achieved.'

31. E.A.Speiser, 'The Biblical Idea of History in its Common Near Eastern Setting', *Israel Exploration Journal* 7, 1957, 201-16. This article reflects in a very clear way the atmosphere and positions of Albrightian fundamentalism at the time of its greatest success; some apodeictic affirmations can only raise a smile today ('the Bible is first and foremost a unique distillation of history', 202; 'the deep, indeed the unbridgeable, chasm between the civilizations of Egypt and Mesopotamia – the one with its static and the other with its dynamic world-view – should now be fully apparent', 206). Many problems of Hebrew historiography have been discussed, with a quite excellent presentation of the state of studies, in the book by J.van Seters quoted in n.30.

32. See Ch.12, especially n.56.

33. On which the annalistic information to which I have referred in n.27 is to be based.

34. The majority of Jewish history is narrated in the Bible as a uniform repertory of disobedience and consequent punishment, but detached from a real historical development, because when certain promises become reality no one seems to accept them; this is truly a cyclical pattern and apparently without a goal. It was only Christianity which gave sense to the events narrated in the Jewish texts, by considering them all as the necessary premise of redemption.

35. Y.H.Yerushalmi has written some penetrating pages on the significance of the almost total lack of a Jewish historiography before the last century in a book from which I have learned a great deal (*Zakhor. Storia ebraica e memoria ebraica*, Parma 1983: I have not been able to see the English original, *Zakhor. Jewish History and*

Jewish Memory, University of Washington Press 1982). I would like to quote two statements from this book, which I feel to have a position close to my own: 'Modern Jewish conceptions of the past have not been formed by historiography; much more decisive in this sense has been the contribution of literature and ideology' (107); and again, 'now as then [viz., in the sixteenth century], it could be said that when the Jews did not reject history out of hand they preferred not to confront it directly, seeing it as a new metahistorical myth' (109). I have been glad to learn from Yerushalmi's study that it was an Italian Jew, Azariah de' Rossi, who for the first time, in the sixteenth century, 'examined the legendary rabbinic degrees not in the light of philosophy or the Kabbalah... but through secular history, unacceptable to all even as a criterion for evaluating the words of the ancients. Even worse, Azariah did not hesitate to resort to non-Jewish sources' (85).

INDEX OF TEXTS DISCUSSED

INDEX OF MODERN SCHOLARS

219